ROUTLEDGE LIBRARY EDITIONS: URBAN HISTORY

Volume 1

DACCA

DACCA

A Study in Urban History and Development

SHARIF UDDIN AHMED

Routledge
Taylor & Francis Group
LONDON AND NEW YORK

First published in 1986 by Curzon Press Ltd.

This edition first published in 2018
by Routledge
2 Park Square, Milton Park, Abingdon, Oxon OX14 4RN

and by Routledge
711 Third Avenue, New York, NY 10017

Routledge is an imprint of the Taylor & Francis Group, an informa business

British Library Cataloguing in Publication Data
A catalogue record for this book is available from the British Library

ISBN: 978-0-8153-5316-4 (Set)
ISBN: 978-1-351-13718-8 (Set) (ebk)
ISBN: 978-0-8153-9407-5 (Volume 1) (hbk)
ISBN: 978-1-351-18675-9 (Volume 1) (ebk)

Publisher's Note
The publisher has gone to great lengths to ensure the quality of this reprint but points out that some imperfections in the original copies may be apparent.

Disclaimer
The publisher has made every effort to trace copyright holders and would welcome correspondence from those they have been unable to trace.

PREFACE

Of the forty-nine postgraduate students I have supervised, two future vice chancellors among them, Professor Sharif uddin Ahmed is one of the most interesting and able.

His intellectual abilities were early demonstrated when he stood first in First Class in MA History at Dhaka University. That achievement secured him a major award taken at Balliol College, Oxford, where in 1972 he did a B.Litt. by thesis on 'The Peasants of Bengal' under John Gallagher and C.C. Davies with whose commendations he came to *School of Oriental and African Studies* – SOAS- University of London. There he found a conference on *The City in South Asia* in preparation. Professor Ahmed attended it, contributed to it and made it the subject of his Ph.D. thesis.

This was a courageous move, for South Asian cities had not often been studied as subjects in themselves, other than by writers of tourist guides. Few competent secondary studies were available and no specialist journals. Only one full blown study on any major city of South Asia was carried out till that date was on the *City of Ahmedabad* and that was done by a geographer Kenneth L. Gillion.

The thesis thus had to be written from original records both of the provincial and local government, widely scattered across many departments and continents, rarely coordinated and subject to "weeding" and neglect. Happily one of Professor Ahmed's great strengths was his decisiveness in setting out lines of enquiry and their boundaries. This was matched by clearly marshalled arguments, set out in concise effective English.

The thesis, analysing changes in the life of Dhaka from 1840 to 1885 was warmly received by his examiners, Dr. P.J. Marshall and Dr. C.A. Bayly whose enthusiasm encouraged SOAS to publish it as the fourth volume in their *London Studies in South Asia* series. It has remained the standard work in the field to this day.

Since breaking new ground with his thesis Professor Ahmed has pursued his study of Dhaka city, exploring the responses to western ideas on education, medicine and civic organization and with several chambers of commerce the commercial history of his country.

After his return from the UK and joining the Dhaka University as Assistant Professor he became more involved in research works particularly with the Asiatic Society, the leading intellectual, academic and research body of Bangladesh. His first venture with the Asiatic Society was to make an effort to turn *Urban History* a more multi-disciplinary field. He thus organised the scholars from different disciplines from all over the world to make a multidisciplinary study of the capital city of Dhaka already in the process of becoming a mega city to present its past, existing state and its future.

With the financial assistance from the Ford Foundation he was able, under the auspices of the Asiatic Society, to hold an International Seminar on Dhaka with scholars from around the globe and published an anthology with the contributions of several leading scholars under the title *Dhaka Past Present Future* in 1990. This anthology became instantly a classic work and has so far gone several editions consulted by scholars all over the world who are interested in urban history especially of Dhaka.

However, Professor Ahmed soon realised that in order to understand the faster growth of urban centers in South Asia it is desirable that rural and regional history should be studied anew. Thus soon with the collaboration of the Bangladesh History Association of which he became the General Secretary and later its President, and with the assistance of local Sponsors and Norwegian Government Development Agency, he published two outstanding regional and local history of Bangladesh on *Dinajpur* and *Sylhet* , with the collaboration and help from scholars all over the world in the 1990s. The latter work Sylhet became instantly famous particularly in the United Kingdom where virtually all the migrants from Bangladesh are from Sylhet . The book is not only read and studied by the migrant Sylhetis and their descendants but by the British public and most importantly by the honourable members of the British Parliament in connection with issues of migrant communities of the United Kingdom. The tradition which Professor Ahmed thus had set for local and regional history study is still being followed by the Bangladesh History Association and other bodies.

Behind these urban and local history studies stand a third major achievement, the planning and organising of the National Library and the National Archives of Bangladesh of which he was the Director for ten years from 1997 to 2007. (The Government of Pakistan in 1962 created a National Library in Karachi leaving Bangladesh with no more than a 'Books and Newspaper Collection Branch ". Likewise the National Archives of Pakistan was established in Karachi in1951 under the Directorate of Archives and Libraries, which had no branch whatsoever in East Pakistan till the National Archives was established in independent Bangladesh in 1972))

However, Professor Ahmed's passion for preserving historical documents has never left him to live in peace. Besides his contribution as the Head of the Bangladesh National Archives, Professor Ahmed worked tirelessly to develop awareness about the importance of preserving records and developing archives as the existing scenario in general throughout South Asia is deplorable . This led him to establish with likeminded enthusiasts a society called *Bangladesh Archives and Records Management Society* in short BARMS of which he is now the President.

The Society besides working as a pressure group to see that the public records are well kept and sent to the National Archives on a regular basis also worked tirelessly to increase public awareness about the importance of archives by holding seminars, workshops, training programmes and even working in the rural areas where there are depositories of records like in old educational institutions and of course public offices since the days of British rule and even earlier. In this particular instance BARMS work closely with the archivists and archives of Europe especially of the Netherlands.

When in 1997 Professor Ahmed was put in charge of the National Library and Archive he could draw upon his acquaintance with the Indian Institute and Bodleian at Oxford, the India Office Library and British Library and the holdings of SOAS. But Professor Ahmed was also equipped in an unexpected way. For some years after 1978 he had worked for Coopers and

Lybrand, in London, receiving a thorough training in the statistical manipulation of complex facts and an understanding of business methods and attitudes. Indeed, he was being prepared for middle management when he felt impelled to return to Dhaka and to teaching, joining also in the collection of government records for the infant National Archives.

I have not used these archives myself but have heard nothing but praise for them, both the design of the building that houses them – opened in 2006 – and the arrangement of the records themselves. The modernising of the administrative offices which support them benefitted particularly from Professor Ahmed's business experience. To have cajoled and manipulated an impoverished government into providing funds and materials to build and equip the new archives and to have driven departments to forward their files with some regularity are major feats. Professor Ahmed's comment "The National Archives today are as I created them" – if bold seems justified.

Professor Ahmed had an unusually long and varied experience of university and business life in Britain – one shared with his wife who herself had taken an MA and would work in the City for Hong Kong Shanghai Banking Corporation and later in Swedish Embassy in Bangladesh. They became regular commuters between Cheam and the City, both very much at ease in English society. However, they remained good Bengalis too, active in the South London Bangladesh Welfare Association of which Professor Ahmed became General Secretary, very much as he had done as a student at Oxford. With the Welfare Association, however, he organised Bengali and music classes, sports and lectures (which I much enjoyed), and acted as their spokesman with the Local Council on health and welfare issues.

Finally, for anyone in London, staff or student, who is interested in the history of Bengal/Bangladesh there can currently be no-one better informed about what records, formal and informal, are available and where to find them than Professor Ahmed. To his ten years at the Directorate of Libraries and Archives must be added his close involvement with the Bangladesh Historical Society as also with the Asiatic Society of Bangladesh, which in its refurbished building has created an impressive library and meeting place. His links with both have been active, as is his interest in the urban archaeology of Dhaka. Nor has he been content to enjoy a well-deserved retirement, instead he has played an active role as Chairman of the Department of History and Philosophy in the new, prestigious North South private University in Dhaka. And it's no wonder that soon he seized the opportunity of writing the institutional history of the first Private University of the country in collaboration with his colleagues under the title *Road to Excellence- the History of North South University* which will go down as the permanent historical document of educational development of Bangladesh. Just his works on institutional history of *Dhaka College* (*1841–1921*) and *Mitford Hospital and Dhaka Medical School (1858–1947*) have lighted the modernisation of Bangladesh through British rule and culture.

It would be absolutely unfair and incomplete if I fail to mention the monumental works that he along with his colleagues at the Asiatic Society and abroad have produced recently while celebrating the **400 Years of Capital Dhaka.** As many as twenty –two (22) volumes of books on multi -dimensional aspects of Dhaka's history and heritage have been produced and published under his leadership many of these have already been reprinted.

Personally I have met few guides to a city more involved and involving than he. His remark on return from Dhaka to London in 1976, that he had explored "many parts of the city previously unknown to me but now given a wholly new interest by my research" is typical of the man. But I believe that is equally true of Professor Ahmed as an historian.

In short both as an historian and as an activist of education, culture and heritage, Professor Ahmed has established an unique place for himself both among his peers and the public at large both at home and abroad.

John Harrison, 2017

LONDON STUDIES ON SOUTH ASIA NO. 4

DACCA

A Study in Urban History and Development

SHARIF UDDIN AHMED

CURZON PRESS
THE RIVERDALE COMPANY

First published 1986 in the United Kingdom by
Curzon Press Ltd., 42 Gray's Inn Road, London WCl
ISBN 0 7007 0180 X

First published 1986 in the United States of America by
The Riverdale Company, 5506 Kenilworth Avenue, Riverdale, MD 20737
ISBN 0 913215 14 7

British Library Cataloguing in Publication Data
Ahmed, Sharif Uddin
Dacca: a study in urban history and development
(London Studies on South Asia, ISSN 0142-601X; No. 4)
1. Dacca (Bangladesh) — Social conditions
I. Title II. Series
954.9'22 HS590.6.03
ISBN 0 7007 0180 X

Printed in Hungary

CONTENTS

ILLUSTRATIONS

between pp. 124 and 125

MAPS

ABBREVIATIONS

ARDM	Administration Report of the Dacca Municipality
BAR	Report on the Administration of Bengal or Bengal Administration Report
BCJC	Bengal Criminal Judicial Consultations
BEC	Bengal Educational Consultations
BJP	Bengal Judicial Proceedings
BOCSOP	Board of Customs, Salt and Opium Proceedings
BPP	Bengal Past and Present
BRP	Bengal Revenue Proceedings
BT	The Bengal Times
Coll.	Collection of Records of the Dacca Municipality
Div. Comm.	Divisional Commissioner
DMRR	Dacca Municipality Record Room
DP	Dhaka Prokash
DPI	Director of Public Instruction
DPI'S Report	Report of the Department, and Director of Public Instruction, Lower Bengal
GCPI	General Committee of Public Instruction
GCPI'S Report	Report of the General Committee of Public Instruction
GB	Government of Bengal
GI	Government of India
HMS	Home Miscellaneous Series
Municipal Proc.	Proceedings of the Commissioners of the Dacca Municipality
NAI	National Archives of India
Report	Annual Report of the Municipal Committee
RNN	Report of Native Newspapers
RSC	Annual Report of the Sanitary Commissioner of the Lower Provinces of Bengal

PREFACE

Dacca, like many other cities in the Indian subcontinent, is steeped in history. It was a Mughal metropolis before it passed into British hands. The transition was painful, and there was much economic and social decay before the dawn of renewal set in.

Politically, socially and culturally, Dacca grew stronger and more vibrant as the nineteenth century wore on. Its development reflected the gradual ascendency of Indian nationalism with its numerous cross-currents of reform and religious revivalism. But Dacca is as indelibly Bengali as, say, Lucknow or Delhi are Hindustani. That Bengali identity has remained unshaken through the severest trials and tribulations and nothing is likely to change it now.

Dacca's old landmarks are fast disappearing; new ones are taking their place. Buildings and monuments that have gone are, however, stepping stones to the past. Thanks to historical reconstruction they live on in the popular imagination and make a people aware of their deepest roots. The present may be viewed as a sort of fulcrum between the past and an evolving future. I hope this study by lighting up some of the successes and failures of Dacca's past will contribute constructively to the debate on its possible future.

I have used in this book the old spelling of Dacca for obvious historical reasons instead of that (Dhaka) adopted recently.

The book owes much to the help and encouragement of Mr J. B. Harrison, my supervisor at the School of Oriental and African Studies, London. I am indebted, too, to Dr Peter Robb, also of the School, and to my friend, Dr Premen Addy, for reading earlier versions of the manuscript and making valuable comments and suggestions. Thanks are due to Dr David Taylor of SOAS for helping me get it ready for the press.

I wish to express my appreciation to the authorities and staff of the British Library, the India Office Library and Records, London, the Baptist Mission Libary and Archives, London, the National Archives in New Delhi, the West Bengal State Archives and the National Libary in Calcutta, the Bangladesh Secretariat Libary in Dacca and the Record Department of the Dacca Municipality, for permission to consult their books and papers and extending to me every facility in my work.

Miss C. Da Silva, who typed the manuscript in record time, put me especially in her debt, and I am also grateful to Miss E. Johnson, cartographer at the School of Oriental and African Studies, for providing the maps. I should say a word about friends and colleagues for being generous with their time and discussing almost every aspect of the subject with me. The responsibility for the final product, however, rests solely on my shoulders.

My last acknowledgement is to my wife, without whose cheerfulness and patience this work might never have been completed. My debt to her is more than any words of mine can express.

NINETEENTH-CENTURY DACCA: SOME VIEWS

'The most salient feature in the history of modern Decca [Dacca] is its rise into prominence, as the metropolis of a new province [of Eastern Bengal and Assam in 1905] after decades of comparative oblivion.' (Ghulam Ambia Khan, 'Dacca, Past and Present', *East and West*, Vol. X, No. 111, Part I (Bombay 1911), p. 58).

'Why should not Dacca, the capital of Eastern Bengal, have its Museum?... Argument is not needed to give weight to this matter; city and Museum are kindred and associate names, and reflect lustre the one upon the other. Dacca is the metropolis of the Province, the seat of energetic thought, the centre of action; it has its college, its press, its bank, and numerous well-endowed public institutions and charities.' (*The Dacca News*, 1 November 1856).

'By the nineteenth century its population had declined to 69,000. For a century and a half it has been called the city of the great sleep. Travellers have spoken of it as a city of ruins... Only once between the departure of the Viceroy's court and the establishment of Pakistan has it shown signs of awakening. That was in 1905 when for a brief span of seven years it was reinstated as the capital of a new province of Eastern Bengal and Assam... Generally speaking, however, the nineteenth century was the most peaceful that Bengal had known. But for Dacca it was the peace of death.' (G. Ruddock, 'Capital of East Pakistan', *Pakistan Quarterly*, Vol. VII (1957), pp. 50, 56.)

'Punctually at half past four [on 8 August 1874]... the Viceroy [Lord Northbrook] landed [at the Sadar Ghat], the left-wing of the 16th Native Infantry, under the command of Major Cubit, V.C., forming the guard of honour, and the National Anthem being played by Khawja Ahsanoolah's band. He was received and conducted to the reception tent by Mr F. C. Cockerell, Commissioner of Dacca. Here were gathered the leading members of the European and Native Community to present His Excellency with an address of welcome from the citizens. Conspicuous among [them] were Khwaja Abdool Ghunny, C.S.I.,... [and] Rajah of Sooshung... [The] address of welcome was read... by Mr Rampini, the Secretary to the Reception Committee. It pointed to Dacca as having been, in days gone by, the seat of independent government under the Muhammedan Rulers, and as now rightly claiming to be the educational, intellectual, and commercial capital of eastern Bengal.' (Report by a Special Correspondent, *The Pioneer*, 13 August 1874, p. 3).

INTRODUCTION

It was a series of seminars on the 'The city in South Asia' at the School of Oriental and African Studies in London that prompted me to specialize in urban history. One of the prime objectives of that seminar was to attract more scholars to this field, for South Asian urban history had till recently been a relatively neglected subject. Kenneth L. Gillion in his pioneering work on the city of Ahmedabad made the apposite observation that 'those who wish to read about Indian cities are more likely to look to the works of geographers and sociologists than to those of historians'.[1] Howard Spodek in a recent article on 'Studying The History of Urbanisation in India' makes a similar remark, though he finds it gratifying that more and more scholars are now working in this field.[2]

As in Europe and America, towns and cities in the Indian subcontinent have played and are playing a significant role in the political, military, economic, social and cultural history of their region, although not necessary in exactly the same way.

Evaluating the importance of cities in world history Rodney W. Jones has observed, 'Cities have traditionally been centres of civilization and power, the abodes of gods and men. Their glories inspired awe and endowed their chieftains with command. They were the vehicles of recorded history, the repositories of learning and conservators of law and custom.' He went on, 'Cities have nurtured most of man's creations, social and technical, and witnessed their elaboration on ambitious scales. Cities have sustained variety and specialty by promoting intramural harmony, and yet they have also served as launching pads for imperial conquest and territorial domination.'[3]

Dacca, the object of my own study, is a city with which I have long personal association, and which today is the capital of a free and independent country.

Its late eighteenth and early nineteenth century decline has attracted considerable attention. Early nationalist writers in India and Marxist historians, including Karl Marx himself, have cited this decline as an example of the destructiveness of Western capilism on India's social and economic life. R. Palme Dutt wrote,

The old populous manufacturing towns, Dacca, Murshidabad (which Clive had described in 1759 to be as extensive, populous, and rich as the city of London), Surat and the like were in a few years rendered desolate under 'the pax Britannica' with a completeness which no ravages of the most destructive war or foreign conquest could have accomplished.[4]

The fact of Dacca's decline can scarcely be disputed, nor that the collapse of its cotton manufactures was due principally to the introduction of machine-made textiles from Great Britain. In 1836, the Board of Customs, Salt and Opium was found pleading for the abolition of town and transit duties in Dacca in order to reduce the economic pressure under which it was sinking:

Dacca is notoriously an impoverished and declining city, and its decline may be mainly traced to that vast increase in the import of British piece-goods which must have greatly promoted the prosperity of the Cotton Manufacturing duties (*sic.* industries) in Great Britain. Neither, of course, do we question the advantages of that importation to this country at large, but still it is beyond a doubt that Dacca and its neighbourhood have suffered from it to a very deplorable extent, and therefore more peculiarly entitled to consideration from a British Government.[5]

It may well be questioned whether this industrial and commercial intrusion from abroad was the sole cause of Dacca's decline, but even a cursory perusal of Dr James Taylor's *A Sketch of the Topography and Statistics of Dacca*, published in 1840, will show how steep was its decline.

What particularly intrigued me, however, when reading Taylor's perceptive and sympathetic account was that he seemed to hold out so little hope for the blighted city. Yet it did revive and grow, awakening to a new life well before the dramatic years of 1905–11. As early as 1874 *The Pioneer*, the leading Allahabad daily, recorded an address of welcome presented by a Reception Committee to the Viceroy Lord Northbrook when he visited the city, it being claimed that not only did Dacca have a glorious past, but that it was also currently 'the educational, intellectual and commercial capital of Eastern Bengal'.[6] Even discounting the euphoria created by this first ever visit of a British Viceroy, I found it difficult to reconcile such a claim—or the fact revealed by the 1881 census that Dacca was then the third most populous city in Eastern India after Calcutta and Patna[7]—with the usual picture of a decaying and stagnant metropolis.[8] When contemporary sources were examined there seemed little doubt that by the 1860s or 1870s the city had emerged from its darkest shadows and was again an important urban centre. The main aim of this book, which has grown out of my doctoral thesis, is to throw fresh light on this vital phase in Dacca's history, to examine the stages and the chief factors responsible for its revival and to assess the true significance of this historical process.

When the British began seriously to tackle urban problems in the mid-nineteenth century they did so with mid-Victorian notions and ideas, and designed their remedies accordingly. This foreign transplant on a country and people so vastly different often led to conflict and tension. Nevertheless, these measures laid the foundations of a new urban order and started a new process of modernization in the subcontinent. In the second half of this book I have examined the living conditions of Dacca's people, the various urban problems that surfaced during the last century, the manner in which these were faced by government and citizenry alike, and the eventual emergence of an urban administration unique in the history of that area.

I found it possible quite early on in my research to decide upon the date at which this study could be conveniently closed without arbitrarily distorting the development of events. The year chosen was 1885, when the newly-constructed Dacca and Mymensingh State Railway began to operate between Narayanganj, Dacca and Mymensingh; the year also when Dacca became a self-governing municipality with an elected chairman and a majority of elected municipal commissioners. This railway development had opened up a more expeditious link between Dacca and the principal parts of its hinterland; a high point in the history of the city's commercial revival. Indeed, so confident were the British officials of a bright future for Dacca after the opening of this new rail link that even as early as 1885 they were prophesying that the city would become the official capital of a new province comprising East Bengal and Assam.[9] The change in status of the municipality from subordination to the Magistrate-Collectors to independence and self-government was in its own way scarcely less momentous. Henceforth the economic and social progress of the city became the responsibility of the city fathers. To carry the study of the history of the city, economic and administrative, beyond 1885 would obviously have meant moving into completely new territory.

The choice of a starting date was less easy to determine, but the existence of Taylor's work, written some time about 1840, seemed an appropriate point. Moreover, certain developments at about that date did put the city on the road to renewed activity; a new era was beginning with 1840 as the watershed.

The themes of this study have been explored almost entirely from original contemporary sources. There are a number of secondary works on Dacca already in existence, and these have been drawn upon whenever useful. Most of them, however, deal with the antiquities of the city, its architectural remains and its Mughal past. Those which do treat of the British period—with particular attention of course to the years 1905–11—are rarely based on any considerable original research, often repeat erroneous or stereotyped judgements, and enter scarcely at all into the details of the city's administration. An extract from Grenfell Ruddock's account of Dacca in *Towns and Villages of Pakistan—A Study*, will illustrate how insecurely based many such accounts are:

> Further improvements were made to the city in 1829, when Mr Walters [the District Magistrate] widened a number of streets, but what was perhaps the most notable event in this period occurred the following year when the Dacca Committee was formed, with Walters as Chairman, thus laying the foundations of what was later to become the Dacca Municipality ... In 1835, the Khas lands in Wari [were] let out and within five years, housed a substantial colony of government officials.[10]

This small extract contains many factual errors. For instance, Ruddock writes that the Dacca Committee was established in 1830. In fact no such committee was formed in that year to deal with the municipal problems of the city. Several committees were, however, formed in Dacca during the early nineteenth century to deal with the urban problems of the city—sanitation, health, communications for example. The last of these—the Committee for the Improvement of the City of Dacca—was founded in 1823. This committee lasted several years and it carried out many important works. It was, however, dissolved in 1829. Thereafter, no other committee was established in Dacca until 1840, when the Municipal Committee was formed.[11] Ruddock's further statement about the development of a new residential area at Wari in the period 1835–40 is also apparently at variance with the facts. This was a period of serious depopulation when properties were changing hands at very low prices and tenants were hard to come by. F. D. Ascoli, the Settlement Officer of Dacca, recorded that by 1837 the value of landed property and houses within the city had greatly depreciated and that owners were anxious to dispose of them, as exemplified in the latter instance by the frequent property sales in the town during the early nineteenth century.[12] In such circumstances, the growth of a new residential area seems rather odd, and indeed admits of no reasonable interpretation. My searches through the contemporary revenue records and municipal files solved the riddle, however. A residential area was indeed developed at Wari during the ninteenth century but in the 1880s, not the 1830s, a much more likely event in view of the rapidly improving situation of Dacca at that later period. Even the more scholarly work of A. H. Dani, *Dacca—A Record of its Changing Fortunes*, is not without slips and errors, as witness the following:

> From 1830 to 1850, Dacca felt the impact of new changes. This was the period which saw the growth of civil institutions like the Dacca Municipality, the Dacca District Board, and also the foundation of [the] Government School and College in Dacca. All these were due to the efforts of four officials—Walters, Taylor, Grant and Skinner.

That the dating of these events is incorrect is clear even from subsequent paragraphs in the same book,[13] but more disturbing is the narrowness of interpretation which would attribute the development of major social and political institutions to the work of four particular men, gifted though each was in his own way. The establishment of the Dacca Municipality was not a purely local event but part of a much wider post-mutiny policy of devolution, given shape by experience in the government of Calcutta and beyond that by the process of local government reform in Britain. In the same way the development of educational institutions in Dacca, if assisted at their birth by individual officials, owed their conception to the wider policies of government and to the geographical pull of Dacca on those in the city and all Eastern Bengal who sought an English education. I have attempted to set individuals and local events in the wider context of government administrative, social and educational policies and of the economic growth fostered by new developments in international trade and commerce, affected as these were by fierce competition from Calcutta, a mere 187 miles away.

I believe that the period under review is of great significance in the history of Dacca. It is not, however, one which readily lends itself to the fashionable study of the rise of new élites and changes in the class structure or of group rivalries and city politics. Indeed, to borrow the words of Gillion, this book 'is not intended to be a contribution to urban theory. It draws to some extent on work in the other social sciences... and the pertinence of general theoretical concepts is kept in mind (if not always explicitly discussed)'.[14] For in the absence of reliable secondary works on nineteenth-century Dacca, it has seemed to me that the first priority should be to establish in detail what happened to the city in this formative period by a thorough investigation of the original records rather than to proceed to theory and analysis of any complexity.

The materials bearing upon the history of Dacca are in fact very voluminous, and because there was no single department concerned with local government they are scattered over many departmental records. Besides those available in Great Britain, I have also made use of the records of the West Bengal State Archives and the National Archives of India, and of the records to be found, often only roughly arranged and classified, in the archives of the central government of Bangladesh and in the record room of the Bangladesh Secretariat. In Dacca itself I consulted the records of the Magistrate-Collector and of the Municipality, together with the newspaper and journal holdings of the University of Dacca (the most important being the almost complete run from 1863 onwards of the *Dhaka Prokash*, the first vernacular newspaper of Dacca), and of the Asiatic Society of Bangladesh; I also consulted the holdings of the Calcutta National Library—all of these during overseas study leave in 1975–6, when I also interviewed a number of older Dacca residents and familiarized myself with many parts of the city previously unknown to me but now given a wholly new interest by the progress of my research. A complete list of all the unpublished and published sources has been given in the bibliography. A location is also given for some reports, books and journals which are not generally available.

The research is thus as complete as I could make it, but even so there are important gaps in the sources, and some vital records are missing. There is little statistical data on trade and production particularly for the latter half of the nineteenth century. Detailed statistical figures for the trade and commerce of the city—its exports and imports—are available only from 1876–7, but regrettably these statistical data soon become fragmentary, only showing the figures for the trade of Dacca with Calcutta and Chittagong. I was unable to discover any nineteenth-century records of the Commissioner of the Dacca Division on the life and administration of the city of Dacca. The extensive correspondence between the Commissioner and the city authorities and numerous reports regularly submitted to the Commissioner by the city authorities, had they been found, would have been extremely useful for the present study, but none seem to survive. Likewise, the bulk of the nineteenth-century records of the Magistrate-Collector and Judge of the city of Dacca has not survived. There are even important gaps in the records of the Dacca Municipality. For example, those which could have given the fullest account of Dacca's economic growth, of the increase of its population, and its wealth and housing, namely the tax records and the assessment books of the Municipality, and the papers of the 1871–2, 1881 and 1891 censuses, were destroyed early this century together with the voters' lists of the earlier period. Information about the business activities of the city's influential bankers and financiers is also scanty because of a similar destruction of the relevant files of the Government of Bengal containing statistical materials on trade, commerce and taxation.

The term 'city' throughout this work has been applied in a non-technical sense. It is applied because all the contemporary sources use the term and because Dacca possessed the population and the urban qualities which made it appropriate. Where Indian terms and titles have been used a reference will be found in the glossary. The transliteration of such terms and of place and personal names has been modernized.

NOTES TO INTRODUCTION

1 Kenneth L. Gillion, *Ahmedabad—A Study in Indian Urban* History, 1.
2 Howard Spodek, in *Journal of Urban History*, Vol. 6 No. 3, May 1980, 251–2.
3 Rodney W. Jones, *Urban Politics in India—Area, Power and Policy in a Penetrated System*, 3.
4 R. Palme Dutt, *India Today*, 102.
5 Board to Government of Bengal, 15 Mar. 1836, Board of Revenue (Miscellaneous) Proceedings, Customs, Range CVIII, Vol. 2, 18. Mar. 1836, No. 30.
6 *The Pioneer*, 13 Aug. 1874, 3.
7 *Report on the Administration of Bengal or Bengal Administration Report* for for 1882–3, 102.
8 See the extracts quoted in the opening pages of this book.
9 See the speeches of the Commissioner of Dacca and others at the opening ceremony of Dacca-Mymensingh State Railway on 3 Jan. 1885, *The Bengal Times*, 7 Jan. 1885; see also chapter IV.
10 Grenfell Ruddock, *Towns and Villages of Pakistan—A Study*, 87–8.
11 For a detailed account of these committees and their activities, see my article 'Urban Problems and Government Policies: A Case Study of the city of Dacca, 1810–1830', in K. Ballhatchet and J. Harrison (eds.), *The City In South Asia*, 129–65.
12 F. D. Ascoli, *Final Report of the Survey and Settlement Operations in the District of Dacca, 1910–1917*, see appendix XII, p. XXXVII.
13 Ahmad Hasan Dani, *Dacca—A Record of its Changing Fortunes*, 116.
14 Gillion, *Ahmedabad*, 1. In this connection the following works have been consulted: H. J. Dyos, *The Study of Urban History;* R. L. Park (ed.), *Urban Bengal;* R. E. Park, E. W. Burgess and R. D. Mackenzie, *The City;* G. Sjoberg, *The Pre-Industrial Society;* R. Turner (ed.), *India's Urban Future;* L. Wirth, *On Cities and Social Life—Selected Papers*.

CHAPTER I

DACCA: THE HISTORICAL SETTING

The city of Dacca, on the northern bank of the river Buriganga, lies at the heart of the region which now constitutes the People's Republic of Bangladesh and which in the British period was commonly known as East or Eastern Bengal. More technically, in the late nineteenth century, it might have been described as the dominant urban centre of the two divisions of East Bengal—Dacca and Chittagong—an area of nearly 40,000 square miles, with a population in 1872 of about 14 million.[1]

This region, Eastern Bengal, is a great alluvial and deltaic plain[2] and includes the lower reaches of the Ganges and Brahmaputra and their tributaries, most notably the Surma, Sitalakhya and Barak which drain the Khasi and Jaintia hills and the ranges dividing Bangladesh from Burma. These rivers provide an annual enrichment of silt to a delta still growing, so that Eastern Bengal is extremely fertile. The Mughals had described the province as a 'hell full of bread'; once the wars and revolutions of the eighteenth century had ended and cultivation had been resumed and extended, the region again came to be called 'the granary of Bengal'.[3]

Even during the early nineteenth century Eastern Bengal was a highly-populated area, and although no accurate figures for the earlier periods are available, from 1872 the decennial censuses show it to have been one of the most densely populated areas of the world. Thus the census of 1881 returned the density as being 756 per square mile in Dacca district; in Mymensingh 485; in Faridpur 719; in Bakerganj 520; in Chittagong 441; in Noakhali 500; and in Tippera 609.[4]

The great rivers, the Ganges and the Brahmaputra, which with their tributaries so enrich East Bengal, also provide admirable cross-country communications. Even when roads were few, and railways undreamed of, James Rennell, busy surveying the rivers in 1765, could observe,

The Kingdom of Bengall, particularly the Eastern part, is naturally the most convenient for trade within itself of any country in the world; for the rivers divide into such a number of Branches that the people have the convenience of water carriage to and from any principal place.[5]

Situated in the centre of East Bengal, Dacca was able to command all these great water routes. Through the Buriganga and the Dhaleswari, to which the former is a loop, Dacca is connected by permanently navigable waterways with the Padma, the Brahmaputra and the Meghna rivers and thus with all the neighbouring districts. The Buriganga, some twenty-six miles in length, rejoins the Dhaleswari near Narayanganj, twin city and in some sense port of Dacca.

Dacca city was also comparatively well placed for landward communications being on the southern edge of an old alluvial terrace. Here it was 'considerably above the highest level of the surrounding rivers in ordinary seasons of inundation',[6] on a laterite plateau which broadens out northwards towards Mymensingh. South-east of this plateau across the Buriganga to the Dhaleswari, and eastwards from the Sitalakhya to the Meghna, are two much lower tracts of alluvial soil which are deeply inundated almost half the year but agriculturally are very productive.

Dacca city not only stood upon the Buriganga but was itself criss-crossed by minor rivers and creeks, the most notable of which was the Dulai. Although by the nineteenth century the Dulai, better known as the Dulai *khal* or canal, was silting up, it had given, and in the rains still gave, the city an excellent network of internal waterways of great strategic and commercial importance. It was this geographical location of Dacca, upon the last bluff of higher ground in a low-lying region, and its commanding position on the water-routes of the country as a whole, which in 1610 moved Islam Khan, the Mughal Subahdar or governor of Bengal, to transfer his capital there from Rajmahal.[7]

This move was made in order to intensify the campaign against the independent and rebellious Afghan chiefs, Hindu princelings and *zamindars* of lower Bengal and so to establish Mughal hegemony in the area.[8] Once that hegemony was established, Dacca became a provincial capital. It would also, later in the century, become the base from which river defence against Portuguese and Magh raids was organized and the Mughal advances north into

Cooch Behar and Assam, and south-east to Chittagong and Arakan, were launched.

As an administrative and military headquarters Dacca expanded rapidly, a whole Mughal town growing round the old fort—now the Central Jail site. At the same time it also grew into a great commercial centre largely through its establishment as an inland port or *shah bandar*.[9] This imperial port was designed to control the trade and commerce of the eastern part of Bengal, inland custom duties being collected and *rawanahs* or permits issued to the merchants and traders by the officials of the bandar. Dacca thus became the chief centre of trade and commerce in the area, handling the rich harvests of Eastern Bengal, collecting manufactures, especially cotton-goods, for export to the Ganges Valley and also overseas, and acting as distributor for the raw materials and imports flowing in. Foreign and Indian merchants, traders and bankers—Europeans, Armenians, Mughals, Pathans, Turanis, Marwaris and other up-country Hindus—came to Dacca to do business. The organized European Companies, the English, French and Dutch, also established their factories in the city.

Dacca also became a large manufacturing centre. As the city grew, artisans, craftsmen and manufacturers came to settle there, buying raw materials and selling finished goods to the local people as well as to merchant-exporters. The Mughal rulers encouraged these people by granting them rent-free lands for habitation.[10] The manufacture of gold, silver, brass, wood and shell-work flourished, but the production of cotton-goods outshone all others. Eastern Bengal had long been famous for the manufacture of cotton and silk goods and the weavers of the area were renowned for their skill in producing the fine and delicate cotton cloth generally known as muslin.[11] With its establishment as the capital Dacca itself became a great centre of textile manufacture, and the production of muslins flowered under the patronage of the Mughal rulers.[12] A state *karkhana* or factory was established in the city where weavers were employed to produce the finest varieties of muslins for the imperial courts at Delhi and Dacca. The textile industry, thus encouraged, became the prime industry of Dacca and one of the chief sources of its wealth and prosperity, catering for markets as widely separated as Southeast Asia and Europe. Dacca's merchants and financiers also contributed greatly to the growth of cotton manufactures throughout East Bengal, advancing money to the thousands of weavers and embroiderers in the neighbouring districts. The visiting Portuguese monk Sebastian Manrique noted,

> The finest and richest muslins are produced in this country, from fifty to sixty yards long and seven to eight hand-breadths wide, with borders of gold and silver of coloured silks. So fine, indeed, are these muslins that merchants place them in hollow bambus, about two spans long, and thus secured, carry them throughout Corazane, Persia, Turkey and many other countries.[13]

By the seventeenth century Dacca was queen of the cities of Eastern India. As Manrique observed in 1640,

> This is the chief city in Bengala and the seat of the principal Nababo or Viceroy, appointed by the Emperor, who bestowed this viceroyalty, on several occasions, on one of his sons. It stands in a wide and beautiful plain on the banks of the famous and here fructifying Ganges river, besides which the City stretches for over a league and a half.
>
> Many strange nations resort to this City on account of its vast trade and commerce in great variety of commodities, which are produced in profusion in the rich and fertile lands of this region. These have raised the City to an eminence of wealth which is actually stupefying especially when one sees and considers the large quantities of money which lie principally in the houses of the Cataris [Khatris], in such quantity indeed that, being difficult to count, it used commonly to be weighed. I was informed also, that the indigenous population of this Gangetic emporium and its suburbs, exceeded two hundred thousand irrespective of visitors who come on mercantile business in order to take advantage of the great facilities offered by the place; others followers of Mars, attracted by the high minas that is monthly pay and allowances which are given on those frontiers. Nor was one less astounded at the great profusion to be found there of every kind of useful article and every species of food which a human being could desire, especially in its numerous Bazars or markets ... The vast pecuniary advantages derived by the Emperors and Mogol Rulers from this city are incredible. I will, therefore, leave it there, merely stating what I have had it told me as an indisputable fact, that from the Betel or Indian leaf alone they received in dues four thousand rupees a day, that is two thousand pesos in our money.[14]

At its Mughal peak Dacca city, with its suburbs, may have had a population of some 900,000.[15] The city proper stretched seven to ten miles along the Buriganga and up to two and a half miles inland. The suburbs extended from the Buriganga to the Tongi Bridges, fifteen miles to the north, and from Mirpur-Jafarabad on the west some ten miles east to Postogola.[16]

In 1715–16, however, the capital of the Bengal *subah* or province was shifted to Murshidabad by the newly-appointed Subahdar, Nawab Murshid Quli Khan. In consequence, Decca lost its provincial status, and its further growth and development was checked. Dacca did, however, remain the headquarters of administration for the Dacca *niabat* or sub-province,[17] headed by the *naib-nazim* or deputy governor, the jurisdiction of which extended over half the area of present-day Bangladesh. The city also remained the headquarters of the Mughal army and navy in Eastern Bengal, and it was from here that the Mughal general Mir Habib, under the deputy governorship of Mirza Lutfullah (Murshid Quli Khan II), launched his campaign in 1728 for the conquest of Tippera. After its conquest, Tippera also came under the jurisdiction of the Dacca niabat under the name of Chakla Raushanabad. Moreover, Dacca's commerce and manufactures increased by leaps and bounds, as the European trading companies gave a new dimension to the export trade in textiles. No major decline of the city other than a political one occurred therefore after 1716,[18] though undoubtedly with the departure of some of the provincial administrative establishments and a large part of the army, the city lost a part of its population.

In 1757, however, the British gained military control of Bengal and in 1765 took over the civil administration of the country. Henceforth both Dacca and Murshidabad declined rapidly. Political, military and administrative power shifted to Calcutta, the rising capital of the province, around which trade and commerce now came increasingly to gravitate.[19]

Soon after its assumption in 1772 of the *diwani* or civil administration of Bengal the East India Company began to reorganize the governmental structure. As a result, Dacca gradually lost many of its administrative functions and with these its revenue, police and judicial staff. The *nawara* or Mughal naval establishment at Dacca had already been abolished in 1768–9 and part of the land allotted for its maintenance resumed.[20] Then from 1787, several smaller districts were successively carved out of the old Dacca niabat. By 1828 the city had been reduced to a mere district headquarters, though retaining its position as a provincial Court of Circuit and Appeal. At the same time the importance of Dacca as a centre of cotton textile manufacture and trade had also sharply declined, a consequence both of shrinking Mughal markets and also, in the nineteenth century, of the competition of machine-made cottons from Britain.

In 1765 James Rennell reported that Dacca had an estimated population of 450,000 and stretched nearly four miles along the river and two and a half miles deep.[21] By 1801 the population of the city, including the suburbs, had declined to an estimated 200,000 while the limits of the city proper had shrunk to three and a half miles by one and a quarter.[22] The population of the city continued to fall sharply during the 1810s and 1820s with the closure of the English factory in 1817, so that a census of the city and suburbs carried out in 1838 showed only 68,610 inhabitants. By 1840 this decline had reached its nadir and most of the former Mughal city had either been deserted or had fallen victim to the encroaching jungle.[23]

Dacca society on the eve of our period defies precise definition owing to a dearth of adequate historical documentation. The city, however, could still be described as pre-eminently Islamic as in the Mughal days; a majority of the population was Muslim, and Urdu and Persian were the languages spoken and cultivated by the upper classes of society.[24] Indeed the dominant spoken language of the city was not Bengali but Hindustani—that mixture of Hindi, Urdu, Persian and Arabic which became a lingua franca in many Indian cities under Mughal rule. Mughal etiquette, dress and tastes in food set the social tone of urban life. At the apex of the society were the aristocratic Muslims—mostly Shias—represented above all by the Nawab's family. But many of the Shia families had left the city at the turn of the century, when they lost their official positions together with their *jagirs* or assigned lands, for other Shia-dominated cities such as Lucknow or Murshidabad where they had relatives.[25] This Shia migration continued throughout the early nineteenth century. With the death in 1843 of the last Nawab of Dacca, Nawab Ghaziuddin Haider, the Shia dominance of Dacca came to an end. The surviving Shias were descendants of old Nawabi administrators, courtiers, scholars, zamindars, and merchants who lived off the family inheritance and whose life-style generally failed to adjust itself to the changes of the time.[26]

Most Dacca Muslims were Sunnis, usually natives of the region, though there were a few of foreign origin like the Kashmiris. The Sunnis comprised the bulk of the service community, the Muslim artisans, the shopkeepers and the labourers living in various parts of the city but particularly in the western and the north-western areas.

Table 1 (see p. 16) provides a broad breakdown of the Muslims of Dacca by occupation based on a census taken in 1830.

It was the Sunnis who from the early nineteenth century gradually came to dominate the Muslim community in Dacca, and one of them, Khwaja Alimullah, a Kashmiri trader turned zamindar, became one of Dacca's most wealthy and influential citizens in the 1830s. In 1843, when Nawab Ghaziuddin Haider died, he took over the responsibility for the upkeep of the Husaini Dalan, the shrine built in memory of Imam Husain, and also agreed to bear the expenses connected with the Muharram festival hitherto paid by the Naib-Nazim.[27] Alimullah's son Khwaja Abdul Ghani founded the new Nawabi line of Dacca which through wealth, influence and patronage rose to the premier position in the city from the mid-nineteenth century. It was this family, together with other wealthy Muslim families, like that of the zamindar Mirza Ghulam Pir, which provided the financial support for the celebration of many Muslim social and religious festivals like 'Id-i-Milad-un-Nabi, Shabibarat, 'Id ul-Fitr, 'Id ul-Azha and Muharram. On these occasions the city wore a festive look with the common people displaying considerable community spirit. The houses were cleaned, roads illuminated and community feasts organized. But beyond this the Muslim like the Hindus took little interest in the general well-being of their city, or in the improvement of its environs.

However, there was among the Muslims of Dacca another social organization known as the *panchayat* through which community leaders regulated the social and religious life of their members. A separate communal identity was thereby maintained at a grass-roots level, and this, translated later into a political form, had a deep and abiding effect on Dacca society as a whole.

Table 1. *Occupational distribution of the Muslim*

Occupation	Number of Houses	Total Inhabitants
Zamindar	74	1,065
Service	2,067	9,065
Physician	9	45
Mullah (priests)	23	99
Merchant	126	286
Grihasta (land and property owners)	1,070	3,879
Baker	16	34
Bricklayer	117	475
Bangle-seller	42	204
Coolie	461	1678
Fisherman	90	329
Grave digger	11	36
Jardozi (Embroiderer)	107	426
Kashdadoz (Kassida Embroiderers)	89	123
Ivory-seller	56	180
Kutti (Corn thrasher)	2,055	8,742
Oilman	16	114
Shoeseller	63	76
Shopkeeper	1,080	4,020
Tailor	188	855
Tinner	103	369
Trader	121	472
Washerman	14	67
Water-carrier	10	49
Weaver	18	65
Total	8,026	32,753

Total Number of Muslim householders: 8,825
Total Number of Muslim inhabitants: 35,238

(*Source:* H. Walters, 'Census of the City of Dacca', *Asiatic Researches*, XVII, 546–8.)

For the community leaders, the panchayat was a mechanism through which they kept control of their social and political constituencies.

Each *mahalla* or ward had its panchayat which engaged much of the people's attention and drew on their community spirit, since all could participate in its deliberations.[28] The day-to-day functioning of the system, however, was in the hands of a small body, the Panch Laeq Beradar or five wise elders under the guidance of a *sardar*, the *mir-i-mahalla* or ward leader. (It was this body which technically formed the ward panchayat.) Ceremonies relating to important domestic events such as births, marriages, deaths in the family of any of its members, were regulated and conducted by the panchayat. The panchayat was, moreover, an institution calculated to maintain social and moral discipline among the members and to preserve peace and unity among the community, often acting as a body of arbitration.

The sardar was assisted by a deputy, the *naib-sardar*, by a *sakhidar*, literally one who gives evidence, and by a *gorait* or messenger. Prior to the 1880s the office of the sardar was hereditary, then from 1890s the system of election was introduced, and the sardar was elected for life. It was through the sardar that all the functions of the panchayat were performed. He summoned the panchayat, ordered whatever religious or social ceremonies had to be observed at the birth of a child; arranged the marriage ceremony by personally attending it; gave direction about funerals. In all domestic and private quarrels he was consulted and in cases of assault and crime full details were generally submitted to him for his decision. It was he who decided what subjects or cases were to be laid before the body of arbitration. Here, after careful cross-examination and investigation, the sardar and the panchayat decided the case and gave a verdict. Any one refusing to accept their verdict was at once excommunicated from the panchayat. This social ostracism was applied by the whole community against the offending individual or family. In most cases the punishment proved so severe that the offender soon acknowledged his transgression.[29] The Magistrates of Dacca often encouraged the panchayats to settle small disputes, a recognition of their usefulness and social influence.

The panchayats also performed certain other duties in connection with the celebration of the great religious festivals like the Muharram which were organized on a city-wide scale. Each mahalla panchayat had to contribute its share by offering manpower and finance for the illumination of the city and the entertainment of the poor. It had an office called Bangla situated in a conspicuous part of the mahalla. It was in this Bangla that many of the social and religious ceremonies of the mahalla were performed, and it was here also that the body of elders met whenever necessary. Sometimes during the day the Bangla was used as a *maktab* or elementary school and at night as a social club for adults of the locality. The panchayat owned immovable and movable properties mostly marquees, utensils, lamps and such other materials required in connection with the celebration of marriages and other social functions, which were put at the disposal of its members when needed. The expenses of the panchayat were borne out of fines, fees and donations.

The Muslims of Dacca had yet another distinct system of panchayats. These were the panchayats or associations of the trades and professions, and might be called the Muslim trade guilds of Dacca. Each trade and profession had a panchayat of its own, designed solely to look after the professional and trading interests of its members.

The Hindus formed the second largest community in Dacca. With the departure of many of the leading Marwari and other up-country bankers and businessmen in the early nineteenth century, the bulk of the Hindus on the eve of our period appear to have been Dacca-born. A sizeable section of the community consisted of high-caste Hindus—Brahmins, Kayasthas and Baidyas—but the majority were low caste like the *nabasaks* among whom the *tantis* or weavers formed a considerable number. These low castes were mostly followers of the Krishna-cult, and were generally known as Vaishnabs. It was the worship of Krishna and the celebration of Janmashtami or the festival of the birth of Krishna which were the hallmarks of the Hindu society. Occupationally the majority of the Hindus of Dacca were businessmen, manufacturers, artisans, clerks and labourers. There were also a considerable number in the city and its environs of landholding zamindars and *taluqdars* who, though shorn of their Mughal function as tax-collectors, remained powerful elements in society. They formed the nucleus of a new élite, the *bhadrolok*, based upon their possession of land under the Permanent Settlement. Soon they also moved into government service, the judiciary and professions opened up by the British administration.

Traditionally, the zamindars were leaders of society, *dalpatis*, whose role was given visible expression at the time of the great religious festivals, the Durga puja particularly. B. C. Allen, the compiler of the first *Dacca District Gazetteer*, wrote that the success of these pujas naturally 'depends to a great extent on the support accorded to them by the wealthy zamindars, and from the point of view of the poorer members of the Hindu community it is a matter of congratulation that different families have devoted special attention to different pujas'.[30] He listed the contribution of the zamindars of Joydebpur, Kashimpur and Srinagar, the Baliati Babus, the Pal Babus of Lohajang, the Bhagyakul family and the Nag Babus of Kalakopa, adding, 'the Kartik puja is specially affected by the wealthy money-lenders of Dacca'. This became a particularly distinctive feature of Dacca Hindu society in the middle and later years of the nineteenth century and thereafter.

Table 2 (see pp. 20-1) gives a broad breakdown of Dacca's Hindu population by caste and occupation based on the 1830 census.

Like the Muslims, the Hindus of Dacca, too, had their mahalla and guild panchayats. But the social life of the Hindu population was more rigidly regulated due mainly to caste rules. Although there was no Brahminical stranglehold on Hindu society the prevailing caste rules did divide it, thus preventing the growth of a genuine community spirit in the city and indeed also preventing the development of an urban Hindu culture. The establishment of secular British authority, and the introduction of Western knowledge and education did a great deal, as we shall see later, to prise Hindu society from the encrusted norms of caste and religion.

Among the smaller communities in the city were the English, French, Greeks, Portuguese and Armenians. Of these the English, particularly the officials, held a privileged status being the rulers of the country. From the beginning of the nineteenth century, however, there started a steady flow of non-official Englishmen into the city as businessmen, traders, agents, indigo planters and missionaries. This group, together with the Armenians who numbered 126 in 1830, played an especially notable part in the life of the city.

Table 2. *Occupation and Caste distribution of the Hindus of Dacca, 1830*

Occupation & Caste	Number of Houses	Total Inhabitants
Zamindar–		
Baidya	1	3
Baisya	2	15
Khettri	6	42
Saha	1	90
Kayastha	13	147
Tanti	1	7
Service–		
Baisya	4	23
Banian	112	531
Brahmin	103	543
Chandal	12	70
Garuriya	2	8
Jant	1	3
Kahar	8	23
Kundu	9	34
Khettri	182	523
Kurmi	5	13
Saha	195	974
Kayashtha	500	2,557
Toyepal	11	29
Physician–		
Baidya	48	215
Barber	13	37
Brahmin	2	47
Chandal	1	3
Khettri	1	1
Saha	1	4
Kayastha	3	11
Jajman–		
Brahmin	107	426
Shopkeeper–		
Baisya	11	22
Banian	128	617
Brahmin	7	11
Gunri	6	27
Kundu	20	80
Khettri	118	349
Kayastha	878	2,643
Saha	646	2,187
Tambuli	1	3
Tanti	1	11
Toyepal	103	509

Table 2. *(cont.)*

Occupation & Caste	Number of Houses	Total Inhabitants
Merchant–		
Brahmin	6	29
Khettri	54	138
Trader–		
Khettri	2	7
Saha	5	31
Tanti	89	288
Toyepal	4	23
Shroff–		
Saha	29	54
Tanti	3	21
Milkman–		
Gowala	382	2,055
Thread-maker–		
Brahmin	1	14
Chandal	2	77
Kayastha	3	7
Tanti	12	22
Weaver–		
Jogi	1	4
Saha	9	36
Tanti	376	2,392
Toyepal	35	155
Embroiderer–		
Sudra	2	2
Washerman–		
Dhobi	188	810
Cloth-seller–		
Toyepal	19	111
Currier–		
Chamar	175	943
Coolie–		
Kundu	42	235
Khettri	6	10
Potter–		
Kumar	143	665
Sweeper–		
Dome	2	8
Mehter	27	103
Total	4,880	21,008

Total number of Hindu householders: 7,327
Total number of Hindu inhabitants: 31,429

(*Source:* Walters, 'Census of . . . Dacca'. 1830).

NOTES TO CHAPTER I

1 *Report on the Census of Bengal, 1872*, 6–7.
2 O.H.K. Spate & A.T.A. Learmonth, *India and Pakistan—A General and Regional Geography*, 571–4.
3 *Census of Bengal, 1872*, 105.
4 *Report on the Census of Bengal, 1881*, II, 5–6.
5 Letter from J. Rennell to the Reverend Gilbert Barrington, Vicar of Chudleigh, Devon, 31 August 1765, 'Rennell's Letters', Home Miscellaneous Series, Vol. 815.
6 James Taylor, *A Sketch of the Topography and Statistics of Dacca*, 2.
7 Abdul Karim, *Dacca the Mughal Capital*, 6–8.
8 For details of this Mughal campaign see Tapan Raychaudhuri, *Bengal Under Akbar and Jahangir*, 49–52; also J. M. Sarkar (ed.), *History of Bengal*, II, ch. 11, 211–15.
9 The exact location of this port is not known. Dr Dani says that it was situated opposite Narayanganj (p. 110) while Dr Karim remarks that it was situated at Mirpur (p.63).
10 About three-quarters of the land in the old city of Dacca was held on rent-free tenures. See Ascoli, *Final Report*, appendix, XII, p. XLIII; see also the petition of the inhabitants of Dacca to the Governor-General, Lord Auckland (no date), ibid,. appendix XII, pp. XLV–XLVI.
11 Anjali Chatterjee, *Bengal in the Reign of Aurangzib, 1658–1707*, 86–9; also Sushil Chaudhari, *Trade and Commercial Organisation in Bengal 1650–1720, et passim.*
12 Yatindra Mohan Ray, *Dhakar Itihasa* (History of Dacca), 190–5.
13 Sebastian Manrique, *Travels of Fray Sebastian Manrique*, I, 43–5.
14 Ibid., 43–5, 56–7.
15 Syed Hossain, 'Echoes From Old Dhaka,' *Bengal Past and Present*, 111 (April-June 1909), 231, quoting Rahman Ali Taish, *Tarikh-i-Dhakha.*
16 Charles D'Oyly, *Antiquities of Dacca*, ; also [J. Taylor], 'Notes by the [Commercial] Resident', HMS Vol. 456 (f), footnote to p. 289; Karim, *Dacca*, 37–8.
17 A. L. Clay, *Principal Heads of the History and Statistics of the Dacca Division*, 36.
18 Karim, *Dacca*, 40–1, 57–8.
19 See Raja Binaya Krishna Deb, *The Early History and Growth of Calcutta;* also L.S.S.O'Malley, *Murshidabad District Gazetteers.*
20 S.N.H. Rizvi (ed.), *Bangladesh District Gazetteers, Dacca*, 71; also Ray, *Dhakar Itihasa*, 132–3.
21 Rennell's letters, HMS Vol. 815.
22 West to east from Enayatganj to Faridabad, and south to north from the river to Dewan Bazar.
23 For details see chapter V.

24 For a review of the state and culture of Urdu and Persian literature in Dacca in the nineteenth century see Rizvi, *Dacca*, 344–55.
25 J.A. Wise, *Notes on the Races, Castes and Tribes of Eastern Bengal*, 107.
26 For an account of the life-style of some of these Muslim 'chieftains' see Bishop R. Heber, *Narrative of a Journey through the Upper Provinces of India*, I. 140–2; also II, 340–2.
27 Dani, *Dacca*, 117–18.
28 Khan Saheb Khwaja Mahomed Azam, *The Panchayat System of Dacca*, 5.
29 Azam, *The Panchayat;* Wise, *Notes*.
30 B. C. Allen, *The Dacca District Gazetteer*, 67.

CHAPTER II

A CENTRE OF PROVINCIAL ADMINISTRATION

In the early years of its rule the East India Company had no positive policy towards Dacca. Nevertheless the city's general importance forced the government to institute measures which ultimately proved beneficial, pre-eminently in the field of administration. For despite Dacca's dramatic decline, it is significant that even at its lowest point, in about 1840, there was no other urban centre in East Bengal that was capable of becoming an administrative and commercial regional centre. So Dacca steadily rose to become the unofficial and undeclared capital of East Bengal and was so described throughout the nineteenth century.[1]

As the capital of the Mughal subah of Bengal, Bihar and Orissa, Dacca had been a vital centre of political life and of provincial civil and military administration; within its walls also lay the imperial exchequer, the repository of all the public revenues. The Subahdar who headed the provincial government administered and controlled a wide territory in conjunction with a host of other officials,[2] most of whom had jurisdictions beyond the city boundaries. The provincial government establishment stationed in the city included some fifty to sixty thousand officers and men.[3] The transfer of the capital in about 1716 meant a reduction in the city's civil and military establishment to that appropriate for a niabat capital.

Dacca as a Mughal capital also had an important revenue role. The provincial Diwan who was entrusted with the management of the imperial revenues, i.e. land revenue and *sair*[4] duties, collected in 1658 crown revenues worth some Rs. 8,800,000. Even during the period of the Dacca niabat—the jurisdiction of which extended 'from the Garrow Hills on the north to the Sundarbunds on the south, and from the Tipperah Hills on the east to Jessore on the west'[5]—the public revenues collected amounted to some Rs. 2,700,000.

However, after 1765, the East India Company made several experiments in the mode of revenue collection which steadily reduced the city's position as an administrative centre. These experiments led to the establishment of small fiscal areas, stabilized by 1787 in the system of district administration. This was followed by the abolition of most sair duties in 1790,[6] and, more importantly, by the Permanent Settlement of land revenue in 1793 which made unnecessary the maintenance of any major centre other than Calcutta for revenue purposes. Thereafter the only revenues collected at Dacca were those of the districts of Dacca and Dacca-Jalalpur, which included parts of the modern Faridpur and Barisal Districts. Under these settlements Dacca was charged with the collection of only Rs. 1,205,000.[7] Even this amount was later reduced as new districts were carved out, incorporating segments of the original Dacca jurisdiction. However, the administrative significance thus lost came soon to be more than compensated by Dacca's growth as a regional centre of control and supervision.

Shifts in the theory of how best to govern a foreign people and experience of the practial problems of administering the land revenue through a highly centralized Board of Revenue and a thin scatter of often young European Collectors, each isolated in his district, both prompted closer supervision.[8]

'From a report of Secretary Holt Mackenzie', as B. B. Misra noted, 'it transpired that cases of embezzlement and defalcation of public money frequently occurred from continued neglect and the prevalence of abuses which could have been detected in time had a controlling authority been resident in the vicinity'.[9]

By Regulation I of 1829, therefore, a system of Divisional Commissioners was created to provide control and supervision of the administration of revenue over more manageable areas than the province. When the Eastern or Dacca Division was formed, consisting of the districts of Dacca, Dacca-Jalalpur, Tippera, Sherpur and Mymensingh, it was the city of Dacca which was chosen as its headquarters because of its past role, its central position and its excellent water communication to all parts.[10]

From 1829 the city of Dacca thus became the headquarters of a Commissioner who although not directly involved in collecting revenue had full responsibility for its efficient management throughout a very large, productive and yet problem-stricken division. The new Commissioner of Revenue and Circuit was also invested with judicial and police responsibilities for the whole division. From the 1830s Dacca thus embarked upon a new life as the headquarters of a regional administration, gaining in staff and offices as the district and divisional systems developed. Not only did Dacca regain some of its former status, its people also enjoyed a modest addition to their employment prospects. In 1829–30 the Commissioner had a staff of 23, drawing monthly salaries amounting in total to Rs. 543; by 1867 the staff had increased to 31 and the salaries to Rs. 1,059.[11]

In course of time the Dacca Division came to include many other districts of East Bengal and even Assam. The inclusion of Assam territories increased the importance of the Dacca Division and the city of Dacca even further. For after the absorption of Assam into British India in 1826 a considerable amount of British capital came gradually to be invested there in business and in tea plantations. The security and proper use of this investment required the backing of an adequate and efficient administrative structure which Dacca was called upon to provide, and for which Dacca was steadily equipped with additional administrative machinery and personnel. In the 1860s the Dacca Division comprised the districts of Dacca, Faridpur, Bakerganj, Tippera and Mymensingh of East Bengal, together with Sylhet and Cachar of Assam. By 1870 the office of the Commissioner of Dacca had become the most important post in East Bengal, being the chief executive position in a very extensive region which commanded the vital water route between Calcutta and Assam. The post was usually given to the most experienced civil servants of the government.

This remained true even though in 1874 the Commissioner's jurisdiction was curtailed by the separation of Sylhet and Cachar from the Dacca Division and their annexation to the newly-established Chief Commissionership of Assam. One further set of changes occurred in our period: the addition to the Dacca Division of Tippera in 1875 and its return to the Chittagong Division in 1880, leaving Dacca with four districts only—Dacca, Mymensingh, Faridpur and Bakerganj. It was a large enough charge, for by 1885 the population of the area had risen to over 8,700,000 paying a total revenue of Rs. 6,911,883, including municipal taxes.[12]

From the 1850s Dacca was the headquarters of another department connected with revenue administration and having divisional jurisdiction. This was the Department of Survey for the Third or Eastern Division. Though the Permanent Settlement had ensured the realization of a secure revenue, the government knew practically nothing about *zamindaris*, *taluqdaris* or other estates except their annual assessment. The lack of detailed surveys of estates and their assets led to frequent and violent disputes over the boundaries of estates between contending landlords; the tremendous rise in criminal cases after 1793 was largely the result of disputes over undefined lands occasioned by the absence of records of lands and landrights. Government also found it hard correctly to apportion the revenue demand on the subdivisions of estates when these were put up for sale for the recovery of arrears.[13] The high level of the revenue demand in relation to the net rental meant that if demand was not allocated correctly, one sale of land for arrears was only too often followed, because of over-assessment, by yet another sale for the recovery of a new balance. Similarly the government had little idea of the location, boundaries and extent of its own lands, known as *khas mahals*. The office of *qanungo*, which in Mughal times had been responsible for the maintenance of accurate records of revenue and its apportionment, had long since been abolished.[14] It was therefore necessary to create afresh a system for surveying the land and preparing maps and records showing every detail of the land and landholding structure in the country.[15]

The survey began in earnest from the 1840s when the whole province was divided into survey divisions, the districts of Eastern Bengal being put under the charge of a Superintendent of Survey with Dacca as his office headquarters, from which survey parties went out for a large part of the year for field-work into the interior.

It was a lengthy business surveying the whole division, since there were several surveys to complete, beginning with the *thakbast* or demarcation survey, and for the whole period Dacca remained the headquarters of the department. As the superintendent explained in 1854, Dacca was the ideal centre, being the only town which could provide suitable accommodation for his *cutcherry* or office and for housing his staff, while it was also in close proximity to the last court of appeal for survey and settlement matters, i.e. the office of the Divisional Commissioner.[16] In the district of Dacca itself the Survey Department began the thakbast survey which determined the boundaries of *parganas* or fiscal divisions (which ordinarily included several estates) and *mouzas* or villages by preparing regular village maps in 1859; it completed the operation in 1878.

Below the division came the district of Dacca, today some seventy miles by sixty-five[17] but till 1871 much larger, as has been seen.[18] Over it presided the Collector, an official first appointed in 1781 after the abolition of the Provincial Council and entrusted with the collection of all government revenues from the district. His office was more than once united with that of District Magistrate, the two coming together permanently in 1859. The land tax formed the primary source of public revenue in the early days of British rule, as in Mughal times, but growing costs—of war, of military and civil establishments and of public services—soon forced government to impose new taxes,[19] which though fluctuating in form and duration, came to yield substantial revenues.[20] Their collection necesitsated the creation of new offices and the appointment of further staff which generated new economic activities within the town of Dacca.

By 1836–7 the principal items of government revenue in the Dacca district were land revenue, excise, stamp duties, police tax, postal receipts and ferry tax; of which land revenue yielded Rs. 430,500; stamp duties Rs. 83,265 and excise Rs. 40,765. To handle their collection the Collector's office was organized into seven minor departments; Treasury, *diwani-sherista* or revenue accounts; *munshikhana* or correspondence; *nazarat* or establishment and supervision; Records; Excise; Stamp. In 1839 the number of people employed in the office, including the Collector and Deputy Collectors, was ninety-three, drawing a total monthly pay of Rs. 4,100.[21]

In course of time the revenue of the district came to be collected under two broad heads, namely Imperial and Provincial Funds, which included such main items like land revenue, excise, stamp duties and police tax; and Local Funds like pound and ferry fund, road cess, *chaukidari* tax, convict labour fund, registration fees, fisheries licences and judicial fees. In 1865–6 the imperial and provincial revenues amounted to Rs. 907,700 and local revenues to Rs. 120,489 or a total yield for Dacca amounting to Rs. 1,028,189.[22] By 1884–5 the total revenue of the district had risen to Rs. 1,485,641, excluding municipal taxes.[23]

The growth and proliferation of the revenue resources and administration of the district would form a study in itself. It is intended here, however, to view the process as it enhanced the importance of Dacca, enlarged employment in the city and led to the creation of a group of English-educated Bengali officials with a distinctive social and cultural role in the city and region.

First we may consider the impact of administration on Dacca's importance and prestige. The settling of the land revenue in 1793, and the absence in Bengal of the close village-level investigation which periodic resettlement required in North India, did not mean that the Collector as revenue administrator was not a figure of great moment to the 9,000 or so zamindars and taluqdars of the Dacca district. It was to his office that they paid in their Rs. 405,000 of land revenue; it was he who put their lands up to auction in case of default. In the early 1840s he had been responsible for conducting the investigation of *inam* or revenue-free land and for the resumption of much of it and even when that process ceased it was the Collector who dealt with all revenue-free estates in the district and who had to manage the permanently settled estates whose administration for such reasons as the minority or mental incapacity of the zamindar fell to the care of the government. It was the Collector who dealt with the losses and gains to cultivated land caused by the constant shifting of river beds and who as Magistrate prevented club law settling all boundary disputes.

Upon the Collector, too, devolved the supervision of the very important office of the Registry of Deeds. On the abolition of the office of qanungo in 1793, the duty of registering deeds connected with landed properties was vested in the Registrar of the Court of *diwani adalat* or civil justice.[24] The Registrar was authorized to effect 'the registration of wills, deeds of sale and gifts of real property, mortgages, limited assignments or temporary transfer of lands', and people came from all over the district to have their property deeds registered at his office in Dacca. The Registrar's office afterwards came to form an important part of the Collectorate and was headed by a permanent Sub-Registrar, the District Collector being ex-officio Registrar of Deeds. Moreover, the government came to believe that the permanent settlement had singularly failed to protect the interests of cultivators,[25] and responded to the situation with the Bengal Tenancy Acts of 1859 and 1885. The administration of these measures, touching the interests of landholders and tenants alike, also fell on the shoulders of the District Collector.

The system of land revenue administration thus led zamindars, taluqdars, *ijaradars* or revenue farmers, the tenure-holders and even the ordinary peasants to look to the city, the seat of the Collector, as the place with which their fortunes were bound up.[26] Here was the office complex where complaints were to be lodged, justice sought against the highhandedness of landholders or collusion of ryots against the zamindars, claims stated under the Tenancy Acts, and lands were bought and sold. Disputes arising out of rival claims among co-sharers of estates, and questions of inheritance also came to be settled here, with reference to the deeds in custody of the Registrar of Deeds. The presence in Dacca of the office of the Commissioner of Revenue, the supreme revenue officer of the division, added further weight and importance to Dacca in the eyes of all those with interests in the land.

Secondly, we may see the impact of administration on the residents of Dacca. It was for zamindars and other landholders a common practice in Mughal times to station an agent in the provincial capital to oversee their interests. Conversely certain landholders took up residence in Dacca, leaving the administration of their estates to *naibs* or deputies. Under the British, this practice was less needed; nevertheless many zamindars and taluqdars continued to maintain a naib in Dacca so as to keep their relations with the Commissioner or Collector in good working order. The goodwill of these officials, it was realized, could be the source of profitable governmental patronage, being particularly indispensable for those hungry for Rai Bahadurship or some similar honour involving a seat on a local board or municipality. In return men so beholden to the government would become a bulwark of authority both in town and countryside.[27]

A classic case was that of the Bhawal zamindar whose rural seat was at Jaydebpur, but who none the less kept a full complement of naibs and staff in Dacca. The later zamindars moved into the city themselves, investing heavily in land and property, thereby acquiring considerable powers of social and political patronage.[28] They were joined by other notables such as the Khwajas, Pogoses, Mitterjeet Singh and J. P. Wise, who having made their mark initially in commerce gradually began investing their wealth in urban land and property. Together with the migratory zamindar element they transformed Dacca into a stronghold of rentier class interests.[29]

At the same time the inevitable expansion of the administrative machinery centred around the Collector and Commissioner lent fresh weight to the English-educated class in Dacca society. From 1833 Regulation IX provided for a superior cadre of Indian Deputy Collectors who, naturally, were Bengalis. As a class their role in the seeding of Dacca's new social and cultural life was significant; the currents originating from there slowly spreading to the hinterland of East Bengal. In 1840 another impetus was given to the recruitment of English-educated Indians to government services through Governor-General Lord Hardinge's resolution of that year, leading to the further appointment of Western-educated Bengalis to high office in Dacca. This privileged élite then introduced the less educated and well-off members of their families, relatives or friends into the lower ranks of the administration.[30]

However, the communal dimension in this development must be kept in mind: the overwhelming majority of this new élite of civil servants were Hindus who had adapted themselves more readily to the government's change from Persian to English as the official language, while their Muslim compeers were less inclined psychologically to accept the reality of British rule after the Islamic millennium. This disparity between the communities soon characterized the administration as a whole, with far-reaching consequences for their future social and political relations.

The impact of land revenue administration was reinforced by that of other revenue sources. The stamp duties were the next most important. The sale of revenue stamps and stamped papers had been introduced in Bengal in 1797 'to make good the deficiency in the public revenue caused by the abolition of the police tax'.[31] Suits filed in the courts, the sale or transfer of lands, the licences for the manufacture or vend of spirituous liquors and many other public transactions were all to be set out on stamped paper.[32] Stamp duty was the one head of revenue which in Dacca showed a steady and large increase. In 1836–7 the stamp duty receipts from the district were Rs. 83,265, in 1865–6 Rs. 215,536, but by 1884–5 they had jumped to Rs. 626,083. They reflected, it has been argued, the growth of population, an advance in material prosperity and in business transactions, and an increased resort to the courts, in preference to private settlement of cases or village arbitration. All these changes enhanced the importance of the administrative centre.

Abkari or excise, imposed mainly on the sale of liquors and various intoxicating drugs, formed the third most important source of government revenue, and the city of Dacca played a significant role as centre for the excise administration not only of the Dacca district but also of many other neighbouring districts during the 1840s and 1850s.

From its introduction in 1790 the management of abkari revenue was vested in the District Collector. The staff he controlled was certainly inadequate. The Abkari Department, it was declared, was 'left to collect an Excise without Excisemen'.[33] In consequence excise duties came to be effectively levied only within the boundaries of the principal towns of Bengal. The remedy proposed in 1839 was the appointment of a larger staff—'an Establishment competent to enforce and protect an Excise'. The Governor-General-in-Council agreed, resolving, however, that the abkari revenue should be supervised not by the Collectors but by specialist Excise Commissioners.[34] On 26 February 1840 a Regulation was passed appointing a first Commissioner of Abkari in the Alipur or Calcutta Division with the possibility of an extension of the scheme to other areas.

The first two Commissioners were diligent and energetic and both administratively and financially the scheme proved a success. A report of 29 August 1843 proposed, therefore, that Bengal be administered as two Abkari Divisions with Commissioners based in Calcutta and Rajshahi, the latter being central and particularly suitable since all 'the Ganja [hemp] cultivated in Bengal comes from that and in the neighbouring districts'.[35]

The plan was sanctioned by the Governor-General-in-Council but with Dacca as headquarters of the second division, the city of Dacca being considered more suitable for administrative reasons than the town of Rajshahi.[36] The new abkari division was thus formally constituted in August 1844, consisting of ten East and North Bengal districts, with Alexander Frederick Donnelly as Commissioner.

In the wake of these changes, the city of Dacca gained three new Abkari offices—those of the Divisional Commissioner, the District Superintendent and the City Darogah. Between them these three officials employed a subordinate clerical staff of eighteen, and thirty-two menials and guards, with salaries totalling Rs. 1,173 a month. (The Commissioner, Superintendent and Darogah drew Rs. 2,950 a month between them.)[37]

The selection of Dacca as the Divisional headquarters of an Abkari Department responsible for nearly half Bengal gave an additional importance to the city, further increased when in 1848–9 the districts of Tippera, Chittagong, Cachar and Sylhet were added to the jurisdiction of the Dacca commissionership.

The new establishment proved a success, largely halting smuggling and the illicit sale of liquor and drugs, and pushing up the net receipts from the Dacca division from some Rs. 193,000 in 1839–40, to Rs. 243,000 in 1848–9.[38] However, the cost of collection also rose very sharply, so that the net gain was reduced to only Rs. 50,000 or so. It was therefore proposed in 1849 to dismantle the elaborate establishment and return to management of excise by the District Collectors, supervised by the Divisional Commissioners of Land Revenue.[39]

The two Commissioners at Dacca and Calcutta differed in their views, but the Board of Revenue, balancing the immediacy of a Collector's supervision against the undivided but more distant attention of the Commissioner, argued that with the system now well established and with efficient agents the Board itself should be able to provide regularity of supervision. So, when J. Atherton, the Dacca Excise Commissioner, was appointed Judge of Tirhut in 1852 his excise post was left vacant. Some of the abkari establishment were also discharged, and the Collectors were once again given charge of the Superintendents, now designated Deputy Collectors. The reorganization was a setback in the city's development though the subordinates of the excise department now formed a much more ample force than in the 1830s.

Since the creation of the Dacca Excise Division virtually coincided with the declaration by Lord Hardinge that the government would favour the English-educated in future public appointments, it also gave its own useful fillip to English education in the region. As Donnelly built up his staff he had applications from all over Bengal and he responded splendidly, appointing a large number from among the Dacca College students.[40] Indeed, as the Hon. J.E.D. Bethune remarked at a prize-giving ceremony at the Dacca College, Donnelly had 'openly avowed and acted' on the principle of bestowing every situation in his power or influencing the disposal of it in favour of the English-educated.[41] Donnelly himself reported that in 1845–6 the yearly salaries of the English-educated Indians employed in the Dacca abkari commissionership amounted to

Rs. 31,620. Most of these jobs went, however, to the Hindus who were at the time almost monopolizing English education.[42]

Other taxes did not contribute to Dacca through their administration to the same extent as the land revenue, the stamp duties and the excise. They do reveal, however, other features about the city. For example, in 1860 in the wake of the Mutiny a tax on non-agricultural incomes was introduced by the Government of India in order to offset heavy deficits and to meet growing administrative outlays; income tax was introduced on a permanent basis in 1886.[43] Such taxes, between 1860 and 1886, were levied by district rather than by division, and their administration did not therefore add to the regional importance of Dacca though they served to enhance in some degree its employment opportunities for educated youths.

More interesting, the inhabitants of Dacca city who were liable to income tax in 1860 did not pay through individual assessment. Instead a delegation led by Khwaja Abdul Ghani asked the government to allow them to pay a lump sum which they themselves would apportion among those liable to tax. If this was agreed, they stated, they would pay a consolidated sum of Rs. 50,000 levied by an assessing panchayat which they would appoint.[44] Though initially reluctant, government agreed to this mode of assessment and collection when the offer was raised to Rs. 65,000.[45] The residents thus avoided any close scrutiny of their financial affairs while government, without cost or exertion, secured a sum which the Commissioner thought fairly to represent the capacity of the city, being equal to a tax of two per cent upon income 'to the amount of 16 and a quarter lakhs of rupees.'[46]

It appears that the system of self-assessment and lump-sum payment by the city was discontinued after 1863–4, but by then the income tax itself was under attack, and in 1865 it was abolished altogether. In its place a Licence Tax (a registration tax on artisans, businessmen, bankers, professional people and others) was imposed from 1867–8. The system suggests none the less that British rule in Dacca imposed a superstructure on existing dispositions of economic and social power, through which indeed the rulers were often content to work.

The same point is clear in the administration of the *chaukidari* tax, levied in Dacca after the passing of Regulation XIII in 1813, for the local purpose of maintaining bodies of *chaukidars* or nightwatchmen, and later in other towns and villages of the district. Though the Magistrate or Collector was responsible for its collection, he operated through ward panchayats not his own officials. Only a small establishment was maintained within his office to keep the accounts and records. In this instance, however, it is apparent that those bodies which were employed by the British were liable to institutional change. The chaukidari panchayats were nominated by the Magistrate and consisted of people with some influence in the mahallas. It is not known whether these included members of the traditional mahalla panchayats, but later it was repeatedly alleged that the chaukidari panchayats were a den of lowly and selfish people. Respectable citizens, it was declared, shunned any association with this body; nor did they participate in the assessment or collection of the chaukidari tax.[47] Yet the tax was a first step towards the establishment of local self-government in Dacca, and indeed from 1840 the surplus of the tax was utilized for sanitation and other civic improvements. In 1864, a Municipality was established in Dacca, and the chaukidari tax, which had caused problems for the Collector,[48] was replaced by a house tax and other cesses collected by the municipal commissioners.

The effect of the expansion of administration on Dacca was therefore both to enhance its prestige and to change its character. This dual impact may be seen also in one last tax, the Ferry Fund, which built upon and then altered existing practices and which contributed both to communications centring on Dacca and later to development within the city. It derived from the dues taken by the zamindars in Mughal times from boats using the *ghats* or landing places within their jurisdiction. They continued to collect such tolls and to run and profit from ferries even under the permanent settlement, and it was not until 1819 that district authorities were empowered to take over the management of ghats and ferries and the collection of dues, any surplus from which might be spent on the improvement of local communications. This power the Dacca authorities did not choose to exercise until 1830 when Henry Walters applied to the Commissioner for permission to do so. Walters pointed to the great military routes from Calcutta to North-East Frontier, 'the medium also of considerable commercial intercourse', which depended upon zamindari ferries across the series of rivers in the district. Proper ferries managed by the police were needed 'to promote the efficiency of the police, to facilitate the passage of troops, and to secure the safety and convenience of travellers, who from the smallness of the boats, and the inefficiency of the crews are constantly exposed to accident'. Under efficient management the ferries would yield a handsome surplus revenue which could be utilized for the construction of roads, bridges and the general improvement of internal communications.[49]

Persuaded perhaps by the last part of Walters' argument, permission was given to take over nineteen ghats, five of them on the northern bank of the river Buriganga at Dacca itself, and to put them under the management of the Dacca Magistrate. Soon additional establishments were instituted to run the ferries. In subsequent years more ghats were made public, their management being placed under various official authorities at different times, including some participation by local dignitaries in the 1840s and 1850s.

The Ferry Funds, some Rs. 7,000 per annum in the 1850s, were then utilized to improve communications within the district. Several roads, bridges and culverts were constructed, particularly to improve communications with the city of Dacca. These works were carried out under the guidance of the Magistrate-Collector who appointed a Superintendent of Roads, usually a European or Eurasian, to execute them. A small establishment was also attached to the Collectorate to run the Ferry Funds Department. In 1867 tolls were established under Act V of 1864 upon the Dulai Khal in Dacca. The tolls were levied upon large country boats and other vessels which entered the city through it. The District Collector gathered the tax through a small band of clerks and toll collectors. Eventually the Dulai Khal tolls, averaging some Rs. 13,000 between 1867 and 1871,[50] were handed over to the Municipality in 1872 for the development of the city.

A final revenue function emphasized Dacca's slow renewal. This involved the despatch of surplus revenues from Dacca and other districts of East Bengal to the Treasury in Calcutta.[51] The task of despatching was initially undertaken by the Dacca Collectorate itself but later the responsibility was given to the newly-established branch of the Bank of Bengal.[52]

For revenue purposes Dacca had thus declined from Mughal capital to niabat sub-capital and so to British district centre before beginning to reassert a regional dominance. This process was paralleled in judicial and police administration too.

The process was not so rapid on the judicial as it had been on the revenue side, however, for until 1832 Dacca remained the seat of a Provincial Court of Appeal and Circuit, with jurisdiction over Bakerganj, Chittagong, Dacca, Dacca-Jalalpur, Sylhet and Tippera.[53] As a contemporary wrote,

> Dacca was the seat of a court of appeal consisting of four judges; there were generally attached to the station ten or twelve Gentlemen of the Civil Service, till the changes introduced by Lord William Bentinck in 1830–32, when the functionaries were reduced to a Commissioner . . . ; a Sessions Judge; a Collector and Magistrate in one, and two or three young Assistants; . . .[54]

From Bentinck's day Dacca had no regional judicial role.

After 1832 the judicial administration of Dacca district was headed by the District Judge. His court, the Zilla (district) court, held in the city, was the highest in the district, and the Judge tried both civil and criminal cases. Because of his double functions, he was called the Civil and Sessions Judge. Below the Zilla court, on the civil side there were in the city in 1840 the further subordinate courts of the Principal Sadr Amin, the Additional Sadr Amin, and the Munsif. Of these the first two had jurisdiction over the whole district while the last had jurisdiction over the city and its immediate vicinity. The Zilla Court of Dacca also had jurisdiction over the district of Faridpur until a separate Judgeship was created in 1875.[55]

The load upon the District and Sessions Judge, responsible as he was for Faridpur as well as Dacca, eventually proved too great to be carried singlehanded. In 1851, use was made of the provision of Regulation VIII of 1833 for the appointment of an Additional Judge at Dacca, to help clear off the heavy arrears on the civil side.[56] This post was at intervals abolished and then, as arrears mounted, again restored. What is significant is that the Additional Judge, though posted at Dacca, was frequently made responsible for other districts—Bakerganj in 1853, Faridpur in 1860, Tippera,

Bakerganj and Chittagong in 1872. In the last of these cases the Additional Judge, H. B. Simson, made an interesting comment on his reasons for choosing Dacca as his headquarters. Thus he reported to government:

> Dacca appears to be the natural headquarters of this part of the world. It is certainly more centrical than any other of my districts... It is alone easily accessible from other parts of India and a great point hereabouts where locomotion is often both difficult and dangerous, there are various means of leaving it which are generally wanting elsewhere. Dacca alone is at all within easy reach of Calcutta.[57]

The same forces which had made Dacca a regional Court of Appeal were clearly still at work. Dacca was a sub-capital in practice, if not in name—and the city was the gainer as in 1860 by one Judge, on Rs. 2,166 a month, and thirteen writers, clerks and menials at a monthly salary of Rs. 171.

A more permanent relief was also attempted by the establishment under Act XLII of 1860 of Small Cause Courts in Bengal to try suits involving trifling amounts other than for land. In 1861 they were given wider powers allowing them to try rent cases and suits for real property.[58] In that year the Dacca Small Cause Court was established for the three *thanas* which constituted the city of Dacca: Kotwali, Faridabad and Lalbagh.[59] From 1863 the Court also held periodical sittings at Narayanganj to which its jurisdiction had been extended.

It was on the criminal side, however, that the work of the District and Sessions Judge proved most appallingly heavy. His jurisdiction was partly original, restricted to persons committed by the Magistrate to stand trial at the Sessions,[60] and partly appellate. His appellate jurisdiction extended to all judicial sentences and orders passed by the Magistrate or his subordinates.

Because of the great prevalence of crime, government was early forced to appoint additional magistrates and to invest a variety of judicial officers with criminal powers. From 1833 a covenanted Assistant Magistrate was appointed in Dacca who exercised criminal jurisdiction in cases referred to him for trial by the Magistrate. Under Act XV of 1843, such uncovenanted officers as Deputy Magistrates, Muhammadan Law Officers,

Pundits, Principal Sadr Amins and Sadr Amins were given similar powers. The city of Dacca thus became the main centre of criminal justice in the Dacca district.

The administration of justice was much modified upon the assumption by the Crown of the government of India. In May 1861, the Calcutta High Court replaced the old Sadr Adalats, and between 1859 and 1861 three great Codes were enacted. The last of these, the Code of Criminal Procedure, enaced under Act XXV of 1861, modified criminal judicial administration, recognizing existing subordinate criminal courts but extending the jurisdiction of the Sessions Courts to larger divisions embracing two or more districts. Below the Courts of Sessions were those of the Magistrates, divided into three classes, with full, first-class and second-class powers.

From 1862 the Civil and Sessions Judge of Dacca was given the criminal or sessions charges of the districts of Dacca, Faridpur, Bakerganj, now known as Barisal, and Mymensingh. An old resident of Dacca recalls the pattern thus established.

> In the early sixties I saw the Courts of the Circuit-Judge and of the Ala Sudder Amin, an equivalent to the present Subordinate Judge, located in the big building in the Wise Ghat Street. The Circuit Judge meant the District and Sessions Judge who used to go about the Districts of Mymensingh, Barrisal, and Faridpore and sit as the Sessions Judge for administering Civil and Criminal Justice in these Districts and ultimately come down to Dacca to clear the file in the Sudder Sessions cases and criminal appeals against the decisions of the District Magistrates and Deputy Magistrates of the First Class powers and the probate cases.[61]

The Criminal Procedure Code of 1861 also provided for the appointment of Honorary Magistrates and for the formation in the towns of benches of Magistrates, honorary or stipendiary, to try minor offences. In Dacca such Honorary Magistrates were first appointed in 1861, the first two Honorary Magistrates of Dacca being Khwaja Abdul Ghani and J.G.N. Pogose, the Armenian zamindar.

The growth of the British system of civil and criminal courts centred on Dacca was also accompanied, there as elsewhere, by the development of a body of legal practitioners. The engaging of *vakils* or pleaders by plaintiffs and defendants became a regular judicial practice in Bengal from 1773. Until 1814 the licensing of such pleaders was governed by rules laid down in 1793 by the Sadr Diwani Adalat. Thereafter the power to appoint vakils to all courts from the Provincial Court of Appeal and Circuits downwards was vested in the Provincial Court of Appeal, and upon that Court's disappearance in 1832 the authority passed to the District and Sessions Judge.

Originally the courts merely selected vakils from among persons of education, ability, good family and character, but from the 1840s would-be pleaders were examined and the successful issued with pleadership certificates, allowing them to practise. Dacca was selected as one of the examination centres, and examinations were conducted almost every year by a Local Examination Committee. If this added to the consequence of the city it also imposed further administrative burdens on officials and created a social problem for the town. Accommodation was often arranged by relatives resident in the town, but even so temporary hostels and boarding houses had to be set up to provide lodging and food for hundreds of candidates who came from as far as Chittagong and Rangpur.[62] The occasion was thought worthy of comment in the press; the weekly *Dacca News* reported in its issue of 30 January 1858: 'The great event of the week has been the examination of candidates for pleadership certificates. About 220 came up for examination.' But it also gave rise to wider ambitions. Next week, finding that there was little in Dacca—'no news, no ladies,[63] nothing but would-be pleaders and dust', raised by 'disagreeable dry west wind'—the same paper was moved to remark that:

> ...only 18 or 19 of the 220 candidates have passed the ordeal of the pleadership examinations. If it is really wished to train up pleaders for our courts, there ought to be a law class attached to our colleges which should be taught by some one having some knowledge of the law, not by a mathematician, or a chemist, or a poet[64]

The suggestion was taken up by the Dacca people four years later and a law class at the Dacca College was opened in 1863 to prepare students for the degree of Bachelor of Law and Licentiate in Law. The numbers attending rose from fifteen in 1864 to eighty-one in 1871, many of the successful candidates going on to practise in the Courts of the Dacca Division.[65]

Meanwhile, however, the old system of pleadership certificates continued. But the candidates from 1861 were required to pass the University Entrance Examination and from 1868 the First Arts Examination in order to qualify for the entry to the pleadership examination,[66] until finally in the 1880s Law degrees came to be required to practise at the District Courts.

Similarly, examinations were also held in Dacca for candidates wishing to practise as *mooktars* or legal agents in the Collectorate Courts.[67] In the same way Dacca for many years served as examination centre for the post of munsif and for the Subordinate Executive Agency.[68]

As in the judicial administration, there had been significant changes in the direction of police administration under the British which not only affected the importance of Dacca but also produced institutional shifts for the maintenance of law and order within the city itself. Initially the District Magistrate (or the Collector-Magistrate as he came to be known from 1859) in addition to his judicial powers was vested with administrative authority over the local police force. This involved the grafting of British concepts on to a Mughal stem: henceforward a professional body of policemen was to function under the traditional darogahs in charge of rural *thanas* (circles), while the Kotwals remained their equivalents in the towns, both being subordinate to the District Magistrate, aided by a body of covenanted and uncovenanted assistants.

In the city of Dacca, however, the pruning of the Mughal system cut deeper. The Kotwal's office was abolished in 1814 and the District Magistrate became the head of the police administration. Below him were the darogahs, each with his own staff in charge of a thana. By 1838 the number of darogahs had been reduced to ten, six Hindus and four Muslims.[69] In November 1838, James Grant, the Magistrate, remarked that there were too many darogahs and thanas, and called for their reduction in the interests of administrative efficiency. Consequently the number of darogahs was reduced from ten to three, as were the thanas and attendant outposts, these being placed under the control of the District Magistrate.

The controlling police authority above the district level from 1808 to 1829 and from 1837 to 1854 was the Superintendent of

Police. In the intervening years, and from 1854 to the great reorganization of 1861, it was the Revenue Commissioner. Thus, from 1854, Dacca became the centre of a police administration stretching over six revenue districts.

The changes at the supervisory level had not altered the basic pattern of police recruitment, training or deployment. In 1860, however, the Government of India appointed a Commission to review the whole police structure. Its proposals contained an emphatic plea for a police department clearly separated from the magistracy and the establishment of a single homogeneous force of civil constabulary for the performance of all general police duties. The discipline and internal management of the force so established was to be vested in an Inspector-General of Police. He was to be assisted by a District Superintendent in each district with an Assistant Superintendent in case the size of a district happened to be very large. The subordinate force within the district was to consist of Inspectors, Head Constables, Sergeants and Constables; the Head Constable being in charge of one police station, the Inspector of a group of such stations.

The Commission specially stressed that the Divisional Commissioners should cease to be Superintendents of Police; 'but so far as the District Magistrate was concerned, his immediate control over the police was to continue, for he was the person who had the charge of district administration in its totality, especially in matters of law and order'.[70] The Commission submitted the draft of a Bill to give effect to its recommendations and this was passed as Act V of 1861.

In Dacca the District Magistrate lost all direct responsibility for the training, discipline and efficiency of the police, while the Commissioner of Revenue, too, lost his police powers. But the deployment of the police was still very much within the say of the District Magistrate, and the Commissioner as executive head of the division continued to act as co-ordinator for the entire police force and continued to write to government suggesting changes and reforms. The city however gained a new police department headed by a European District Superintendent. A police hospital was also established.[71]

In this reorganization, however, the strength of the regular police force for both the city and the district was largely reduced, the theory being that a small band of qualified and well-paid police would be more effective than a large body of ill-qualified, ill-paid and generally ill-disciplined men. The annual cost of this smaller force in Dacca was increased, however, by Rs. 12,540, mostly by way of European officers and English-educated Indian Inspectors.[72]

Major changes were also introduced in the chaukidari police of Dacca, marking a new milestone in the city's history. The chaukidari police was now called the Municipal Police Force or City Constabulary. Its strength like that of the regular police was also reduced from 166 to 129 men.[73] One important feature of its reorganization was the appointment of a European Inspector who became the immediate chief of the new Municipal Police Force.

The evolution of the chaukidari police into a Municipal Police Force was closely tied up with the local self-government legislation of the Bengal Government. In March 1864, the Bengal Government passed the Municipal Improvement Act, Act III, which led to the transformation of many of the cities and towns in the province, including Dacca, into municipalities. As a price for this privilege Dacca, like other towns, was obliged to bear the cost of its city police.[74]

The newly-created Police Department of Lower Bengal was soon representing to the Bengal Government, however, the anomaly of the existence of two separate police forces in many towns and cities, and the Inspector General of Police suggested that in order to increase efficiency and avoid confusion, the two forces in Dacca, as in other towns, should be amalgamated—a suggestion, he added, which the Commissioner of Dacca fully supported.[75]

The Bengal Government agreed and in 1867 an Act was passed, Act VI, authorizing the amalgamation of the Imperial and Municipal Police. In Dacca, for the two bodies was substituted one, under the name of Municipal Police, with jurisdiction both over the city and the immediate countryside, under the general control of the District Superintendent of Police. The new force consisted of one Inspector, two Sub-Inspectors, eight Head Constables and 191 Constables, and cost Rs. 20,068 annually, towards which the Dacca Municipality paid some Rs. 17,000. The Municipality continued to pay for the city police until 1882 when the government itself took over the charge of the entire force.[76]

For those criminals whom the Dacca Police, old or new, apprehended, and whose conviction followed, Dacca further provided. From the very beginning of the East India Company's rule, Dacca had been chosen as the site for a major jail. For a long time the only building activity of the Company in the city was the conversion of the old Mughal fort of Dewan Bazar into a secure prison, capable by 1837 of holding 800 prisoners and actually housing a daily average of 526.[77] For many years thereafter the Dacca jail also acted as an unacknowledged central prison for all Eastern Bengal. Indeed until the 1860s prisoners were brought from as far as Sylhet, Tippera and Faridpur for confinement at Dacca, the jails of those districts being overcrowded and unsuitable for housing dangerous criminals.[78] In 1864, when it was considered necessary to establish a central jail for the Dacca and Chittagong divisions, the Inspector-General of Jails and the Lieutenant-Governor of Bengal both reiterated that it should be housed in Dacca, though C.T. Buckland, the Dacca Commissioner, wanted to have it in the town of Comilla.[79] In 1873 the Dacca Jail was selected as one of the places where European British subjects could be kept in custody.[80] Six years later it was finally elevated to the status of a Central Jail. The elevation led to further expansion and development[81] and reorganization in its management.

Originally it was the District Magistrate who was responsible for the running of the jail acting through a gaoler, usually an Armenian or Eurasian, who undertook the immediate superintendence of the prisoners and the jail. The Civil Surgeon of Dacca was charged with the medical supervision of the prisoners and of jail sanitation[82] and was briefly in 1868–9 given administrative charge of the jail on the mistaken assumption that he would have more time to spare from his other duties than the Magistrate.[83] From 1879, however, after its elevation to a Central Jail, a specialist Jail Superintendent took charge.

The jail administration in Dacca was quite elaborate and provided employment, directly or indirectly, to many residents in the city. Moreover, the prisoners sentenced to labour were employed in manufacturing jute-bags, canework, woodwork, clothes and blankets which were then sold in the Dacca markets and elsewhere. The average number of prisoners also rose from the 526 of 1837 to 635 in 1873-4 and to 803 by 1883. The annual cost rose sharply, too, and by 1883 totalled Rs. 51,328 for food, clothing, charges for prison guards, hospital and contingencies.[84]

Under the East India Company, Dacca did not play the important military role it had done under the Mughals. Nevertheless, a body of troops was always maintained in the city, and after the Mutiny there were always two or three companies and at times an artillery unit at Dacca, employed on occasion in subduing the hill tribes of the North-East. In 1879, however, the troops were replaced by Special Reserve Police.

If the East India Company's forces had no very active military role at Dacca they did have a valuable if limited civil role since public works, mainly road construction and public buildings, were managed by military engineers. The Public Works Department until 1859 was under the Military Board, the whole country being divided into Executive Divisions under Military Engineers. From about 1830 the city of Dacca became the headquarters of one such division, the Dacca or 18th Division comprising Dacca, Barisal and a few other districts of East Bengal. From Governor-General Dalhousie's day, however, public works in the province increased greatly and in 1859 a separate Public Works Department was established. Under the Department came a provincial system of PWD Circles, each under a Superintending Engineer, these Circles in turn were then divided into Executive Divisions under an Executive Engineer, and from 1872 each district received its own District Engineer. From 1859 Dacca thus became headquarters of a PWD Circle and an Executive Division, and from 1872 of a District Engineer also. Under the Road Cess Act of 1871 the District Engineer was given the additional charge of such local works as were financed by the Road Cess funds, hitherto supervised by the Magistrate and sub-divisional officers.[85] For a brief period in the 1860s Dacca also became the headquarters of a Forest Division which included Sylhet and Cachar.[86]

Another, very curious and distinctive link with Dacca's military past was provided by the Kheda Department. Since Mughal times Dacca had been the centre from which the capture of wild elephants and their taming and training had been organized, and the Kheda department survived into the nineteenth century as a direct link with the Kheda Afyal of earlier days.[87] The elephants were captured in the jungles of the Chittagong Hill Tracts by *koonkees*, who drove them into great traps or *kheda*. They were then taken to a large area west of Dacca, then and now known as the Peelkhana or Elephant Depot, which was earmarked for their breaking in. Once tamed they were marched through the main thoroughfares of the town to pasture in the Ramna area. There was much complaint from the public about serious nuisance caused by their movement, and so, soon after its establishment, the Municipality built an alternative road through the northern outskirts of the city. Elephant Road, running from the New Market to Ramna, still survives. Individual zamindars from the surrounding districts also used to send their elephants to the Dacca Peelkhana for training and maintenance on payment of fees.

Elephants from the Dacca Peelkhana were used by the government during the 1860s and 1870s in the expeditions against the hill tribes of the North-East Frontier. They were also used for transport of district officials and in the city of Dacca itself for parade and show on such state occasions as the visits of the Lieutenant-Governors and Viceroys.[88]

In 1881 the Kheda establishment at Dacca included one Superintendent, one Head Assistant, two Veterinary Surgeons, three clerks, one cattle *gumashta* or accountant and a number of *syces* or elephant drivers.

A third field with which the Army was closely connected was that of medical provision, since Army surgeons provided much of the medical care available: indeed the Civil Surgeon who was found at most district headquarters was curiously misnamed since he was a military officer seconded for civil duties but liable to recall to the Army in time of war. In Dacca the first step in providing medical aid was, however, the establishment of a Native Hospital in 1803, which was followed in 1819 by a Lunatic Asylum. By 1839 the medical establishments in the city consisted of the Native Hospital, the Lunatic Asylum, a Jail Hospital, a Military Hospital and the Vaccine Departmnt.[89] The Lunatic Asylum treated patients from the Dacca and all the surrounding districts. It was one of the few such institutions in the Bengal Presidency, and grew rapidly as it began to accept patients from the whole of East Bengal and Assam. The average number of patients between 1831 and 1837 was 53, rising to some 300 a year in the decade 1857 to 1867. In the latter year the Asylum establishment, under the Civil Surgeon as Superintendent, consisted of an overseer, one native doctor and a menial staff of forty-eight. In the 1830s the government had also established charitable dispensaries throughout the country, and one such dispensary was established in Dacca in 1839. It was through these dispensaries that the government ran its campaign to vaccinate people against smallpox, and a Vaccine Department was attached to the newly-established Dacca Dispensary in 1839.

The most important medical institution of the city, however, was the Mitford Hospital opened in 1858. It was built with a bequest left by Robert Mitford, once Collector and Judge of the Provincial Court of Appeal of Dacca. The old Native Hospital and the Government Charitable Dispensary were absorbed into the Mitford Hospital, government providing a monthly grant of Rs. 453. (The total cost of the hospital in 1871 was Rs. 14,210.) It had two surgical and two medical wards for males, and one for females, providing accommodation for ninety-five patients. In the decade after it was opened the hospital also treated an average of 10,000 out-patients yearly. Soon the Mitford Hospital became the premier medical institution in East Bengal and people from all over the region came to receive treatment there. In 1867, Arthur Lloyd Clay, the Joint Magistrate of Dacca, described the hospital as the best in Lower Bengal outside Calcutta and Howrah.[90] In the 1860s Dacca also became the headquarters of the Deputy Inspector-General of Hospitals who was entrusted with the supervision of the hospitals and charitable dispensaries in charge of the Civil Surgeons and Assistant Surgeons in the Dacca Circle. This Dacca Circle was one of the three such Circles into which the whole province was divided and comprised almost the whole of East Bengal and Assam.[91] By the 1870s Dacca had also become the headquarters of the Superintendent of Vaccination for East Bengal.

Many of the administrative departments which centred upon Dacca grew out of older Mughal structures, some like the elephant depot being rather unexpected survivals of the past. Education in Dacca was, by contrast, very much a harbinger of change. The development of educational instutions and their major contribution to the life of East Bengal are discussed in the next chapter. Here, however, it is necessary to note the rise of Dacca as the administrative centre of educational development.

The East India Company did not take any substantial steps towards the education of the Indian people before 1835.[92] But thereafter a policy of establishing government schools and providing scholarships to needy and meritorious students was followed, implemented at first in the district headquarters and other important towns through local educational committees and the district authorities. In Dacca a Local Education Committee was organized in 1835 for the town, while the District Magistrate looked after educational development in the district, and the Divisional Commissioner in the division.

In the 1850s Sir Charles Wood's Education Despatch, and Dalhousie's working out of its proposals, encouraged the spread of privately established Anglo-Vernacular and Vernacular schools, both primary and higher, under the system of grants-in-aid by government. These schools were inspected as a condition of their receiving a grant and a body of Inspectors of Schools was created under the Department of Education for the purpose. The whole province was divided into several Educational Circles in 1855, each of which was put under the charge of an Inspector with a number of Deputy Inspectors stationed at important centres in the circle,[93] a shift away from the amateur local educational committees and civil servants to a professional educational department. The city of Dacca was made the headquarters of such a circle comprising twelve East Bengal districts. Some of the most eminent educationists of the time were appointed Inspectors of Schools for the circle, men whose zeal and efforts were mainly responsible for the great educational development of East Bengal during the nineteenth century. It was of course partly the existence of so many government offices and officials which made Dacca so appropriate as an educational centre. In one more way, too, the impact of administration was cumulative.

It will already have been noted that the Surveyor who chose Dacca as his headquarters did so partly because there it was cheek by jowl with the office of the Commissioner to whom appeal would lie in survey cases. Each successive addition to the administrative structure at Dacca made it easier and more useful to centre further departments there too. A dramatic change however had meanwhile occurred in the economic scene of the region with the plantation of tea in the recently acquired areas of Assam and the international demand for jute. Vast amounts of capital had been invested in the trade of these two items which obviously required an administrative centre nearby well equipped to oversee the region's economic growth and stability. But it should be noted that administrative needs meant Dacca's locational advantages were growing also. The value of its nodal position on the river system remained, but the growth of the postal and telegraphic systems of East Bengal were scarcely less important since they centred on Dacca. A modern postal system was introduced in Dacca early in the nineteenth century,[94] and as the system was extended the city became the main nerve centre for East Bengal, under a separate Postal Department. When in 1878 East Bengal was made a separate postal circle, Dacca was formally named as its headquarters under a Deputy Postmaster-General in charge of the Dacca, Mymensingh, Tippera, Chittagong and Noakhali districts.[95]

An even more powerful element in the transformation of medieval Dacca into a modern city was the installation of the telegraph, destroying as it did Dacca's partial isolation. The telegraphic system linking the Presidency towns was working by 1854 and by 1855 over forty telegraph offices had been opened to the public,[96] none as yet at Dacca. The new economic reality and above all the Mutiny of 1857 served only to intensify government's anxiety to extend the system: for days together Calcutta heard nothing from the Dacca authorities about the safety of the city, though rumours were flying that the troops there were mutinous. And as such a mutiny became increasingly probable the Dacca officials had no means of seeking urgent support,[97] though Dacca was almost defenceless until British sailors arrived in November 1857.

The telegraphic link between Dacca and Calcutta was installed and working by 18 October 1858, and a year later a further link between Dacca and Chittagong was established.[98] Business and commercial interests and the general public soon began to utilize the new service,[99] and in numbers which justified the hopes with which Dalhousie had entered upon his original plan for an Indian telegraph system. Until all the districts in East Bengal had been linked together telegraphically, moreover, important administrative messages between Calcutta and these districts were exchanged by way of the telegraph office in Dacca.

An equally powerful element in the transformation of the city was the building of a railway line connecting Dacca with Narayanganj and Mymensingh.[100] The work on the line began in December 1882 and in January 1885 the first passenger service between Narayanganj and Dacca started. The city of Dacca was made the headquarters of this newly constructed Dacca-Mymensingh State Railway under the charge of an Engineer-in-chief.

The final effect of all these accretions of departmental offices was to make the city of Dacca by 1885 the largest civil station, after Calcutta, in the province of Bengal.[101] It was not only the headquarters of a Divisional Commissioner of Revenue but also the regional centre of many other government departments—Public Works, Post and Telegraph, Education and Medical. These regional establishments together with the various district offices—civil, police and military—provided direct and indirect employment to large numbers of people. There are no detailed figures available of the staffs employed at the end of the period, but even in 1867 they numbered some 980 in all,[102] to which must also be added those departments whose Dacca offices were established after 1867. The population of Dacca city was enumerated at 69,212 in 1872 of which 37,395 were male. Assuming that half that figure represented adults in employment, then perhaps one in twenty was directly employed in government offices, a figure which takes no account of the pleaders, mooktars and their clerks, the contractors who supplied the jail and the hospital, the employees of the municipality, and the shopkeepers and craftsmen whose livelihood largely depended upon the presence of so many elements of government administration.

Historians have tended to ignore the importance of Dacca as a centre of provincial administration, only giving it serious attention after its formal emergence in 1905 as the short-lived capital of Eastern Bengal and Assam. One historian dismisses these pre-1905 institutions as the 'rudimentary jacket of the new administration'.[103] Rudimentary, they certainly were not; they were well tested, for well before the end of the nineteenth century Dacca had recaptured most of the regional dominance and power it had enjoyed in niabat days. It was already a regional capital in practice before it became the constitutional capital of East Bengal.

The growth of Dacca was a case of trade and the flag marching hand in hand. The absorption of Assam into British India in 1826 and the subsequent development of the tea industry which soon attained a global dimension was coupled with the equally spectacular rise of jute manufactures. An enormous amount of British capital was sunk into both. Each of these commodities had to be transported through the waterways of East Bengal to the environs of Calcutta where they were processed for export to markets overseas. Dacca was advantageously placed in the bowl between the two main rivers in the system—the Brahmaputra and the Padma. With a hinterland of such massive potential, it followed naturally that the city should be provided with an administrative structure to match the economic reality. It is perhaps this more than anything else that prevented it from ending up, like Murshidabad, as a fading relic of Mughal grandeur. Just as Calcutta emerged from rural obscurity to become the second city of the British Empire, so Dacca emerged from the shadows of its post-Mughal decline to become the second city of Bengal. The scale may have varied, but each city developed a comparable web of commercial, industrial, administrative, cultural and political relationships.

NOTES TO CHAPTER II

1 See Richard Temple, *Men and Events of My Time in India*, 145.

2 Besides the Subahdar, popularly known as the Nawab, there were in the city the Diwan or the Finance Minister, 'responsible for revenue and civil justice'; the Bakhsi or pay-master; the Sadr or head of the religious department, charity and grants; the Qazi or judge; the Kotwal or city-superintencent of police; the Mir-i-Bahr or admiral; the Waqianavis or news-reporter; and the Quanungo or the 'expounder of the law' and keeper of the land revenue registers.

3 Karim *Dacca*, 91.

4 Under the Mughal Government all revenues other than those from land were called *sair*. The word sair thus connoted various items of collection—duties on imports and exports, on goods brought to the market for sale, duties on shops in the markets and so on.

5 A.L. Clay, 'Principal Heads of the History and Statistics of the Dacca District in '*Principal Heads of the History and Statistics of the Dacca Division*', 36.

6 Pramatha Nath Banerjee, *Indian Finance in the Days of the Company*, 251; also F. D. Ascoli, *Early Revenue History of Bengal and the Fifth Report, 1812*, 247, n. 1.

7 Rizvi, *Dacca*, 362.

8 For the theoretical and often romantic considerations which led to significant changes in the administrative policy of Bengal during the nineteenth century, see Eric Stokes, *The English Utilitarians and India.*

9 B. B. Misra, *The Central Administration of the East India Company, 1773–1834*, 149.

10 For the background of this Regulation and various reports and minute on the subject, see Bengal Revenue Consultations, Range LX9, vol. 45, 10 December 1828, Nos. 32–56; and 30 December 1828, Nos. 20–22.

11 Bengal Revenue Consultations, LX1, 50, 12 May 1829, 9; Clay, *Principal Heads.*

12 BAR for 1884–5, appendix C.

13 Similar difficulties were also faced in tracing the invalid *lakhiraj* or revenue-free lands which were to be resumed.

14 The office of the qanungo was abolished in 1793; it was re-established in 1819, but abolished again in 1828; see Ascoli, *Early Revenue History*, 247, n. 1.

15 BAR for 1921–2, 703–4.

16 C. H. Cambell to GB, 21 August 1854, Bengal Revenue Consultations, LXV, 76, 23 November 1854, 15.

17 The present limits of the district of Dacca came to be fixed in 1871 after the transfer of the Thana Mulfatganj to Faridpur in exchange for the Thana Manikganj of that district.

18 For details see Rai Bahadur Monohan Chakrabarti, *Summary of the Changes in the Jurisdiction of Districts in Bengal, 1757–1916;* Nabakanta

Chattapadhaya, *Dhaka Zelar Bhugal Abong Shankep Aitihasik Bibaran* (A Short Account of the History and Geography of Dacca District); Ascoli, 'The Jurisdiction of the District of Dacca from the Earliest Times', *The Dacca Review*, 1916–17, 15–23.

19 P. Banerjee, *A History of Indian Taxation*, 23–5, *et passim*. Some of these taxes tapped new sources, for example, the incomes of professional people and the profits of industry and commerce in the towns hitherto scarcely touched.

20 Income tax, for example, was introduced in 1860, abolished in 1873 and then reintroduced in 1886.

21 Taylor, *Dacca*, 220.

22 Clay, *Principal Heads*, 92.

23 BAR for 1884–5, appendix, C, sec. V.

24 Misra, *Central Administration*, 165.

25 Ascoli, *Early Revenue History*, 81, *et passim*.

26 This is not to deny the continuance of customary ties in the countryside or the importance of the zamindars' cutcherries for the tenure holders and ryots, but to emphasize the growth of the Collectorate as a rival seat of authority and justice, within reasonable distance of every village in the district.

27 J. B. Harrison and R. Hunt (eds.), *The District Officer in India*.

28 Nabin Chandra Bhadra, *Bhawaler Itihasha* (History of Bhawal); also [Graham, G], *Life in the Mofussil; or the Civilian in Lower Bengal*, II; 160–3.

29 In 1879 an East Bengal Landholders' Association was formed in Dacca under the presidentship of Nawab Khwaja Ahsanullah to protect the interests of the zamindars of East Bengal, see *Dhaka Prokash*, 29 Poush 1285 (12 January 1879).

30 M. S. Islam, 'Mufassal Towns of Bengal' in K. Ballhatchet & J. Harrison, (eds.), *The City in South Asia*, 233–4.

31 Banerjee, *Indian Finance*, 241.

32 The Collector acting through a darogah, kept the stamp and stamped papers of various denominations in his treasury, and arranged the sale in commission through numbers of private vendors who took post outside the various offices and courts.

33 Minutes of Henry M. Parker, 23 October 1839, Board of Customs, Salt and Opium Proceedings, XVIII, 33, 7 November 1839, 5, para. 38.

34 Resolution of 26 February, 1840, Bengal Separate Consultations, CLXIV, 79, 26 February 1840, 6.

35 Commissioner of Excise to GB, 15 September 1843, Bengal Separate Consultations, CLXV, 5, 8 August 1844, 21.

36 Bengal Board of Revenue Proceedings (Misc.), CVIII, 73, 15 August 1844, 65.

37 Bengal Separate Consultations, CLXV, 6, 27 November 1844, 4; also BOCSOP, CIX, 4, 6 March 1845, 7–9.

38 BOCSOP, CX, 10, 15 August 1850, 19.

39 The probable excise revenue yields, it was argued, had been based on experience in Bihar—a mistake since Bengal did not consume so much as Bihar. See BOCSOP, CX, 10, 15 August 1850, 32.

40 For the history of this College see chapter III.
41 *Annual Report of the Council of Education* for 1848–9, 275.
42 See Annual Report of the Dacca College in *Education Reports—Bengal Schools & Colleges* for 1853–4, appendix 1.
43 For the background of this tax see R. J. Moore, *Sir Charles Wood's Indian Policy, 1853–66*, chapter XI, *et passim;* also Mrs J. A. Rahman, *Some Sspects of the Indian Viceroyalty of Lord Elgin I, 1862–63*, (Unpublished Ph. D thesis). The tax was, however, vigorously opposed by European and Indian vested interests and was repealed at their instance in 1872–3, but modified versions continued to be imposed. See [Graham], *Life in the Mofussil*, 186–9.
44 Abdul Ghani to GB, 9 February 1861, Bengal Revenue Proceedings, Finance, LXVI, 36, March 1861, 4–6.
45 BRP, Finance, LXVI, 36, March 1861, 115–17.
46 Commissioner of Dacca to GB, ibid.
47 For details see chapter VI.
48 See chapter VI.
49 Walters' letter, 30 April 1830, in the Commissioner of Dacca to GB, 29 June 1830, Bengal Criminal Judicial Consultations, CXXXIX, 53, 13 July 1830, 20.
50 Bengal Judicial Proceedings, 251, December 1872, 246.
51 For an illustration of this shipment see A. L. Clay's sketch in his *Leaves From a Diary in Lower Bengal*, plate 15 facing p. 78.
52 [Graham], *Life in the Mofussil*, 190–1.
53 This court was first established in 1793.
54 The Rev. Owen Leonard to Baptist Missionary Society, 23 May 1838, Leonard Papers.
55 Allen, *Dacca*, 138.
56 654 suits—8 original, 278 appeals and 368 labelled miscellaneous—were pending at the close of 1850.
57 Simson to GB, 20 February 1873, BJP (Appointments), 257, March 1873, file 3–5.
58 BJP, CXLVI, 39, April 1861, 344.
59 BJP, CXLVI, 41, June 1861, 36.
60 The crimes for which the Magistrate was by law bound to commit persons for such a trial included treason, murder, robbery, arson as well as serious cases of burglary and theft.
61 Hriday Nath Majumdar, *The Reminiscences of Dacca*, 82.
62 BJP, CXLVI, 21, 22 September 1859, 57.
63 This was a reference to the wives and children of Europeans resident in Dacca who had been sent to Calcutta during late 1857 as a precaution against any possible rebellion of the native troops in the city.
64 *Dacca News*, 6 February 1858, 72.
65 For details see chapter III.
66 BJP, CXLVI, 70, February 1864, 102.
67 Clay, *Leaves From a Diary*, 130–1.
68 BJP, CXLI, 75, 3 April 1843, 39; BAR, for 1872–3, p. 9.
69 Report of D. J. McNeil, 22 May 1866, BJP (Police), CCCXXXIII, 12

September 1866, appendix A, 126–7. In 1794 they had all been Muslims; see Report of the Dacca Magistrate, September 1794, BOR, LXXII, 35, 28.

70 Misra, *Administrative History*, 539.

71 For details on the reorganization of police in Bengal, see C. F. Carnac, *Report on the New Police in Bengal from the Date of its Organisation under Act V of 1861 to the Close of 1862*.

72 BJP (Police Branch), CXLVI, 71, March 1864, 6.

73 Ibid.

74 For details see chapter VII.

75 Inspector-General of Police to GB, 8 June 1866, BJP (Police), CCCXXXIII, 11 July 1866, 17–18.

76 See chapter VII.

77 Allen, *Dacca District Gazetteer*, 145.

78 See for example, BCJC, CXLV, 10, 10 May 1855, 147–9.

79 BJP (Jail), CXLVII, 8 March 1865, 60–1. Buckland only considered the central position of Comilla town within these two divisions, but overlooked the advantages of establishing a central jail in a growing administrative centre like Dacca.

80 BJP (Jail), 253, January 1873, 144.

81 Between 1880 and 1883 rupees 74, 437 were spent to develop it into a Central Jail, see BAR for 1883–5, 56.

82 There was a small hospital attached to the jail.

83 BAR for 1867–8, 50–1.

84 Based on figures in BAR for 1883–4, appendix C, statement X.

85 BAR for 1872–3, 253; also BAR for 1873–4, 132–3.

86 From this time a Government Timber Depot was also established at Dacca.

87 See Karim, *Dacca*, 61.

88 Lady Dufferin, *Our Viceregal Life in India*, 401–2.

89 Taylor, *Dacca*, 356.

90 Clay, *Principal Heads*, 59–60.

91 BAR for 1870–71, 35, appendix VI A.

92 See S. Mahmood, *A History of English Education in India (1781–1893)*.

93 *Annual Report of the Director of Public Instruction* for 1854–5, p VII.

94 For details see Misra, *The Central Administration*, 430–2, *et passim*.

95 *Dhaka Prokash*, 25 Kartik, 1285 (10 November 1878).

96 M. N. Das, *Studies in the Economic and Social Development of Modern India: 1854–56*, 147.

97 Editorial, *Dacca News*, 19 December 1857, 544.

98 Clay, *Principal Heads*, 47.

99 *Dacca News*, 6 November 1858, 534.

100 See also chapter IV.

101 The total expenditure on the civil and police establishments of all kinds in 1884–5 in Dacca (including some mofussil establishments) was the highest in the province after Calcutta and its suburbs; see BAR for 1884–5, appendix C, IV–V.

102 Clay, *Principal Heads*, statement 14. This figure, however, includes some staff who were not actually mentioned in the list of officials given by Clay.

103 Dani, *Dacca*, 97.

CHAPTER III

A CENTRE OF EDUCATION

Probably the most significant factor behind Dacca's rejuvenation in the nineteenth century was its emergence as an important seat of education. So great was the spread of education that by the end of the century Dacca had not only become the main centre of English education in East Bengal, but also the second largest centre of education in the province ranking only after Calcutta.

Dacca's emergence as an educational centre owed much to its geographical location and to the cultural heritage of its hinterland.[1] This hinterland contained a substantial number of the Muslim aristocracy—the descendants of Afghan, Turk and Mughal rulers and their nobility—who, though not economically well off, valued Persian and Arabic education as aids to religious instruction and, in the case of Persian particularly, as the hallmark of the cultured gentleman. The other cultural heritage from the Mughal past was the presence of large numbers of Hindus belonging to the literary castes—the Brahmins, Baidyas and Kayasthas—they were high officials, priests, teachers, physicians, professional and service people as well as landholders. Besides knowing Sanskrit they learnt Arabic, Persian and Urdu, essential if they were to hold administrative, professional and service positions under an Islamic administration. Knowledge of languages fitted men for employment—but it also brought social and intellectual prestige.[2] Vikrampur, the ancient capital of Bengal,[3] situated some fifteen miles south-east of Dacca, had over time become the principal stronghold of these high-caste Hindus. With the establishment of British rule and the introduction of English as the language of business and administration, these castes came to see the language of their new masters as the key to worldly success. But English education offered not just career prospects; it also provided entry into an exciting new world of intellectual discovery and challenge. Moreover, because of the secular, liberal framework within which the British introduced the new learning it was open to other castes too, the Basaks and the Nandis, the lowlier weavers and shell-cutters of the city, for example.

Western education scarcely got under way before 1835, however. Till then education remained traditional in content[4] and method and in the clientele it served[5]: only a small proportion of the population received any formal education, Hindus at *pathsalas*[6] and *tols*[7] (seminaries) supported by zamindars and merchants, Muslims at home (for upper-class families[8]) or at maktabs generally attached to mosques and supported by mahalla panchayats.[9] British rule saw a decline in Persian and Arabic studies for want of patronage. There was an unsatisfied demand for education appropriate to government service.

The first people to meet the new educational needs of Dacca were the Baptist Missionaries of Serampore. In 1815 they sent the Reverend Owen Leonard, an Irishman, to Dacca to establish a branch of the Calcutta Benevolent Institution 'for the education of the children of poor Europeans and Eurasians';[10] and in April 1816 he opened the first English school near Chauk Bazar, in the Chota Katra building.[11] Thirty-nine Christian boys and girls including Greeks and Armenians were admitted. The children were given lessons in English, grammar and arithmetic, the Bible, Watt's Hymns and the Catechism.

Not content with providing education for Christian children only, Leonard also founded seven Bengali schools,[12] and in 1817 started a Persian school to attract Muslim pupils. His most interesting experiment, however, was the opening of his English school to Indian, non-Christian children. It is not certain when this began, but initially numbers of local boys sought and gained admission. But despite a promising start the school did not flourish and when Leonard died in 1848 it had to be closed.

Two factors prevented the school from becoming a success: Leonard's increasing evangelical zeal, which frightened away many non-Christian parents and made them withdraw their children from his charge, and the establishment of a secular government school in the city. This school was the product of a twenty-year official debate about the content and medium of instruction which had been largely resolved by the Governor-General Lord William Bentinck's intervention in favour of European science and literature taught through the medium of English.[13]

In a report submitted to Bentinck on 20 April 1835,[14] the General

Committee of Public Instruction proposed that schools should first be instituted (as far as government funds would permit) 'for teaching English literature and science in the principal cities and towns' of the Presidency, commencing 'with the populous cities of Patna and Dacca'. The Committee had earlier written to the local officials in Dacca asking them to report whether Dacca would be a suitable place to establish a government school, and whether subscriptions could be raised from the inhabitants to support it if necessary. Dr James Taylor, then Assistant Surgeon of Dacca, and others replied enthusiastically, declaring that the city was not only an ideal place for such an institution but that its establishment would be greatly appreciated by the inhabitants who were ready to raise subscriptions to defray its expenses. This encouraging reply led the General Committee to ask the Government of India to institute a government school at Dacca immediately and to allot Rs. 6,000 a year for its maintenance.[15] On 24 June 1835 the Government of India accepted the Committee's scheme.[16]

Meanwhile the Committee, without waiting for formal sanction, had gone ahead with its plan to establish a school at Dacca, sending two distinguished teachers, Mr Ridge and Babu Parbati Charan Sarkar, from Calcutta early in June 1835.[17] The old Factory of the East India Company at Dacca was rented and the school formally opened on 15 July 1835. It was thus in the city of Dacca that the first government English school in the Bengal Presidency was established. The people of Dacca responded generously to this. Ram Lochan Ghosh of Bairagidi near Dacca and the Sheristadar of the Sadr Board of Revenue at Calcutta, donated Rs. 1,000[18] and others, Europeans and Indians, soon raised the sum to Rs. 5,000.[19] The school's administration was entrusted to a Local Committee of Public Instruction.

The newly-established English school and its subsequent growth proved a catalyst not only for the social and cultural renewal of Dacca city but for its hinterland as well. The curriculum apart from providing a useful facility in the new rulers' language,[20] exposed students to Western liberal arts, sciences, religion and philosophy. Many among them wished to refashion and modernize their society in the light of this learning.[21] But the school's success in these early years was chiefly attributable to people's eagerness to learn English as a means for securing jobs.[22] The demand for such education exceeded the facilities available and new premises had very soon to be sought; but the bulk of the students came from the city and its suburbs, and were Brahmins, Baidyas and Kayasthas, the Hindu service castes.[23] It was nonetheless a demand the government was ready to meet, on both practical and (according to the ideas of the time) moral grounds.[24]

In 1841, as part of a programme of concentrating on English education in preference to the wider dissemination of instruction through the vernacular languages, and indeed of 'rendering the highest instruction efficient in a certain number of Central Colleges, rather than... in the extension of... ordinary Zillah schools',[25] a collegiate section was grafted on to the school at Dacca[26] and the city became the focus of English education in East Bengal. The Dacca Central College, as it was now known, was divided into two departments, Senior and Junior, each with its own headmaster, under a single principal, one J. Ireland, from Cambridge and the Hindu College, Calcutta.[27] In the Senior Department the higher branches of European science and literature were taught and in the Junior, English, Bengali, Arithmetic, History and Geography at a lower level. In 1844 the college had fourteen European and Indian teachers on its staff, a librarian and clerk, besides a complement of darwans and peons.[28]

Dacca College contributed to the development of the city in several ways. It gave support to certain sections within the community, it introduced Western ideas to those sections, and reinforced the centrality and prestige of the town by attracting outsiders to it. The college added therefore a new dimension to the cultural, social and intellectual character of the city, and gave it a new role to perform in the region. Although initially the college's success was registered in its student numbers—from 344 in 1842 to 455 in 1856[29]—the composition of the student body became if anything more restricted during the early years of its existence. It was, however, a deliberate policy, though one opposed by the Local Committee at Dacca.

At their inception in the 1830s all government institutions had provided free instruction, even to the books required. However, the limited funds available led the government to modify this policy in the early 1840s. Firstly, in 1843 it decided to stop the supply of free books and then resolved to demand school fees from the students. In 1844 the government instructed the Dacca College authorities gradually to reduce the number of free students and to levy a monthly fee of one rupee from the Senior and eight annas from the Junior Department students.[30] Most of the newly-admitted boys were obliged to pay the fees and in 1844 of the 308 boys 124 were paying fees.[31]

The success of the fee-system led the government to resolve in January 1846 that 'the schooling fees should be demanded from everybody without exception'. Moreover in March 1846 it was further decreed that the Senior Department students should pay a fee of three rupees per month and Junior Department students two rupees per month.

These rules and instructions, coming as they did one after another, greatly alarmed the Local Committee at Dacca who immediately protested.[32] They asserted that the abolition of the system of free scholars was not only harsh but also discriminatory in view of the government's clear commitment towards the education of every class in society. They also argued that the level of fees in the government colleges might be reasonable for other places like Calcutta, but was not so for Dacca, a decaying city where even the slightest increase in fees would be an impossible burden. The Committee's experience led them to plead that at least for some time the fees should be half those proposed by government and that at least fifty students should be allowed to join the college as 'Free scholars'.[33]

The authorities, however, ordered the strictest implementation of the new rules. They explained,

> . . . where millions need instruction and the government is in a position to afford it only to hundreds, it is obviously proper to begin with those whose circumstances will probably enable them to turn their advantages to the best account, and who are willing in return to provide the Government with the means of extending its operations.[34]

As a result fees were increased and payment made mandatory. The consequences were disastrous. In 1846 ninety-nine students were expelled from the college 'for neglecting to pay the increased fee demanded for their schooling'.[35] A crisis had occurred but fortunately it led to Dacca's further growth as a centre of English education through the foundation of a new English school. At the critical juncture when the doors of the college were closed to many boys, certain ex-students of the college, together with some of those forced by poverty to leave, with the help of their former Principal, Dr. T. A. Wise,[36] founded a new school in the city, on 12 June 1846, under the name of the Union School. The school was founded for the express purpose of imparting English education to the needy.[37] Within two years however it became clear that the school could not be continued for lack of funds. At this juncture another ex-student of the Dacca College, N. P. Pogose, a rich Armenian zamindar, came to the school's rescue. The still famous Pogose School thus came into being. A philanthropist and keen educationist, 'Nickie' Pogose took up the management of the school himself, and largely thanks to his efficiency the school within a decade had grown to be one of the most celebrated institutions of Bengal.

Meanwhile, the Dacca Central College had recovered from the shake-up of the 1840s. The popularity of the college was ensured by the increasing opportunities which were opened up to the English-educated in the administration and in commerce,[38] but its social exclusiveness remained, mitigated only slightly by a scholarship system. The result, for Dacca, was the creation of an English-educated stratum of people as officials, clerks, accountants and commercial agents.

However, the city's emergence as a regional centre of education through the growth of the college was already in the making. It began with the scholarship scheme instituted by the Governor-General Lord Auckland to popularize higher English education. Thus scholarships were offered to enable the mofussil students to continue further studies at the Dacca Central College. Initially a single Junior Scholarship of eight rupees, tenable for four years (awarded on the basis of the results of the Junior Scholarship Examination), was allotted to each of the newly-established zilla schools, a number later increased. In addition, the Council of Education also authorized the local committees in the districts to nominate a few meritorious students for free tickets enabling them to study at the college without paying fees and other dues.[39]

The system of scholarships and free tickets at once created a spirit of emulation and fostered an enthusiasm for English education. The scholarship links with the college moreover increased the popularity of the mofussil schools. As the secretary of the Natore School, Rajshahi, remarked,

> The permission to send two boys free to the Dacca College cannot but be attended with highly benefical effects. The very fact of their being a connection with a Government college would be means of extending its sphere of usefulness.[40]

The Dacca College thus not only became the pivot of English education in East Bengal but it also brought prestige to the city.

The earliest information that we have of students joining the college from other districts relates to 1843. In that year the college authorities reported that fifteen such students—seven from Faridpur, two from Barisal, two from Jessore, two from Mymensingh and two even from the Upper Provinces—had entered the college.[41] In 1850, the Local Committee at Dacca, commenting on the esteem in which the college was held, reported,

> Parents and guardians send their sons from distant schools apparently with little hesitation; from Chittagong, Rampore-Bauleah [Rajshahi], Commilla, Mymensingh, Burrisaul, Furredpore, to attend the College.[42]

There were thirty-one non-Daccaite students at the college by 1853. The numbers continued to increase steadily as responsible and remunerative government posts such as Deputy Magistrate and Collector, teachers in government schools, Excise Superintendent and Munsif came gradually to demand a high level of English education.

Dacca's growth as educational centre was further aided by the new educational system of the 1850s. The progress of education in British India in the first half of the nineteenth century had been considerable but haphazard. There had been numerous changes of direction and the system had only been loosely articulated. With the publication of Sir Charles Wood's famous Education Despatch in 1854, and Dalhousie's strong support for the cause of education, however, a more orderly and rapid advance began in all-India education. The aim—to teach the improved arts, sciences and literature—was unchanged, as was the use of English as the medium for higher education. There was additional stress upon professional and technical education, and at the other end of the scale upon mass education and the encouragement of the vernaculars. But the decisive moves were to create the first three Indian universities, to link these with affiliated colleges and the latter to the schools, and through the grants-in-aid scheme supervised by the newly appointed Director of Public Instruction to encourage much greater public participation in the extension of education. Dacca was to take a full share in all the consequent developments.

With the establishment of Calcutta University in 1857 as an affiliating body, the old Dacca Central College was split into two institutions. The old Senior Department was formed into a regular College and the Junior Department into an English High School, both being supervised by the Principal.

The College was affiliated to Calcutta University, and a four-year course leading to the Bachelor of Arts degree was started from 1857–8. In 1862, a two-year course leading to the First Arts Examination was opened, and from 1863 courses were also started for the Master of Arts Examination. Admission to the College was subject to the High Schools Entrance Examination, held for the first time in Bengal in March 1857, when fourteen students passed from the old Dacca Government School. In 1857–8, there were forty-one students at the Dacca College many being students of the former Senior Department.

The foundation of this modern collegiate institution at once raised the importance of Dacca throughout its hinterland. However, as the reorganization of the educational system was followed by a greater demand for English-educated young men in the job market, the Dacca College at first failed to prosper. Students, mostly from impoverished middle or lower-middle class background, left the college for service as soon as they had entered. Few remained to finish the full course of the college. Commenting on the situation, the DPI reported,

> It arises chiefly from the fact that the demand for educated labour exceeds supply, a state of things which leads to tempting offers of salary and independence being placed at the disposal of lads still at school, or in the first year or two of a college career.

He pinned his hope of a remedy on the new 'prospect of obtaining a University Degree'.[43]

That hope, however, seemed at first a very distant prospect, for at the beginning the state of the Dacca College was so bad that ambitious students were reluctant to get themselves admitted into it. Dacca's potential powers to pull students from its hinterland, and its expected rise as a centre of higher Western education were thus threatened. Indeed for a long time the college lacked a good library and an adequate and qualified staff; initially there were not even sufficient professors for all the subjects offered. The result was that most students left the college after completing their first or second year and sought to join the Presidency College, Calcutta, to finish their B.A. course. So desperate was the situation that in 1860 the third and fourth-year classes were abolished for lack of students and professors, and the few students who had been studying in these classes were transferred wholesale to the Presidency College. In 1861, to compete with the Presidency College, the finest institution of higher Western education in the country,[44] the Dacca College had only one regular Principal and a Pundit on its staff, who were supposed to teach four different classes in the six compulsory subjects prescribed for the B.A. examination, so that the Head Master and the Second Master of the Collegiate School had often to be employed to assist them. This deplorable situation was said to be due to a shortage of qualified teachers, but the DPI blamed also the policy of the government which allotted most of its limited funds for higher English education to the Presidency College, leaving little to go round elsewhere.[45]

Then in 1861–2 an unprecedented increase in the number of students entering the Dacca College occurred. The number of candidates from East Bengal successful in the Entrance Examination rose from 34 in 1860 to 74 in 1861 and to 138 in 1862.[46] The DPI, W. S. Atkinson, reported to the government that it had become a matter of great urgency to 'strengthen the instructive staff' of the Dacca College.[47] His intervention led in January 1863 to the appointment of two more professors and one assistant,[48] and in subsequent years there followed further appointments of professors including a number of eminent Oxford and Cambridge men. The college thus grew into one of the best staffed colleges of Bengal, and the enlargement of the staff immediately led to academic success. In 1864, for the first time, two Dacca College students, Akhil Chandra Sen and Rohini Kumar Basak, passed the B.A. examination. The news of this result produced a mood of rejoicing in the city, and the *Dhaka Prokash*, the Dacca-published Bengali weekly, wrote a leader congratulating the college. 'Until today', remarked the elated editor, 'we have been extremely anguished that none of the students of the college had passed the B.A. examination; but we are now delighted that our woes have disappeared.'[49] From 1864 onwards a few students from the college passed the B.A. examination every year, and in 1867 Peari Mohan Biswas and Hari Chaitanya Ghosh passed the M.A. examination in Mathematics.[50] In that year also, Serajul Islam (later Nawab) passed the B.A. examination, winning the distinction of being the first Muslim graduate of the college.[51]

The improvement in the quality of teaching staff and library facilities at the college led not only to higher academic standards but also marked a distinct stage in the development of Dacca's educational system, and its status as a genuine regional education centre. Thus in 1872, the Principal of the college reported that almost all the students in the Dacca Division who had been awarded scholarships had elected to hold them at the Dacca College, indicating 'a growing tendency among the students of Eastern Bengal to stay by their own college, instead of migrating largely to the Presidency College as was formerly the custom'.[52] He also added that of the forty-two newly-admitted students in the college, twenty-eight were from the city and district of Dacca, and the rest came from Barisal, Mymensingh, Faridpur, Comilla, Sylhet and Kuch Bihar. The flow of students from other districts further increased when a separate science department was opened in 1875. From that year the number of students, then 130, also began to increase and in 1883 reached 285, making the college the second biggest Government College in Bengal after the Presidency College.[53]

There was considerable concern in the late 1860s when the Government of Bengal sought to curtail the expenditure of some of the colleges, the thinly-attended degree classes of Berhampur and Krishnagar colleges in particular. This the English-educated middle-class Bengalis and their supporters interpreted as an attempt to check the progress of higher English-education in the country, thereby restricting opportunities for Indians to gain higher positions in the public services. They vigorously opposed the plan.[54] A leader in the *Dhaka Prokash*, the mouthpiece of educated opinion, declared that such a measure would be a death blow to the cause of higher Western education among the East Bengalis.[55] In June 1870, an association, the Sikha Bisayak Sabha (Association for Educational Purposes) was formed in Dacca which protested against any curtailment in the establishment of the Dacca College or the abolition of its degree classes, and withdrawal of government support for higher education in general.[56] However, the government had no intention of closing the degree classes of the Dacca College, holding rather that the college should be maintained, whatever the circumstances, as a key institution for higher English education in East Bengal.

Public concern was more positively shown in 1875 with the opening of the science department, when donations poured in from the zamindars and other notables of East Bengal for a new science building and laboratory. Maulvi Golam Ali Chowdhury, a wealthy zamindar of Faridpur, alone contributed Rs. 10,000 to the Dacca College Extension Fund.[57] Such charities moreover contributed to the economy of the city through aiding development activities.

The success of the Dacca College not only secured Dacca's regional role in educational development but also led to private enterprise in the field of higher education within the city itself. The college being a government institution was looked on by many with great awe. It was regarded as an extended arm of the government machinery with all its bureaucratic control, authoritarianism and fastidious discipline, and hence not much liked by those who wanted a freer atmosphere. But more importantly, the college with its higher fees and limited seats meant no place for less well-off but meritorious students who nevertheless wanted or needed to be given higher education. It was to cater for this group of students, and to play their own role in educational development in competition with government enterprise that many Daccaites contemplated establishing a private college in Dacca. Eventually in 1884, Kishori Lal Chaudhury, the zamindar of Baliati, established the Jagannath College, affiiliated to the Calcutta University with effect from 1883, as a second-grade Arts College.[58] The college over the years grew into the largest private college in East Bengal drawing students from all over the region. Their number rose from 48 in 1885 to 396 in 1889.[59] The phenomenal success of the college not only strengthened Dacca's regional status in the educational sphere, but also provided higher education to many socially deprived students who otherwise would not have received it. By doing so it brought about immense social and economic changes among the community both within the city of Dacca and in East Bengal. Many of its students who originated from humble and poor backgrounds, rose to prominence in later life. It also contributed to the growth of an educated middle class within Dacca itself. Girish Chandra Nag, a former student who joined the civil service and later became the treasurer of Dacca University, declared at a meeting of the old boys association, that his old Alma Mater had caused a social revolution in East Bengal by bringing 'higher education within the easy reach of its poor and backward population'.[60]

As at the higher level, so at the secondary level of education there took place a tremendous growth. In 1841, Dacca had only one English high school—the Dacca Government School—though there were some thirty-one primary schools, viz, eleven pathsalas, nine maktabs and eleven Baptist Mission schools. Apart from the mission schools, they were run in the traditional manner. With the implementation of the government's educational policy, the city's primary schools underwent significant changes both in their organization and curriculum; though maktabs were hardly touched. The city also gained new primary schools run on the state system. By 1867, though Dacca had lost almost all its mission schools (they were closed for lack of funds), it had acquired five new high English Anglo-Vernacular schools, seven middle vernacular schools, five girls' primary schools and two night schools. Some 3,000 boys and girls studied in the day schools.

Reviewing the progress of education in the city, the Comissioner of Dacca recorded in 1873, 'Dacca town has always been an eduational centre with many high class schools to which boys [even] flock from other districts'.[61] Of these schools, the Dacca Collegiate School was the best and most famous. Indeed, such was its reputation that the school was the first choice for every aspiring student. For a time it was also the only school in the city and its environs which furnished students for the Dacca College, as students from other schools regularly failed to pass the Entrance Examination. The number of students of the Dacca Collegiate School rose from 59 in 1858–9 to 319 in 1873. The number in the school could indeed have been even greater had not the authorities rejected many applicants for fear of overcrowding and raised the school fees.

The raising of the fees at the Collegiate School, however, had the same effect as the raising of the fees at the Dacca College had had some ten years earlier in leading private enterprise to fill the gap. The Bangla Bazar Anglo-Vernacular School was founded in December 1855 by Babu Ananda Mohan Das, an ex-student of the Dacca College and a teacher of the Collegiate School, to provide education to students who could no longer afford to study at the government school. He was greatly assisted in this by William Brennand, the Principal of the Dacca College and other residents of the city. In 1856 the school received a government grant and it soon reached the standard of a mofussil zilla school. Despite strong competition from the Collegiate School and Pogose School it progressed satisfactorily and in 1863 it had 208 students on its roll. The Pogose School remained, however, the best private school of the city. Under the able management of its owner, N. P. Pogose, and its Head Master Babu Kashi Kanta Mukherjee, the school flourished, numbers rising from 145 in 1856–7 to 562 in 1867. In the latter year, no fewer than twenty-seven candidates passed the Entrance Examination and between them gained eight scholarships.[62] Until 1878, when he left Dacca for England, the school remained under the management of N. P. Pogose. In that year Babu Mohini Mohan Das, the zamindar-banker of Dacca, took over the school[63] which still survives, however, under its original family name.

The contribution of this Armenian was complemented by that of another worthy citizen of Dacca, Khwaja Abdul Ghani. In 1863 he established a free English school to provide English education to poor Muslim boys. However, Abdul Ghani's Free High School did not thrive, largely owing to bad management, failing even to attract Muslim students. In 1873 the 190 students on its role were mostly Hindus.[64] Though the school survived until the beginning of this century, it never rivalled the Pogose school. Years later Babu Ruplal Das and his brother Babu Raghunath Das, the most wealthy Hindu zamindar-bankers of Dacca, made their own contribution by founding an English high school in 1879. The Ruplal-Raghunath High English School at Dal Bazar survived until 1884 when it was taken over by a new management, which changed its name to Eastern Bengal Academy.[65]

The spread of Western education in Dacca as elsewhere in India produced a group of idealistic and progressive people who regarded education as an important element in the regeneration of their country. Naturally enough they committed themselves to the foundation of educational institutions as part of their broader vision of radical religious, social and cultural reform. It was here that the Brahmos[66] first made their mark. In Dacca the Brahmo Samaj was founded as early as 1846 by a cross-section of Indian officials, school teachers and other enlightened Daccaites, led by Babu Broja Sundar Mitra, the future Deputy Collector of the city.[67] By the 1860s the Dacca Brahmos had grown into a substantial community exercising considerable influence on the socio-religious life of the city. In 1869 they constructed their *mandir* (temple) which as David Kopf records was 'the largest and most architecturally impressive Brahmo Temple in all of South Asia up to that time'.[68]

In 1863, Broja Sundar Mitra together with fellow-Brahmos like Babu Dina Nath Sen, the Inspector of Schools for Dacca, founded a Brahmo School 'with the object of combining a good secular education, with religious instructions in the tenets of the Brahmo creed.'[69] It was a vernacular middle school, and was open for students of all castes and creeds. Instruction was given free, and the school was located inside the Brahmo Samaj House at Armanitola. The subsequent history of the school is shrouded in obscurity. However, it seems that within a few years the school had declined for lack of funds and care. It survived until 1872, when its management was taken over by Kishori Lal Roy Chaudhury who turned it into a fee-paying school, renamed the Jagannath School after his father. This new school proved a very significant addition to the growing number of English high schools in the city. Babu Gopi Mohan Basak, until then the Head Master of Pogose School, joined it as its new Head Master. Under his able supervision and care, the school soon became a flourishing institution, and its student roll grew rapidly. By 1876 it had grown into the largest school in East Bengal with 562 pupils.[70] At one time, its income after all the establishment and other charges had been met, rose to Rs. 1,000 per month.[71] With the increase of students, a strong staff[72] and the financial success of the school, its standard too reached higher levels. It became one of the best pre-university institutions in Bengal. 'In fact for five or six years or more the Jagannath School stood first in the Entrance Examination, and the reputation of Babu Gopi Mohan Basak rose very high, in the whole Dacca Division'.[73] Unfortunately, this continuing success ended with a pay dispute between the proprietor of the school and the staff which led to its closure. When it finally re-opened, Kishori Lal changed its name to the Jubilee School, as it is now known today.[74]

The establishment of these private schools further widened the scope of Dacca's educational role both within the city and outside. Indeeed they provided new opportunities for education especially to the city's lowlier and poorer sections. This helped to bring about a new social and intellectual awareness in Dacca. This was highlighted by the foundation of a girls' high school in 1878.

Female education, socially taboo, had been taken up in Dacca before many other parts of India, though in Calcutta it had been attempted by a group of progressive Bengalis, largely supported by liberal Europeans, early in the nineteenth century.[75] To the emerging group of progressives and social reformers of Dacca the cause of female education became primary objective. The move to set up girls' schools was first made in 1856 by a small group of Brahmos. In that year Ananda Mohan Das and Babu Dina Bandhu Mallick, the Deputy Inspector of Schools, Dacca, encouraged by the Principal of the Dacca College, W. Brennand and Head Master F. Tydd of the Collegiate School, opened a girls' school at Bangla Bazar with twenty-two students. The school soon received a government grant and financial support from a cross-section of Dacca's inhabitants.[76] In the same year another girls' school was established at Lalbagh, chiefly supported by Dina Bandhu Mallick. Within the next few years more such schools were founded.

The establishment of these schools caused great excitement in the city, and even tension between conservatives and progressives. There was, however, great disappointment that the schools failed to grow beyond the primary level due to social pressure. The custom of child marriage proved to be a major stumbling block. 'The girls', commented Henry Woodrow, the Inspector of Schools, East Bengal, 'leave their school as soon as they are married and they marry when almost infants. Our female schools are attended only by children who in England would attend Infant classes'.[77]

The lack of female teachers was another serious difficulty, for parents and guardians disliked the idea of their female wards being taught by male teachers. In May 1862, R. L. Martin, the Inspector of Schools, South-East Division, Dacca, urged by local people, asked the government for a Female Normal School to be established at Dacca where interest in female education especially among the 'Native gentry' was strongest. He added that it was only the want of schoolmistresses that had prevented the establishment of girls' schools even in the interior of the Dacca District.[78]

The question of establishing female normal schools had been under consideration for some time, but the authorities were convinced that a proper class of students would not be available. The conservative attitude of the people, even of the 'gentry' class whose demand was strongest, required that if schoolmistresses were to be employed, they must be of respectable parentage and of unimpeachable character. But in the existing state of indigenous society it was impossible to find women belonging to the higher social classes who were willing to take up careers as teachers. It was only after much debate, therefore, that the Government of India sanctioned 'the establishment, experimentally for one year, of a Normal School at Dacca for the training of Native School Mistresses.'[79] It is interesting to note that about this time the Bengal Government also asked the Bethune School Committee in Calcutta to form a normal class for female teachers in their school. But the secretary of the school, Ishwar Chandra Vidyasagar, who also happened to be the greatest Hindu reformer of the age, replied that in the existing state of Calcutta society, no students of good social background could be found for such a school in the capital.[80]

It was thus in Dacca on 11 May 1863, that the first Government Female Normal School in Bengal was opened, with sixteen students;[81] one was Brahmin, one Kayastha, two Bengali Christians and twelve Byraginis (of the Hindu caste of Byragi or religious mendicants). One Bengali Christian schoolmistress was appointed to instruct the students; a building was rented near Sutrapur which served both as a school and the residence of the mistress. An infant girls' school was also attached to the Normal School for the practical training of the pupil teachers.

For a time the school proved a success, and in 1864 the government increased the annual grant from Rs. 900 to Rs. 1800.[82] In 1864 it decided to make the grant a permanent one. In the end however, the school proved too far ahead of its time; it was attended only by Bengali Christian and a few low-caste Hindu women. The upper and middle-class 'Native gentry' and the managers of schools were extremely reluctant to appoint women of such social and religious background as teachers. The school was declared a failure and in 1872 it closed.[83]

Meanwhile the Brahmos in Dacca had been making their own experiments in female education, including the establishment of a Zenana Education Society, which encouraged female education at home through examination and reward. Babu Nabakanta Chattopadhya, a teacher of Jagannath School, who also taught for some time at Pogose School, was at the time the moving spirit of Brahmo struggle for social and religious reforms in Dacca.[84] Son of a wealthy Brahmin lawyer of Dacca, he formally embraced Brahmoism when Keshab Chandra Sen visited the city in 1869, for which he was deprived of his family inheritance. In 1871, with other progressive Daccaites he founded the Dacca Subha Sadhinee Sabha or Dacca Philanthropic Society for Social Reform, and in 1873 under its auspices established a Female Adult School in Dacca, mainly though not exclusively attended by the Brahmo women. In 1876 Mary Carpenter, English reformer and friend of India's progressive movement, reported,

> Dacca, the capital of East Bengal, though somewhat remote, is considerably in advance of other places in female education, through the efforts of many enlightened Native Gentlemen. Here I found a small adult school, unique in its character, which is chiefly attended by married ladies, whose husbands desire for them intellectual improvement. Some of them learn English.[85]

Encouraged by this report the Bengal Government asked the Dacca Philanthropic Society whether another girls' school could be established at Dacca. In reply Nabakanta proposed to convert the Female Adult School into a girls' school, which was formally opened in June 1878. Within months however, the School Committee, prompted by Nabakanta, decided to hand over the management of the school to the government and to name it the Eden Girls' School after Sir Ashley Eden, as a token of their appreciation of the Lieutenant-Governor's deep interest in the cause of female education in Dacca. The committee's proposals were accepted and so in September 1878, the now famous Government-controlled Eden Girls' School came into existence.[86]

The growth of high schools in Dacca as elsewhere in Bengal was matched by a growth of primary and middle vernacular schools which helped to feed them[87] For all these schools, encouraged after 1854 by grants-in-aid, improvement depended upon the provision of better-trained teachers. Quite early, therefore, the Bengal Government turned its attention to the establishment of Normal Schools for the major centres of education to meet the urgent need for qualified teachers. Of the four Normal Schools founded in 1857 one was in Dacca.[88] The establishment of this school added yet another educational role for Dacca city.

The Dacca Normal School, under its Superintendent Samuel C. Aratoon, an Armenian teacher from La Martinière School in Calcutta, achieved a high reputation[89]. In its first year eighty-nine students joined the school. It was then housed in the Chota Katra building near the Chauk Bazar. A vernacular model school was also attached to the school for the practical training of the teachers, and this soon became the best middle vernacular school of the city. The growing demand for trained teachers in the country was quickly reflected in the increased number of Dacca Normal School students by 1872.[90]

Though an Inspector of Schools referred to the Normal School in 1876 as the 'Vernacular College of Eastern Bengal',[91] it suffered from the preference of managers and proprietors of even small vernacular schools for teachers who could teach 'elements of English'.[92] Only the rapid expansion of the total educational demand enabled the Normal School to hold its own against the competition of teachers drawn from the ranks of English high school and Dacca College students. Between 1857 and 1868, more than 250 teachers[93] from the Dacca Normal School received employment in various schools of East Bengal.[94]

Enthusiasm for English education among the Indians as an entry qualification for government service was followed by their demand for specialist institutions which would teach law, medicine and engineering. Such a demand was made not only to acquire skill for independent and lucrative employment but also to enable them to take up leadership within their own community and help in the general development of the country. The first and most important of these institutions founded in Dacca to meet this new demand was the Law Department of the Dacca College, established in 1863. A systematic study of law had become indispensable when the government, following Wood's Education Despatch of 1854, passed regulations requiring lawyers even in the mofussil courts to qualify by examination.[95] In response, the Government of Bengal opened a Law Class in 1857 in the Presidency College, but made no provision for other parts of the province. In 1862 Babu Brojo Sundar Mitra and other residents of Dacca city petitioned the government to open a Law Class in the Dacca College for the people of East Bengal. They emphasized:

> The general indigence of the people, as well as the distance of Calcutta, prevents them from sending their relatives to the Law Department of the Presidency College. The institution of a Law Class in this College is, therefore, highly desirable.[96]

Fortunately the government was already considering the extension of facilities for legal education 'in several of the provincial Capitals at a distance from Calcutta'.[97] The demand for a Law Class in Dacca thus fell on very willing ears; in July 1863 the Government of India gave its approval and a Law Department opened at the Dacca College that same month,[98] inaugurating a new era in the city's educational development. Upendra Nath Mitra, a distinguished law graduate of the Calcutta University, was appointed its first law lecturer. Fifteen students joined the first year, and by 1867 the number had risen to forty-nine. Even when the government, having decided to make law classes completely self-supporting, then increased the monthly tuition fees from two rupees to five the number of students continued to rise showing the eagerness of the Bengalis to have an independent career in the legal profession. Between 1868 and 1872, for example, forty-nine students qualified from the Law Department as Pleaders of the High Court or District Judge's Court, seventeen as Bachelors of Law, fifteen as Licentiates in Law and seventeen as Senior Pleaders.[99] Many of them were locals, others came from the adjoining districts, but large numbers of them eventually settled down in the city to carry on their practice. The rise of these qualified lawyers not only ensured a better legal service within the city but also introduced a new element in its society —a set of highly-educated professionals who could speak their mind to secure the city's welfare, and whose professional independence ideally placed them to assume community leadership. In 1881, Thacker's Directory listed thirty such graduate lawyers. In the long run they proved to be the core of future politicians in the city and the region.

The success of the Law Department was soon followed by attempts to make similar gains in the medical and engineering fields, thus charting out further roles for Dacca in public health and the general development of the region. By the 1850s, the Western system of medicine as an approved alternative to the indigenous system had taken root in East Bengal, and the opening of the Mitford Hospital in 1858 in Dacca, the only institution of its kind in the region, was a formal recognition of this acceptance. The demand for a medical college in Dacca was thus a logical conclusion.

Western medical education was initially available only at Calcutta where a Medical College had been training Indian students in European Medicine and Surgery since 1835.[100] (A few Dacca College students who had scholarships had also attended the college since the 1840s.) The college at the time offered two different courses—one an undergraduate course covering instruction in all branches of medicine and surgery through the medium of English; the other only in some branches and at a lower level through the vernaculars, Bengali and Hindustani. This second course aimed at raising a body of 'Native Doctors' who would be employed in the army and in government hospitals and dispensaries as Medical Assistants.

Calcutta's distance from East Bengal and the high cost of living in the capital deterred many altogether, and those students who did go mainly attended the Bengali class of the Medical College, since the course was short and inexpensive. Even so, in 1873, one third of all the students then in the Bengali department were from East Bengal.[101] But as early as 1863, the *Dhaka Prokash* voiced the demand for a medical school in Dacca.[102] That demand was later reinforced in 1868 by the Civil Surgeon and the Magistrate of Dacca, who suggested the establishment of a medical college 'if not on an elaborate scale yet one that shall be as useful...'[103] Next year, as part of a general scheme for vernacular medical schools to train 'a body of local practitioners able to supply simple remedies to ordinary diseases such as cholera, small-pox and epidemic fever and who should displace the native Kabirajes', one such school was sanctioned for immediate opening at Dacca. Unfortunately, financial difficulties led to the postponement of the opening, and ultimately the whole scheme was dropped.

It was not until 1873, therefore, when overcrowding in the Calcutta Medical College, particularly in the Bengali class, became a serious problem that the Lieutenant-Governor, Sir George Campbell, took positive steps to implement the medical school scheme. He sanctioned the establishment of a separate vernacular medical school at Calcutta (later known as the Campbell Medical School) and approved the establishment of two others, at Dacca and Patna, designed to cope with the demand of their huge hinterlands. It was stated,

> The School at Dacca will serve the districts of East Bengal with its thirteen million souls, whence already come more than one-third of the Calcutta [Medical] College Students, and where the practice of European medicine has spread as much as anywhere in Bengal. The Dacca School may also serve the province of Assam.[104]

The new vernacular medical school, attached to the Mitford Hospital, finally opened in June 1875.

With the opening of the Medical School, students from all over East Bengal came to study there, as many as 384 joining in the first year. Though this initial enthusiasm was not sustained for very long, as the school proved a poor substitute for a full-fledged medical college, and more ambitious students opted for the Calcutta Medical College, yet it proved to be the key institution in training students in Western medicine for the entire region and laid the foundation of future higher medical institutions in Dacca. Soon new land was acquired and buildings constructed to house the school and accommodate students. The Mitford Hospital was simultaneously modified to fit its new role as a teaching hospital. Of the 136 students who passed the final examination between 1878 and 1885, most obtained jobs in hospitals and charitable dispensaries or chose private practice, many in Dacca. This led to an increase in the number of physicians trained in Western medicine in Dacca which proved particularly beneficial to the city's poor. A similar result was achieved with the establishment of two homeopathic schools in 1883 and 1884 by private enterprise.

The government's need for professionally-trained servants also led to the founding of a vernacular survey school attached to the Dacca College in January 1876, which offered a two-year course in surveying by chain, compass and plane-table and in levelling and the elements of road-making. The school became an instant success as it opened at a very opportune moment when the demand for qualified surveyors was very great owing to the field-work then being carried out for the extension of railways in East Bengal. Qualified surveyors were also eagerly employed by the province's newly-founded municipalities, which needed their skills to implement the water and sewerage schemes and other public works then increasingly being undertaken. In 1876, 29 students joined the Dacca Survey School; the number rising to 52 in 1882–3 and 222 by 1890.[105] Though the school fell far short of the expectations of the people of Dacca, for they had dreamt of an engineering college, yet it trained many young men of the city and the region in a new skill that readily provided them with employment, and also aided in the city's physical development.

The growth of Western educational institutions and the general popularity of English education produced a deep impact on sections of Dacca society. One important result was the rise to position and power of an English-educated middle class with a new intellectual and moral outlook. This class was almost exclusively Hindu. The Muslims generally kept themselves aloof from the new education. The attendance of Muslim students in the various new educational institutions at Dacca was pathetically low. For example, in 1873, out of 319 students at the Dacca Collegiate School, 290 were Hindus, 14 Muslims and 15 Christians.[106] The same year, in a report, Principal A. W. Croft of the Dacca College noted that since the establishment of the college in 1841 there had never been more than three Muslim students at any given time.[107] The statistics of attendance of Muslim students also for that year for the whole of East Bengal showed a similar situation.[108]

The causes of this apathy have been commented on by many historians. Briefly it can be said that the Muslim lack of participation was basically due to their religious and cultural beliefs.[109] They regarded Arabic and Persian as aids to learning the Quran and Islamic principles, and the acquisition of Muslim culture as their primary objective. In the report of 1873, noted above, it was also revealed that in the city of Dacca there were then more than 50 maktabs where some 500 boys were learning to read the Quran, while in the Dacca Collegiate School there were only 14 Muslim boys and in the Dacca College only one. Emphasizing this bias of the Muslims towards Islamic education, Khan Bahadur Syed Abbas Ali Khan, the Principal Sadr Amin of Dacca, had in 1853 observed that the lack of Muslim students in the new institutions was due to there being 'no means. . . for the study of the Urdu and Persian languages.'[110]

However, the Muslims even believed English education to be a source of evil,[111] which could endanger their cultural identity and undermine their Islamic faith. There was also an aversion to Bengali, the medium of the primary and secondary schools, considered a Hindu language, particularly among the urban Muslim élites, the descendants of the old Muslim rulers who spoke Urdu,[112] and among those in the rural areas who sought to imitate them even to the point of accepting their prejudices. Persian continued to be cherished as the hallmark of a gentleman, and Arabic as that of the religious scholar. In Dacca the maktabs continued to be largely frequented, and until the 1870s at least Muslim scholars (*Talb-ul-ilim*) from all the districts of East Bengal continued to flock to Dacca to study the higher branches of Arabic and Persian learning in private under the learned Maulanas and Munshis.[113]

But Muslim dedication to their cultural traditions and their aloofness from English education exacted a heavy price—an increasingly complete exclusion from government service and the professions which became the near monopoly of English-knowing Hindus.[114] By the 1860s, many Muslims had realized the disastrous social and economic consequences of such rigid orthodoxy and those who had benefited from an English education became particularly keen to impress upon the community the vital necessity of learning English. In Bengal, Nawab Abdul Latif, a prominent member of the Muslim community who served the British Government from 1846 to 1884 in various capacities,[115] gave the lead. He urged his fellow Muslims to take to English education and to break out of their isolation from the new India emerging through the British connection, and to exploit opportunities for their own social and economic advance. Through the Muhammedan Literary Society which he founded in Calcutta in 1863, he pressed his views upon the upper and middle-class Muslims of Bengal, much as Sir Syed Ahmad Khan was doing in Northern India.

This regenerative movement gradually spread through the riverine lands of East Bengal. Even the generally conservative upper-class Muslims of Dacca acknowledged the central point of this movement, and admitted the value of an English education. In Dacca its recognition was found in the establishment of a branch of the Muhammedan Literary Society in 1863 by Khawja Muhammad Ashgar (the son-in-law of Nawab Abdul Ghani) and Maulvi Elahabad Khan.[116] However, longstanding prejudices and overwhelming emphasis on Islamic eduction barred the Muslims of East Bengal generally from allowing their children to go to the regular government and private schools for English education, insisting on sending them to separate Muslim schools where they could learn Arabic, and Persian, as well as English. There was, however, at the time a growing awareness among the leading Muslims that Muslim educational backwardness was also due to 'the poverty of many of the Muhammedans of East Bengal. There are many who cannot afford to pay the schooling fees and other expenses for their children'. In 1872, in a petition to the government, the influential Muslims of Dacca, led by Nawab Abdul Ghani, put forward a solution to this intricate problem:

> ...that one simple step of establishing an institution exclusively and independently for the education of the Muhammedan boys like the Calcutta Madrassa and the Hooghly Mahommedan College at a reduced rate of schooling fees will at once remove and obviate all the objections and difficulties on the part of the Mahommedans of this portion of Bengal for the non-admission of their children in Government Colleges and Schools.[117]

The timing of the petition, though not its content, doubtless owed something to provincial jealousy for it followed upon the news that the Bengal Government was considering the establishment of a Government Madrasah at Chittagong, the district where the demand for Arabic and Persian studies was thought to be strongest. The scheme for the establishment of madrasahs by the government was closely tied to the wider question of Muslim educational backwardness in Bengal and indeed in India as a whole. The signatories to the above-mentioned petition, however, made it plain that they held Dacca's claim to be clearly superior.[118] The government also seemed to have been convinced by their argument.

In July 1873, the Bengal Government, prompted by the Government of India, set aside Rs. 10,000 a year from the Mohsin Fund for a new madrasah at Dacca.[119] A committee was formed in Dacca of officials and leading Muslim inhabitants to supervise the madrasah which was formally opened in March 1874. Muslim students from the city and the neighbouring districts at once rushed to seek admission. Four hundred applied, of whom only 104 could be accommodated and even after larger premises had been rented, only 169. Half of these students were from Dacca and the rest from different parts of East Bengal. Most of them belonged to what were called 'respectable families'.

The Dacca Madrasah attracted these large numbers even though it started as a purely oriental institution devoted to Arabic and Persian studies. But the 'Muhammedans of the town of Dacca', the DPI noted, 'and those belonging to respectable families in the surrounding districts, wish their sons to learn English'. The Dacca Madrasah Committee, unwilling to let it become yet another centre for training Munshis and Maulvis, therefore decided to make it a centre of English education too for the Muslim students of East Bengal. This was broadly in line with the contemporary thinking of progressive and liberal Muslims in other parts of India. They were encouraged, too, by the European officials and residents of Dacca, and particularly by the Superintendent of the Madrasah, Maulana Ubaidalla Al-Ubaidi, a supporter of Sir Syed Ahmed. It thus became possible for the Muslim children to learn English, together with the Arabic and Persian so necessary 'to entitle a man to be looked upon as a gentleman in their own society'.[120] From 1875, the new Anglo-Persian Department offered both Arabic and Persian, and English and Western arts and sciences. The department instantly became popular, so that by 1883, 202 of the 338 students in the Madrasah were to be found in it. The Madrasah Committee could say that the Madrasah was valued less as a centre of classical education than as one where Islamic and Western subjects could be studied together.[121]

The Anglo-Persian Department soon reached the standard of an English high school with students sitting for the Entrance Examination for the first time in 1882, when three students passed. An English-educated Muslim middle class and intelligentsia soon appeared on the scene with its focus at Dacca but drawing on the whole of East Bengal.[122] Sir Abdullah Suhrawardy, the eminent educationist, Justice Zahidur Rahim Zahid, and S. M. Taifoor, author of one of the earlier studies of Dacca were among the distinguished old pupils of the Anglo-Persian Department of the Dacca Madrasah.

The Madrasah proved an important addition to the already growing number of educational institutions in Dacca, by 1885 second only to Calcutta. By that date no less than 5,000 students were attending the schools and colleges of Dacca, a quite impressive figure, reflecting the educational advancement of the city itself, and its emergence as the principal centre of Western education in East Bengal, students coming from such distant places as Chittagong, Sylhet, Barisal and Rajshahi. These new educational institutions nurtured generations of young East Bengalis who became high officials, teachers, lawyers, scientists, writers and politicians, and thus bringing about a social revolution in the region. To take an early example, among the 163 students who left the Dacca College between 1842 and 1854, 55 became teachers, two Deputy Magistrates, four Munsifs, five vakils, one Sadr-Amin, fourteen Abkari and Police Darogas, and eighty-two other officials and clerks.[123]

This spread in education led inevitably to the growth of a vernacular press in Dacca which was used particularly by the Western educated class for propagating their social and religious ideas. The first Bengali printing press was founded by Haris Chandra Mitra, once a teacher of Dacca Bansi Bazar Pathsala. In 1860, together with Brojo Sundar Mitra, Bhagwan Chandra Bose, the Deputy Collector, and Krishna Chandra Majumdar, a former teacher of the Dacca Model School, Haris Chandra founded the Dacca Bengali Press. This was used not only for publishing literary works and school books, but also for printing bills and other commercial papers and forms. The press became very successful, and to cash in on such success, five more presses were established in the next few years. In 1874–5, seventy-two Bengali works, in 110,235 copies were printed and published from the Dacca Division, the largest number being of course, from the Dacca presses.[124] Some of the most famous literary works of nineteenth-century Bengal were printed and published in Dacca, including two outstanding works on the social life of the city, *Lakhsmimani Charit* (The Story of Lakhsmimani) and *Balya Bibaha* (Child Marriage) by Somnath Mukhopadhaya, a Dacca College professor. Once printing presses had been established, the publication of newspapers, the most prominent being the *Dhaka Prokash* and *Hindu-Hitoishini*, quickly followed.

New educational institutions, books and newspapers—both English and Bengali—were products of a developing middle class, which was not confined only to Brahmins, Kayasthas and Baidyas, the Hindu castes with traditions of government service and professional occupation, but extended also to lower-caste Hindus like the Nabasakas or the weavers, smiths, shell cutters, and later included Muslims as well. Rohini Kumar Basak of the weaver caste was one of the first two Dacca College students to graduate, and the first student who passed the Law examination. In fact, large numbers among the Basaks took to English education, and later became lawyers, teachers and government servants.

English education and Western influence also changed people's taste and fashions, and on a lighter but significant plane led to the introduction of new sports and games—cricket,[125] football, gymnastics and athletics.

The spread of English education also created a consciousness of individual and national freedom, and hence the earliest efforts at social reform in Bengal were directed against caste restrictions, child marriage, polygamy and many other archaic forms of social and religious custom. Efforts were also directed to encouraging female education, widow remarriage and religious reform. Ananda Mohan Das, Somnath Mukhopadhya, Nabakanta Chattapadya, Krishna Chandra Majumdar, Dino Nath Sen, Dr P. K. Roy, William Brennand, F. Tydd, W. B. Livingstone, V. J. S. Pope and other teachers of the educational institutions of Dacca worked tirelessly to promote female education and their efforts became the source of inspiration for others in Bengal who were similarly engaged. Perhaps the greatest contribution to the cause of female education was the publication of the Bengali work *Nari Jati Bisayak Prastab* or *A Discourse on Woman* in 1868 by Dacca's famous writer, Babu Kali Prasanna Ghosh. His work, which became a classic on the position and status of women in Indian society, emphasized the need to educate them for the moral uplift of the country, and was a powerful weapon for the supporters of female education in Bengal.[126] The teaching fraternity of Dacca, together with their students, enlightened officials and residents, founded debating clubs, societies and associations for the propagation of their views. In 1874–5, there were sixteen such societies and associations in Dacca.[127] Prominent among these were the Aghyan Timir—Nashini Sabha (society for the eradication of illiteracy and ignorance), Desh Hitoishini Sabha (society for the promotion of the welfare of the country), Gyan Dayini Sabha (society for the promotion of learning), Ballya Bibaha Nibarani Sabha (society for the stopping of child marriage), Subha Sadhini Sabha (society dedicated for the suppression of drunkenness, propagation of higher education, promotion of mass education and reformation of the marriage system), and Antapur Stri Sikha Sabha (society for the propagation of female education). In the 1870s the Dacca College teachers and students established a Dacca College Society which organised a series of lectures on different topics, for example in July 1879, Professor Somanath Mukhopadhya gave a lecture on 'The Ancient Hindus'; in September, Babu Ganga Charan Sarkar spoke on Bengali literature; and in October, Principal V. J. S. Pope spoke on university life in England. These lectures were well attended by students and public.[128] But perhaps the greatest socio-religious movement in Dacca during the nineteenth century was the rise of the Brahmo Samaj. The Samaj was founded in 1846, and for some time a great many of the teaching fraternity, their students and other Bengali officials were its active followers and supporters. Their religious and progressive activities shook Dacca's Hindu society and forced the orthodox on the defensive.[129]

It is clear that the growth and expansion of Western education, the intellectual ferment and the deepening movement for social and religious reform, added a new dimension to Dacca's history. Without these Dacca might have remained a divisional administrative centre or at best become a prosperous entrepôt for inland trade like Burdwan and Sirajganj. As it was, it became a focal point second only to Calcutta in the political life and culture of Bengal.

Newspapers, journals, reform associations were the pulse of a new modern spirit: the call for popular participation in the machinery of, say, local government was matched by equally earnest cries in favour of female education. However, this notable undercurrent of change was largely spearheaded by the higher-caste Hindus, who constituted the bulk of the middle-class bhadrolok. Their enthusiasm for English education meant also that they monopolized the ranks of government services. A section of this class was later to articulate their political aspirations through a revivalist idiom, which did little to bridge the Hindu-Muslim divide. Indeed, it played a considerable part in widening communal divisions; as a result the Muslim masses and leaders grew more self-conscious, increasingly assertive of their separate religious and social identity, and it was thus particularly significant that the first public call in 1940 for a separate Muslim homeland in the Indian subcontinent was made by an East Bengali Muslim leader.

Thus a century of evolving ideas and their cross-fertilization with the movement for social reform interacted with the forces of conservative and militant reaction, making East Bengal the primary political base of the Muslim League and a constituent part of the state for which the League had struggled—Pakistan. However, the springs of change in East Bengal society were deep and powerful enough to release it eventually from the fetters of a distorted ideology and state, culminating in the establishment of a free and independent Bangladesh.

NOTES TO CHAPTER III

1 For a detailed survey of the social and cultural history of the region see B. M. Morrison, *Political Centres and Cultural Regions in Early Bengal;* Raychaudhuri, *Bengal Under Akbar and Jahangir;* Clay, *Principal Heads.*
2 See Ramesh Chandra Raychaudhury, *Faridpur Zellar Abdullahbad Gram Nivashi Raychaudhury Banser Itihasa,* 8–10; also Abdul Mannan, *The Life and Work of Khan Bahadur Maulvi Khabirullah of Munshiganj,* 3.
3 For a history of Vikrampur, see Yogendra Nath Gupta, *Vikrampur Itihasa.*
4 For details of the indigenous educational system of Bengal during the early nineteenth century see William Adam, *Reports on the State of Education in Bengal (1835 and 1838),* ed. by A. N. Basu; also A. P. Howell, *Education in British India Prior to 1854 and in 1870–71,* Rev. J. Long, *Adam's Report on Vernacular Education in Bengal and Bihar submitted to Government in 1835, 1836 and 1838 with a brief view of its past and present condition.*
5 W. Adam, *Reports on the state of Education,* 84.
6 Provincial Court of Circuit and Appeal at Dacca to the GB, 9 June 1802, BCJC, CXLVII, 55, 8 July 1802, 22.
7 Taylor, *Dacca,* 272–73.
8 Dacca Provincial Court to Govt. of Bengal, 9 June 1802, BCJC, CXLVII, 55, 8 July 1802, 22.
9 Azam, *The Panchayat.*
10 Harold Bridges, 'The Kingdom of Christ in East Bengal' (unpublished D. D. Thesis), 16. See also H. D. North-Field, *A Front Line Post – Mission Work in Dacca,* 11.
11 Leonard to Serampore Baptist Mission, 23 Nov 1816, Leonard Papers, In/28.
12 Ibid.
13 For details see D. P. Sinha, *The Educational Policy of the East India Company in Bengal up to 1854.*
14 Ibid.
15 General Committee of Public Instruction to Government of India, 20 April 1835, in H. Sharp (ed.), *Selections from Educational Records (1781–1839),* 142. The Committee also asked for a similar school at Patna. For the history of the establishment of the Patna Government High School and College, see J. N. Sarkar, 'The Early History of the Patna College' *BPP,* LXII (1942), 92–115; LXIII (1943), 31–43.
16 Govt of India to GCPI, 24 June 1835, India Public Consultation, CLXXXVI, 68, 24 June 1835, 12.
17 GCPI to GI, 19 June 1835, ibid., 10.
18 *Report of the General Committee of Public Instruction of Bengal,* for 1835, 34. Ghosh was the father of the famous brothers Monomohan and Lalmohan. For details on his life and contribution to the Bengal Renaissance see N. Sinha, *Freedom Movement in Bengal, 1818–1904,* 32–4.
19 Ibid.

20 In the early years the students were taught English, Bengali, geometry, arithmetic, history and geography. In the higher classes they were given lessons at a higher level. They read Richardson's *Selections from Shakespeare, Addison and Pope;* Goldsmith's *History of England, Rome and Greece;* Euclid's *Geometry and Mathematics;* Bacon's *Essays* and Lennie's *Grammar.*

21 For details see G. Chattopadhaya (ed.), *Awakening in Bengal in Early 19th century—selected documents;* also Atul Chandra Gupta (ed.), *Studies in the Bengal Renaissance.*

22 *GCPI's Report,* for 1838–9, 62–3.

23 Ibid; see also *GCPI's Report,* for 1837–8.

24 For details on the government's preference to promote English education and Governor-General Auckland's famous minute of 24 November 1839 rejecting the plea to advance vernacular education, see Sinha, *Education Policy,* 226–7; *GCPI's Report,* for 1839–40, appendix 1.

25 India Public Consultations, CLXXXVI, 95, 16 December 1840, 24.

26 Clay, *Principal Heads,* 38. The foundation stone of the college building was laid on 20 November 1841 on the site of the old English East India Company Factory near Sadar Ghat.

27 Principal's Report, 11 August 1842, India Public Consultations, CLXXXVI, 103, 7 September 1842, 59–60.

28 *Report of the Department of Public Instruction in the Lower Provinces of Bengal,* for 1843–4, 99.

29 *DPI's Report,* for 1856–7; see the Report on the Dacca College, 188.

30 GB to the Local Committee of Public Instruction at Dacca, 5 February 1844, Bengal Educational Consultations, XV, 31, 14 February 1844, 18.

31 Principal's Annual Report, for 1843–4, BEC, XV, 35, 29 January 1845, 28.

32 The members of the Local Committee in 1846 were J. Dunbar (Commissioner), J. Sweetenham (District Judge), A. F. Donnelly (Abkari Superintendent), J. Wheeler (Collector), R. H. Cooper (Magistrate), J. Jarvis and J. P. Wise (Zamindars and Planters), the Rev. H. R. Shepherd (Station Chaplain), and George Lamb (Civil Surgeon).

33 Local Committee to the Inspector of Schools and Colleges, 24 March 1846 in Local Committee to GB, 25 April 1846, BEC, XV, 39, 24 June 1846, 44.

34 GB to the Local Committee at Dacca, 24 June 1846, ibid., 49.

35 Principal's Report in Local Committee to GB, 21 October 1846, BEC, XV, 40, 2 December 1846, 7.

36 He was then the Civil Surgeon of Dacca.

37 Report of the Deputy-Inspector of Schools, Dacca, in the Annual Report of the Inspector of Schools and Colleges, South-East Division, for 1860–1, *DPI's Report,* for 1860–1, 45–6; see also the report of the Dacca College Principal, 21 October 1846, BEC, XV, 40, 2 December 1846, 7.

38 *DPI's Report,* for 1844–5, 2–3.

39 Annual Report of the Dacca College in *Education Reports—Bengal Schools and Colleges,* for 1851–2, 12, 17.

40 Annual Report of the Dacca College, ibid., 19.

41 Principal's Annual Report, for 1842–3, BEC, XV, 31, 18 February 1844, 14.

42 *Education Reports-Bengal Schools and Colleges*, for 1849–50, 5.
43 *DPI's Report*, for 1856–6, para 3.
44 As early as 1859 the Officiating Director of Public Instruction, W. M. Lees described the college as 'the Oxford and Cambridge of the East'; see his report of 26 September 1859 in BEC, XV, 66, October 1860, 111, p. 173.
45 DPI's Report, 20 February 1861, BEC, XV, 68, April 1862, 53, pp. 45–8.
46 A reflection of the improvement already effected in the High Schools of East Bengal since 1854.
47 Atkinson to GB of 4th November, 1862 BEC, XV, 68, Dec 1862, 1–4.
48 *DPI's Report*, for 1862–3, 13.
49 *Dhaka Proksh*, 23 Magh 1270 (3 February 1864).
50 Syed Murtaza Ali, 'Education and Literature in Dacca', in Azimusshan Haider (ed.), *A City and Its Civic Body*, Book I, 16.
51 Ibid. He eventually became a leading lawyer of the Calcutta High Court.
52 Principal's report for 1872–3 in *DPI's Report*, for 1872–3, appendix A, 671.
53 See the statement of attendance in college for General Instruction, *DPI's Report*, for 1884–5, 15.
54 For opposing views on the subject see George Campbell, *Memoirs of My Indian Career*, II, 262, 273–4; also A. Mandal, 'The Ideology and the Interest of the Bengal Intelligentsia: Sir George Campbell's Education Policy, 1871–74', *The Indian Economic and Social History Review*, XII, 1 (1975), 81–98.
55 *DP*, 11 Magh 1276 (23 January 1870).
56 *DP*, 13 Asarh 1277 (26 June 1870); also 20 Asarh 1277 (8 July 1870).
57 BEC, 874, April 1877, file (39–13), 157.
58 *Hundred Years of the University of Calcutta, Supplement*, 46.
59 *DPI's Report*, for 1884–5, 15–16, 28; also for 1889.
60 *A Short History of the Jagannath College and Jagannath Hall Reunion, 1929–32*, 21.
61 Report of the Commissioner for 1872–3 in *DPI's Report*, for 1872–3, 171.
62 *DPI's Report*, for 1866–7, 37.
63 Majumdar, *The Reminiscences*, 8.
64 Report of the Inspector of Schools, Dacca, for 1872–3, being appendix 'A' to *DPI's Report*, for 1872–3, 151.
65 Majumdar, *The Reminiscences*, 11.
66 For a detailed history of the Brahmo Samaj see D. Kopf, *The Brahmo Samaj and the Shaping of the Modern Indian Mind;* G. S. Leonard, *A History of the Brahmo Samaj From Its Rise to the Present Day (up to 1870);* Sibanath Sastri, *History of the Brahmo Samaj*.
67 Dacca Brahmo Samaj, *Dacca Brahmo Samajer Itihasa;* Brojo Sundar Mitra, 'Dhaka Samajer Sambatsharik Karjer Bibaran', Magh 1769 Saka, in Benoy Ghosh (ed.), *Samayik Patre Banglar Samaj Chitra—Tattabodhini Patrikar Rachana Sankalan, 1840–1905*, 504.
68 David Kopf, *The Brahmo Samaj*, 225.
69 DP, 18 Baisakh 1270 (30 April 1863), 73–4; also BEC, XV, 70, April 1863, 69.
70 *DPI's Report*, for 1875–6, 54.
71 Majumdar, *The Reminiscences*, 10.

72 In 1875 it had one Head Master, twelve other teachers and two pundits; see *Thacker's Directory* for 1875, 10.
73 Majumdar, *The Reminiscences*, 10.
74 Ibid., 10–11.
75 For details see Nirmal Sinha, *Freedom Movement in Bengal, 1818–1904, WHO's WHO*, Introduction; R. C. Majumdar, *Glimpses of Bengal in the Nineteenth Century;* A. Poddar, *Renaissance in Bengal—Quest and Confrontation.*
76 *The Dacca News*, 5 July 1856.
77 *DPI's Report*, for 1859–60, appendix A, 20.
78 Martin's letter in DPI to GB, 16 December 1862, BEC, January 1863, XV, 70, 13.
79 GI to GB, 23 March 1863, BEC, XV, 70, March 1863, 140.
80 Letter to GB, 13 June 1863, BEC, XV, 70, July 1863, 167.
81 BEC, XV, 72, August 1864, 8.
82 Ibid., 8–10.
83 During its short existence, the school, however, sent seventeen trained teachers to various girls' schools in East and North Bengal.
84 For details on the life and social work of Nabakanta, see Sinha, *Freedom Movement*, 330–1.
85 Mary Carpenter to the Secretary of State for India, August 1876, BEC, 874, May 1877, 204. For Mary Carpenter's account of the progress of social reform in India, see her *Prison Discipline and Female Education in India and Six Months in India.*
86 BEC, 1154, September 1878, 135–6; also *DP*, 17 Bhadra 1285 (1 September 1878).
87 For a comprehensive report of the development of these schools in the Dacca Division up to the 1870s see *DPI's Report*, for 1872–3, appendix A.
88 The other three were at Calcutta, Hooghly and Gauhati.
89 Majumdar, *The Reminiscences*, 12.
90 *DPI's Report*, for 1858–9, appendix A, 382–5; also *DPI's Report*, for 1875–6 99–100.
91 *DPI's Report*, for 1875–6, 99–100.
92 Report of Inspector of Schools, South-East Division, Dacca, for 1868–9, in *DPI's Report*, for 1868–9, appendix A, 179.
93 Ibid., 43.
94 Ibid., 43.
95 *Calcutta University Commission Report, 1917–19*, III, 27–8.
96 Petition of Brojo Sundar Mitra and others, 9 September 1862, BEC, XV, 68, December 1862, 3a.
97 DPI to GB, 4 November 1862, XV, 68, December 1862, 1.
98 BEC, XV, 70, December 1863, 42.
99 Report of the Dacca College Law Lecturer, for 1872–3, in *DPI's Report*, for 1872–3, appendix A, 672.
100 Sinha, *Educational Policy*, 170–3.
101 See the Resolution of Bengal Government on Medical Education, 18 August 1873, BEC, 163, December 1873, file 72–36, p. 274.
102 *DP*, 22 Jaishta 1270 (4 June 1863).

103 *DPI's Report*, for 1868–9, also BEC, CCCCXXXII, 10 July 1869, 50; also BEC, 163, December 1873, file 72–36, 274.
104 GB to GI, 18 August 1873, BEC, 163, December 1873, file 72–38.
105 *DPI's Report*, for 1890–1, 72.
106 Principal's Report in *DPI's Report*, for 1872–3, appendix A, 676.
107 Ibid., p. 669.
108 Report of the Dacca Divisional Commissioner in *DPI's Report*, for 1872–3.
109 For details see Sufia Ahmed, *The Muslim Community of Bengal;* Pradip Sinha, *Nineteenth Century Bengal—Aspects of Social History;* P. Hardy, *The Muslims of British India;* A. Karim, *Muhammedan Education in Bengal.*
110 See the Dacca College Principal's letter to DPI, 30 July 1866, BEC, CCCCXXXII, 9, No. 15.
111 Taifoor, *Glimpses of Old Dhaka*, 31–2.
112 Sufia Ahmed, *Muslim Community*, 9; also A. F. Salahuddin Ahmed, 'The Bengal Renaissance and the Muslim Community', in David Kopf and Saifuddin Joarder (eds.), *Reflections on the Bengal Renaissance*, 37.
113 Report of the Dacca Normal School Headmaster in Dacca Commissioner's Education Report, being appendix A to *DPI's Report*, for 1872–3, 168.
114 As early as 1845, Edward Lodge, the Inspector of Schools and Colleges reported, 'The Mahomedans who avail themselves of our education bear but a small proportion to the Hindoos whom we are instructing... The circumstances of educated Hindoos filling many situations which they formally monopolised will before long bring them to reason.', *DPI's Report*, for 1844–5, appendix 5, CCVI; see also S. Ahmed, *Muslim Community*, 9–10.
115 S. Ahmed, *Muslim Community*, 18, n. 2.
116 RNN, week ending 31 March 1866, 3 para. 19.
117 Petition of the Muslim inhabitants of Dacca, 5 November 1871, in Commisioner to GB, 28 November 1871, BEC, 163, August 1872, 86.
118 Ibid.
119 Resolution of the GB, 29 July 1873, BEC, 164, August 1873, file 87–6.
120 *DPI's Report*, for 1875–6, 91.
121 *DPI's Report*, for 1877–8, 91.
122 Ibid., 90. In 1878 of the 172 Madrasah students, 86 were from Dacca district, 42 from other districts of Dacca Division, 75 from Sylhet, 13 from Chittagong and 6 from Burdwan.
123 *Education Reports—Schools and Colleges of Bengal*, for 1853–4, see appendix 11 to the report of the Dacca College.
124 *BAR*, for 1874–5 appendix part IV p. CXXXVII.
125 The Dacca College students started playing cricket from the 1850s.
126 Siba Nath Shastri *Ramtanu Lahiri O Tatkalin Banga Samaj* 261.
127 *BAR* for 1874–5 appendix part IV No. C, CXXXII-CXXXVIII.
128 *The Bengal Times*, various dates.
129 For details see Shastri, *Ramtanu Lahiri;* Bipin Chandra Pal, *Memoirs of My Life and Times, 1857–1900;* Dacca Brahmo Samaj, *Dacca Brahmo Samajer Itihasa;* Brojendra Nath Bandhopadhaya, *Bangla Samayik Patra*, 504–507; G. S. Leonard, *A History of the Brahmo Samaj From Its Rise to the Present Day;* Benoy Ghosh, *Samayik Patre Banglar Samaj Chitra—Tattabodhini Patrikar Rachana Sankalan, 1840–1905*, 504–5.

CHAPTER IV

ECONOMIC REVIVAL: TRADE, COMMERCE AND MANUFACTURES

During the Mughal period Dacca was both a centre of trade and commerce, and an important manufacturing town.[1] A centre of consumption and a Shah Bandar (Imperial Custom House), it attracted merchants and traders, Indian and foreign. As the provincial capital and revenue headquarters the city also drew great *shroffs* (bankers), who handled the revenue, acted as army paymasters, dealt in *hundis* (letters of credit) on a nationwide scale, changed coins, provided insurance, and sometimes engaged in commercial activities on their own account. *Poddars* and *mahajans* (small bankers), money-changers and money-lenders also contributed to the growth of trade, commerce and manufactures.[2] The artisans and manufacturers of Dacca supplied the local market with general needs and produced the luxury articles, gold, silver and ivory work, perfumes and the like for the Mughal grandees, rich landholders, merchants and bankers, and also exported their goods to areas in northern India. But the prime manufacture of Dacca and its neighbourhood—Jangalbari, Sonargaon, Baburhat—was cotton-textiles, plain, mixed and embroidered. The muslins of Dacca were world-famous products. In the eighteenth century between twenty-eight and forty lakhs of rupees worth of cotton goods were exported annually from Dacca, much of it to Europe.[3]

Any sharp decline in Dacca's trade and commerce only began from 1765 when the East India Company became the ruler of Bengal. The subsequent replacement of the old Mughal administrative cadre by a new body of government servants caused the city to lose the most notable patrons of its valuable manufactures. While the rise of Calcutta as the new metropolis drew away the bulk of the country commerce, the near monopolistic control of the province's trade by the Company and its officials[4] and their imposition from 1801 of heavy custom and town duties blighted Dacca's trade, forcing many foreign and Indian merchants to leave the city.[5] The decay caused by the fall of the Mughal authorities was then made almost complete by the Industrial Revolution in England.

The manufacture and export of cotton piece-goods which had been the key to the city's commercial prosperity dwindled sharply. 'The export of [Dacca] muslins to England in 1787', reported Taylor, 'amounted in value to 30 lacs of rupees; in 1807 they were only eight and a half lacs; and in 1817 they altogether ceased and the Commercial Residency was abolished'.[6] In 1828, the Board of Customs, reporting on the great influx of British cotton goods in India in recent years, stressed the great harm caused to the indigenous products even in Indian markets.[7]

In consequence of the general commercial stagnation many of Dacca's leading Armenian, Greek, Kashmiri and local merchants gave up trade and invested their capital in land, buying zamindaris and other properties. At the same time reform of the currency of the country,[8] the imposition of a maximum rate of interest and the despatch of revenues through government agency seriously affected the monetary and financial transaction of the shroffs, mahajans and bankers of Dacca, many of whom wound up their businesses and left the city.[9]

Despite the steep decline in its trade, commerce and manufactures, Dacca retained a regional importance as a trading and manufacturing centre and entrepôt. Its hinterland was rich agricultural land even though its true potential remained unfulfilled since large tracts of fertile land lay uncultivated, and its agricultural products and manufactures were in wide demand while its dense population drew in goods from many other areas of India. Taylor's list of 1840 of exports and imports demonstrates the importance of Dacca's role as a central place in the whole region's commerce, as does his observation that 'Dacca and Naraingunge are also markets for the produce of the surrounding districts, grain and oil-seeds are imported from Sylhet, Mymensing and Tipperah and salt from Chittagong and Bulloah to the latter mart, for transmission to different parts of the country'.[10]

Much of this trade followed traditional patterns, though no single item dominated Dacca's commerce as cotton-goods once had. But economic life was sluggish because of the collapse of the old regime, the withdrawal of capital, the disrepair of the transport system, and the lack of security resulting from the growing numbers of dacoits. The journey from Dacca to Calcutta through the rivers of Barisal and jungles of Sundarbans (the usual trade route, especially during the dry seasons) was a hazardous one forcing traders and merchants to pay heavy premiums for the insurance of their merchandise.

However, even during this period of decline, which lasted until the 1850s, there were signs of change; the abolition of inland transit duties and town duties in 1836 finally set in motion a slow recovery. In 1840, Dacca, with a population of some 68,000, was still one of the most populous towns in Bengal. In addition to the settled residents it also had a floating population of traders and labourers, villagers who together gave it continued importance as a centre of consumption, and market for traders and local producers in Bangla Bazar, Nawabpur, Islampur, Urdu Bazar and other bazaars of Dacca.[11] The commerce of the city was still concentrated at the Chauk Bazar—the city's main emporium during the Mughal period. Here, hundreds of wholesale dealers, retailers and small shopkeepers had their shops and *golas* (warehouses), while others for want of room set themselves up on the roads leading to the river ghats on the Buriganga.[12] Villagers from the surrounding areas brought rice, pulses, oil, ghee and vegetables and fish to sell in the city. These they usually exchanged for salt, spices, cloth and other such items. The supply of milk to residents and producers of sweetmeats came largely from the Mirpur area whither the *goalas* (milkmen) of Dacca travelled almost daily to buy milk from the villagers.[13]

With the restoration of Dacca's position as major centre of regional administration, trade and commerce, the city's numbers swelled: by 1881 its population stood at about 80,210.[14] This rise in population further stimulated the growth of Dacca's markets. Old bazaars were restored to life; many new shops were opened and business became diversified and brisk. If the city's own handicraft production had been hard hit by British competition, the import of British cotton yarn served to cut costs for the local weavers; and as a westernized middle class developed, and wealthy zamindars aped English fashions, Dacca became a distributing centre for western goods such as Lancashire textiles, Belgian glass, wines, spirits and the like. Dacca's new Nawabi family furnished their palace in European style; they wore English clothes and shoes; they gave lavish balls in honour of European visitors, and kept a racing stable and English jockeys. Nawab Khwaja Abdul Ghani and his son Khwaja Ahsanullah came to be described by one British official as good specimens of 'Anglicised' natives.[15] And since there was a substantial community of Britons, Greeks, Armenians and Frenchmen—officials, indigo planters, merchants, agents, and their families—in and around Dacca, city merchants quite early on began to import European articles. In 1824, Bishop Heber thus wrote:

> ...in these waste bazaars and sheds where I should never have expected anything of the kind, the dressing boxes, writing cases, cutlery, chintzes, pistols and fowling-pieces, engravings and other English goods or imitation of English, which are seen, evince how fond of them the middling and humbler classes are become.[16]

The Armenian traders of Dacca were among those pioneers who first imported and sold European goods. The shop of G. M. Shircore and Sons in 1857 was a storehouse for varieties of European goods ranging from 'Wines, Spirits, Cigars, Hams, Bacon, Cabin Biscuits, Lozenges, Candles, Patent Lamps and Wicks, Reading Lamps, Shoes, Dolls and Toys, Table Cutlery, Honey Soap, Essence, Shaving Soap, Fancy Note Papers' and other stationery, 'Saucepans and Fryingpans, Travelling Bags, Bathing Towels, Toilet-Glasses, Umbrellas, Fancy Walking Sticks' and so to 'Pigou's Gunpowder' and shot of various numbers.[17] Indian merchants such as Roop Chand De and Co., Ganga Charan Das & Co., Doss Co. became established in the 1860s in Patuatuli, Babu Bazar and Nalgola respectively and N. K. Chattopadhya and Co. in the 1870s in Babu Bazar followed in their wake. Besides selling European goods such as shoes, dresses for children, buttons, socks and stockings, perfumes, patent medicines and umbrellas, these stores also sold articles of local production.[18] The trade in European goods became a new source of wealth in Dacca, many merchants earning considerable profits, while the availability of these fashionable commodities enhanced the importance of the city as the chief emporium in East Bengal not only for foreign but for local goods too.

In his diary Lt. Colonel C.J.C. Davidson of the Bengal Engineers noted in 1840, 'Dhacca has now only three manufactures worthy of name but these are very curious ones'—those mentioned were violins, shell-ornaments and idols. His casual observation need not be given too much weight, but it was at this time that rings and bracelets made from conch shells became a major product of Dacca. There were about 500 *shankaris* (manufacturers of shell-work) using about 300,000 'chankshells' a year imported from Calcutta. Ready-made *shankas* (bracelets) and rings, elaborately carved and painted, were sold in large quantities in the city and at all the great fairs in the district. They formed one of its principal exports.

However, there was also much gold and silver work, Dacca craftsmen being famous for their fine filigree designs for bracelets, there were above 300 goldsmiths and silversmiths in the city. There was also some horn and ivory carving, soap and paper making, and of course boat building, a major industry throughout the Mughal period. Nevertheless, it was the textile industry which in the 1840s remained the most important element in the city's economic life, and employed the largest work-force comprising weavers, embroiderers, darners, dyers, washermen and others. In 1846 there were about 1,500 looms in production in the city itself.[19]

The fine embroidered work, mainly for Indian courts, of which Taylor gives a very full account, was a typical luxury handicraft industry, conducted in innumerable homes upon the putting-out system, merchants issuing the design-stamped fabric and embroidery silks to be worked on at home by Muslim women. The thread used was the fine product of Hindu weavers. There was also much cloth produced of a more ordinary quality, but this, as the Commissioner of Dacca, John Dunbar, in a most valuable report on the means of saving the Dacca industry noted, was woven almost entirely of imported English thread and served a regional market. There was also a declining trade to the Middle East in mixed fabric woven with an English thread warp and a weft of *muga* and *tussar* silk from Sylhet and Assam. Besides its own manufactures, the city also acted as a distributing centre for coarse cloth woven in Faridpur, Tippera and in the Noakhali district. From Dunbar's figures it would seem that the total export of cotton goods in 1844 was down to about Rs. 936,000—a third of the figure for 1747. The export of piece-goods to Europe had entirely stopped. Dunbar also stressed that though weaving as an industry survived, it was hard pressed by English-imported cloth while 'spinning, which afforded employment to a large portion of the population is now almost entirely superseded by the introduction of English yarn which can be purchased here at a cheaper rate than country thread of a similar quality'.[20]

The only trade and manufacture which increased considerably in Dacca in these years was that in cow and buffalo hides and goat skins. Originally an hereditary profession of the low-caste Hindus called *chamars* or *muchis* (skinners), the trade in hides and skins was taken up towards the close of the eighteenth century by the Armenian, Iranian and Kashmiri Muslim businessmen of Dacca,[21] at first from Barisal, and then from Dacca which they made an important centre of the hide trade. They purchased raw hides and skins from various districts of East Bengal, and shipped them to Calcutta for export, principally to England. With the growth of trade, the curing and preparation of hides in the city itself also increased greatly. Dacca became one of the largest manufacturing centres in the region with chamars travelling about the countryside buying up supplies.[22] Although no figures are available regarding the total value of the trade during the first half of the nineteenth century, many hide merchants certainly grew wealthy. The most successful among these businessmen was Khwaja Alimullah, the father of Nawab Abdul Ghani, whose profits were said to have run to lakhs of rupees.[23] From the purchase and rough curing of raw hides to the establishment of tanneries, and a handicraft shoe industry was but a few steps and Dacca might have emerged as centre of a leather industry (like Leicester in England). The pioneer traders in hides and skins, after pocketing their fat profits, chose instead to invest their wealth in zamindaris and other properties which offered secure returns and social respectability, and by the 1850s, most of those prominent Armenian, Iranian and Kashmiri merchants who had been the pioneers of the trade had given it up to become big and powerful zamindars. The most striking example of the process was the transformation of Khwaja Alimullah into a zamindar with large estates. In his son's day the annual income from this biggest of Muslim zamindaris was estimated at eleven lakhs of rupees.[24] The trade in hides and skins continued, with the Hazaribagh area as its centre,[25] under a second generation of Muslim merchants, but with no real breakthrough into leather manufacture.

However the future of Dacca did not lie in the revival of old industries or even in the rapid growth of new ones. Dunbar had seen this quite clearly in 1844. Asked to report on measures to encourage the revival of Dacca's cotton industry, he had replied that since only a prohibitive duty on English cotton goods could do that, what should be assured was the 'providing for the manufacturers of Europe abundant supplies of raw materials'. Indigo and safflower cultivation had already been introduced into the district, hemp and flax might probably be cultivated with success, and above all 'there would appear to be no article of indigenous growth to which the soil of the District is so well suited as cotton'. Enthusiastically he proceeded,

> It is not unreasonable to believe that the decay in the manufacturing prosperity of the city of Dacca will be more than compensated by the prosperity of the District at large arising from the profitable employment of the agricultural portion of its inhabitants and the greatly increased value of its exports.[26]

Dunbar's statement was actually a commentary on the changed economic structure of Bengal brought about by colonial rule in the early decades of the nineteenth century. From the well-balanced economy that had prospered over the years through a happy marriage between agriculture and manufacture, Bengal was gradually reduced to a raw material-producing country—a change promoted by the Company for the sake of its colonial manufacturing and commercial interests. 'The economic changes introduced by the British stimulated both the internal and international market demand for Bengal's agrarian produce...'

Returns from agriculture in the district of Dacca, as in East Bengal as a whole, vastly increased from the late 1850s, but without government assistance other than an experiment in growing American cotton which failed miserably.[27] Development before the 1850s had largely been due to the enterprise of private European traders and planters. Thus the cultivation of safflower for its yellow dye was encouraged by European traders at Dacca, and then by Indians, for export to European markets. The average yield of the crop in the 1830s had been about 4,000 maunds; by the mid-forties this had been pushed up to about 10,000 maunds,[28] and in 1856 the *Dacca News* reported,

> A sort of madness seems to seize the people of Dacca during the safflower season. Carpenters, black-smiths, cooks, table servants, all have their little speculation in the dye. They are the great mixtures [sic] of the good and inferior qualities.[29]

Dacca also benefited to a minor degree from the extension of indigo planting. But the turning point came with the Crimean War in the 1850s. The pace rapidly accelerated in the 1870s when

> ...the revolution in industrial production and world communications —the growth of railways in Europe and North America as well as in India ..., the opening of the Suez Canal drew Bengal into a much more tightly integrated world economy. Agrarian produce diversified and by the late nineteenth century involved a variety of commercial crops such as tea, indigo, rice, opium, jute and sugarcane...[30]

The significance of the Crimean War was set out in an editorial of the *Dacca News* entitled 'Eighteen Hundred and Fifty Six'. The leader commented,

> The War had done a great deal for India. Russia, which had been, up to that time, the source from which England had drawn all her supplies of oil seeds, hides, tallow and fibres, was closed... Hence arose an immense demand for oil seeds from India, which in Dacca doubled the price of the common oils.

Russian flax being no longer available to Britain, the paper added, 'a substitute was required. And hence arose a great demand for Jute and Sunn Hemp.' British shoemakers even preferred 'light and cheap East India hides' to 'expensive and difficult-to-work' Russian hides. 'A great demand for Rice [from Bengal] has lately sprung up. This we believe is caused in part by the rapid growth of the Australian colonies'.[31]

The increased demand for rice, jute, hides, oil-seeds and other country produce both in India and abroad proved providential for Dacca, for most of these could be produced and supplied from East Bengal. The rapid expansion in this same period of steamer services, the opening of a telegraph system and the construction of Bengal railways, together with the first wave of investment in tea planting in Assam and in East Bengal ushered in a new boom.

The key item was jute. Jute had long been grown in Bengal as a fibre for making twist and rope and for weaving on handlooms into sacking cloth, gunny bags, and sails and bedding by the rural population. The potential of the fibre had been recognized by the East India Company as early as 1795, though jute could not then be competitive with the finer hemp produced by Russia. Nevertheless, in 1828, about 500 maunds of raw jute were exported to Dundee,[32] and in 1838 a great impetus to the jute trade was given by the Netherland Government's decision to use jute instead of flax in the manufacture of coffee bags for the East Indies.[33] When the Crimean War cut off supplies of flax a still greater stimulus was given.[34]

Jute, which had formed a minor item of Dacca's trade even as late as 1853, suddenly became a major article of commerce.[35] Exports to Britain boomed, while after 1855 the establishment of jute mills in Calcutta further encouraged cultivation.[36] The peasants in East Bengal diverted more and more land from rice and other food crops to jute, especially in Dacca, Mymensingh, Faridpur and Tippera—districts which formed the jute bowl of East Bengal.

First, local merchants and then agents from Calcutta established themselves at Dacca and Narayanganj as jute shippers. Both the quantities exported and the prices paid rose dramatically so that by 1877 the Magistrate-Collector of Dacca, estimating the output at twelve lakhs of maunds and the price at three rupees and seven annas, of which the cultivator received three rupees and the traders and brokers the remainder, argued that the returns from jute alone had been enough to pay the whole rental of the district, and still leave a surplus of from eight to thirteen lakhs. And as he pointed out, agricultural prosperity had at once pushed up demand throughout East Bengal for salt, for better quality food and cloth, for metal utensils and for ornaments.[37] That demand the merchants and artisans of Dacca soon set about meeting.

Many of the goods for which Dacca became the point of distribution were drawn from Calcutta.[38] Road communications with that city were still appalling, but Dacca had excellent river links which from the 1860s were used by regular steamer services, themselves an adjunct of the Eastern Bengal Railway, incorporated in England in 1857 and completed from Calcutta to Kushtia, on the river Padma, in 1864–5.[39]

The extension of the line from Kushtia to Dacca originally envisaged was not then undertaken. However, a regular steamer connection between Dacca city and the river terminus at Kushtia was established as early as 1862 via Narayanganj, thanks to the constant pressure upon government exerted by C. T. Buckland, the Commissioner of Dacca,[40] and the Assam Tea Company.[41] Initially the Railway Company plied their own steamers, later other navigation companies such as the India General Steam Navigation Company also put their steamers into service.

The river terminus of the East Bengal Railway was moved from Kushtia to Gorai Bridge in 1867 and, in 1871, to Goalundo. The steamer-rail route between Dacca and Calcutta via Narayanganj and Goalundo has been in operation ever since. From the 1860s private steamer companies like the India General introduced direct steamer services between Dacca and Calcutta via Barisal and the Sundarbans, carrying both passengers and goods. At the same time regular steamer services also linked Dacca and its satellite port, Narayanganj,[42] with the tea producing areas of Assam. Plans to build a branch-line from Dacca to Aricha, a small trading centre opposite Goalundo and linked to it by a regular ferry were, however, bitterly opposed by the steamer companies when mooted in 1879 and the scheme was therefore dropped.[43] Even so the existing structure of railway and steamer services encouraged a very rapid growth in trade, and made Dacca the commercial capital of East Bengal. In time, moreover, river links were opened up between Dacca-Narayanganj and Chittagong as an alternative port for the export of jute, rice, oil-seed and tea.[44]

The final act in the consolidation of Dacca's commercial dominance in East Bengal was the construction by government of a new railway line connecting Dacca with Narayanganj and Mymensingh. Work on the Dacca State Railway or Dacca-Mymensingh State Railway began in 1883–4, the Narayanganj-Dacca section was opened for passengers and goods on 4 January 1885, and the entire eighty-six miles between Narayanganj and Mymensingh was opened during the official year 1885–6.

The immediate consequences were important enough, but it is interesting to note the clarity with which a confident nineteenth-century British official visualized the possible political and administrative implications of its construction. The Commissioner of Dacca, Mr Lowis, at the opening ceremony of the Dacca State Railway, declared that

...though only a short length of less than a hundred miles, this line is nevertheless destined to play an important part hereafter, as a developer by itself and through other lines, of the great resources that now lie latent in Bengal and Assam... For this division, and in special [sic] this town, our work of today has a significance almost limitless. A hundred years ago, Dacca was an imperial city ... and may yet, in the years to come regain the splendour which was hers, ... That such a prospect is open to her, may readily be seen, if we examine the country through which this line will act as a feeder of that network of railways, which soon [traverse] Assam and part of East Bengal ... when that day comes ... Dacca may expect to recover some portion of her ancient heritage, not merelly as a trade centre, ... but in political status, as again a seat of Government. It is, I assure you, quite within the limits of measurable probability that East Bengal will, ere many years are past, develop into a Lieutenant-Governorship, with the seat of Government in Dacca, a splendid port at Chittagong and a sanitarium at Shillong.[45]

Even before this crowning act Dacca's renewed importance as a trade centre was very clear. In 1876–7, for example, the total import-export trade of Dacca and Narayanganj was valued at 367 lakhs of rupees, while its rivals Chittagong and Murshidabad, also long-established centres, recorded only 77 and 176 lakhs respectively.[46]

A substantial part of this trade was with Calcutta, the total value of goods moving down to it in 1878–9 being some thirty-two lakhs, while imports from the metropolis were valued at fifty-eight lakhs of rupees[47] The size of the latter figure is a clear indication of the importance of Dacca as a distribution point for the whole region; for many of the imported goods were, of course, re-exported. The Sanitary Commissioner for Bengal, a vigilant observer, commented in 1877, 'the Jute trade has within recent years revived the fortune of this city, making it a thriving and busy commercial town and the centre of all the trade of Eastern Bengal'.[48] The connection he made was a crucial one, for it was the prosperity brought to East Bengal by the jute trade which simultaneously pushed up the rural demand for consumer goods which the merchants and traders of Dacca were quick to supply. The largest items imported from Calcutta in 1881–2, for example, were European (mainly English) cotton-piece goods valued at Rs 4,354,973 (66 per cent of the total imports valued at Rs. 6,550,195); European twist and yarn, Rs. 1,197,755 (18 per cent); salt, Rs. 262,717 (4 per cent); metals and metalware, Rs. 197,010 (3 per cent); sugar, Rs. 118,530 (1.8 per cent); oil, Rs. 67,692 (1 per cent); and spices, Rs. 46,998 (0.7 per cent).[49] Most of the trade was controlled and distributed by Dacca's wholesale traders; lower down the scale were the retail traders from neighbouring districts who came to the city to make their purchases, and then distribute them throughout the country-side. But though trade drew its strength largely from the country-side, it also led to economic renewal within the city itself.

With the departure of the great European and Indian merchants, bankers and financiers from Dacca during the late eighteenth and early nineteenth centuries, the trade and commerce of the city had been left in the hands of local businessmen and financiers, and of a small group of immigrant merchants and bankers, Armenians, Greeks, Kashmiris, Iranians, Punjabis and the up-country Marwaris who had settled in the city. Among the strictly local businessmen the majority were Hindus. By the 1830s they were already the city's main merchants, shopkeepers, wholesale and retail dealers in grain, rice, oil, oil-seeds, money-lenders, dealers in coins, brokers, *paikars* and *beparis* (petty traders) and their trading and commercial activities grew enormously during the second half of the century. Of these Hindu businessmen and traders the dominant groups be-longed to the two great trading castes of Subarna-baniks and Sahas, and to a lesser extent to the weaver caste of Basaks.[50] These Subarna-baniks, Sahas and Basaks, together with other Hindu businessmen and traders, gradually came to control the commercial and financial life of the city, making the most of Dacca's commercial recovery after the Crimean War. The Subarna-baniks, who were general merchants, had large dealings in English goods, cloth and precious stones, and in addition, virtually monopolized the city's money-lending business in the post-1840 period. Most of the poddars in the city belonged to this caste.[51] The poddars were traditionally money-changers but during the nineteenth century transferred their activities to money-lending and providing ad-vances to the city's artisan and manufacturing classes. With the revival of Dacca as the principal commercial centre in East Bengal and the jute boom of the post-1854 period, the Subarna-baniks of Dacca found fresh financial outlets in trade and commerce supplying the city and its hinterland with the English cloth and piece-goods,

8

precious stones, and gold and silver jewellery which both the urban population and the rural folk, particularly the rich peasantry, now demanded. They also provided advances to Dacca's goldsmiths and silversmiths. In the 1870s there were some five thousand Subarna-baniks in the district of Dacca. The number in the city is not known, but urban Subarna-baniks can be assumed to have quickly established close commercial links with their counterparts in the countryside.

The Sahas were the most enterprising business community in Dacca, trading in cloth, grain, salt, wood, betel-nuts and various other country produce. With the boom in jute many of them expanded their business to include jute. In Dacca they were usually known as 'Amda Walah', or traders who imported goods wholesale and sold them to small retailers.[52] According to the census of 1872 there were a total of 225,558 persons of this caste living in the nine eastern districts of Bengal. In 1891, the Sahas of Dacca district numbered 60,537.[53] The Saha merchants of Dacca town in close association with their counterparts in the countryside carried on a brisk business in cloth, salt and jute. Some of the biggest merchants of Dacca belonged to this caste. They were also bankers.

The Basaks were originally tantis or weavers but some of them later became cloth merchants. Many of them were also employed by the English East India Company as paikars, dalals, *jachandars* (apprisers), and *mukims* (supervisors). In the early nineteenth century some of them became the chief country-cloth merchants of Dacca, buying from the weavers of the city and its neighbourhood and then exporting to Calcutta the Daccai saris, *dhutis* and *baftas* (coarse cloth used as wrappers). These were bought wholesale by their kinsmen who traded extensively in Indian and foreign-produced cotton goods. They also made advances to Dacca weavers and embroiderers for the manufacture of silk-embroidered cotton piece-goods for export to the Middle East. Trade in these Kassida cloths proved very profitable and continued throughout the nineteenth century. The most successful Dacca merchant in this line of business was Madan Mohan Basak who amassed a considerable fortune and grew to be the city's leading country-cloth merchant, even exporting Kassida cloths direct to the Middle East.[54] Later he diversified his business, and finally switched to the jute trade. With the wealth thus acquired, he purchased zamindaris in Dacca district and a substantial number of other properties in the city.

He became a very influential social figure in the city because of his wealth, ending up an Honorary Magistrate and Municipal Commissioner. There is still a road in Dacca named after him.

Of the up-country Khatri or Marwari merchants in Dacca in the 1830s, Taylor remarked, 'The merchants that belong to Dacca export their goods to Calcutta while those who are natives of the Upper Provinces and have settled here, carry on a traffic with that part of the country.'[55] It seems, however, that their number was then small, and their activity of little significance until towards the close of the century when the jute trade was at its peak, at which point many Marwari merchants from Calcutta established their firms at Narayanganj and Dacca, and built jute pressing and jute baling mills.[56] In the course of time, however, they succeeded in almost monopolizing the jute trade of Dacca.

While commenting on the business community of Dacca, Taylor noted that there were only four or five Muslims and about the same number of Christian merchants in the city.[57] By this he probably meant that there were only a handful of major Muslim merchants, participants in the import and export trade upon a large scale, for in 1830 Henry Walters had returned the number of Muslim merchant families in the city as 126 besides another 1,080 families of Muslim shopkeepers.[58] (There were no reasons for a fall from 126 to 5 Muslim merchants in a space of less than ten years.) Nevertheless, it is the case that there were only a handful of big Muslim merchants in Dacca at the start of our period. Apart from the great zamindars, a few high government officials, the descendants of the old Mughal families, some priests and physicians, most of the Muslims of Dacca were small traders and shopkeepers, vegetable-sellers, butchers, fishmongers, grain-parchers, boatmen, artisans, bricklayers, day-labourers, cooks, servants, peons and office menials.[59] The Muslim commercial role remained a secondary one. Interestingly however, the Kuttis, a lower class of Muslims, who had traditionally lived by husking paddy (hence their name Kutti from *kutna*, to husk or thresh) succeeded in monopolizing the retail business in rice in the city by the late nineteenth century. So great was their power, that they could easily raise the price of rice or create a scarcity by hoarding. They regularly profited from any shortfall in the harvest or threat of scarcity.[60]

Over one branch of trade in Dacca, however, the Muslim merchants had complete control. This was the trade in hides and skins.

The rise of Khwaja Alimullah, the biggest hide merchant of Dacca, has already been described, as also his achievement of zamindar status. But since no caste Hindu would engage in the hide trade,[61] this branch of commerce remained in Muslim hands, most notably those of Khwaja Abdul Ghani, who finally handed over the family business to his principal manager, Battoo Shaheb, who eventually became the biggest hide merchant of Dacca, amassing huge wealth.[62]

But although they monopolized the hide trade the Muslim merchants had little place in Dacca's most important item of commerce, that of jute, the preserve of the British, Armenian, Greek, Saha and Basak merchants until it finally passed to the Calcutta Marwari businessmen.[63]

The Armenians of Dacca, though only 126 in 1830,[64] of whom 49 were males above sixteen years, played a very significant role in the city's trade and commerce. Being few in number they lived close together as a tight-knit community. They were also a wealthy community, with a close relationship with the British administrators and European merchants in the city and with their kinsmen in Calcutta.

In the early nineteenth century when trade and commerce were declining, many Armenian families, such as the Pogoses, Aratoons, Michaels, Sarkies and Stephens, invested their capital in land and became zamindars. Nevertheless, they did not lose their business skills and when in mid-century a new opportunity offered, they reappeared as pioneers introducing European and British goods to the city's markets and setting up western-style departmental stores. C. J. Manook, G. M. Shircore, J. A. Minas and Anania were prominent in this role, with big shops and stores in Bangla Bazar, Dig Bazar, Patuatuli and other important shopping centres of Dacca. Messrs Anania and Company were great wine merchants who 'removed their extensive depot from Dig Bazar to Patwatolly' in 1850 to open their new shop 'in the two-storied house next to the Kali Baree'.[65] G. M. Shircore and Sons sold such novelties as tea, and were probably responsible for popularizing tea drinking in Dacca. Their Exchange Hall at Shankari Bazar was one of the premier shops of the modern type in the city during the 1870s. However, the most striking contribution to the life of Dacca, from the founder of this business firm, was the introduction of the *ticca-garry* or hackney-carriage, better known in Dacca as *ghorar-gari*.[66] Shircore thus pioneered a transport revolution, and his 'Horse carriage' business became such a great success that his example was soon followed by other Armenian and local businessmen: the ticcagarries rapidly became the chief form of public transport until they were replaced by cycle-rickshaws and buses in the twentieth century. There were 60 ticca-garries plying for hire in Dacca in 1867,[67] but some 300 by 1874,[68] while by 1889 the total number of horse-carriages in the city had risen to nearly 600.

In the 1840s and 1850s many of the Armenians entered into partnership with the growing number of British private traders and indigo planters. J.G.N. Pogose, the Armenian zamindar, was one of the directors of the Dacca Bank established in 1846 on the initiative of European indigo planters and other free traders.[69] The Armenians extended their trading activities in agricultural products such as safflower and grain still further in the prosperous second half of the century. A number of them—notably J. Lucas, Abraham Margar David, A. Thomas and J. Minas—opened commission agencies in Dacca, and bought for or supplied Calcutta firms.

The Armenians were also the first Dacca merchants clearly to visualize the bright prospects of jute and invest capital in it.[70] They purchased jute both at Dacca and Narayanganj, and shipped it to Calcutta, buying sometimes on commission for Calcutta firms. Most of the Armenian families in Dacca became involved, their firms at Narayanganj buying in the interior from the cultivators and small traders. Their jute businesses flourished during the boom of the 1860s and 1870s when there were few competitors, and brought new wealth to the city of Dacca. The most prominent at this period were Abraham Pogose, Margar David, J. C. Sarkies, M. Catchatoor, A. Thomas, J.G.N. Pogose, Michael Sarkies and P. Aratoon.[71] A detailed history of these Armenian firms cannot be reconstructed, but there is information about the commercial activities of Margar David, the biggest Armenian jute merchant in Dacca, a 'merchant prince of Eastern Bengal'.[72] It appears from his own statement[73] that he came to Dacca, probably from Calcutta, in 1852 not as a jute merchant but as a trader in rice, oil-seeds, etc. It is not clear whether he had any relations in Dacca, but soon after his arrival he entered into a partnership with Abraham Pogose. The firm 'Abraham & David' first appeared in the *New Calcutta Directory* in 1857, described as 'Commission Agents'. This partnership split up some time in the 1860s after which M. David carried on business independently until the 1880s when he entered into a partnership with Hendersons, the famous jute merchants of Calcutta and London. Throughout the intervening period he had carried on an extensive business in jute, rice and other country produce and salt, and had acquired considerable wealth. One great stroke which paid off handsomely was his decision to export jute not to Calcutta but direct to Europe by way of Chittagong, recently opened as an intercontinental port.[74] His brigs, and later his steamers, returned laden with salt from Chittagong; this two-way traffic in two of the most important articles of trade in the country was the key to his business success. A vivid glimpse of his activities is given in private correspondence about business at Narayanganj by an anonymous writer, published in the *Bengal Times:*

> The *Celt* – ... and the *Moulmein* [two steamers owned by David] are both hard at work towing, and there is plenty for them to do, their duty being to tow down to Chittagong the country brigs and barques that load with jute here and to return alternatively with those left behind salt-laden. These vessels are easily kept in active employment by your wealthy fellow townsman, Mr David, the merchant prince of Eastern Bengal, whose shipments of jute are simply gigantic.[75]

David also founded steam presses at both Dacca and Narayanganj for pressing and baling jute. Another Armenian who also founded a hydraulic jute press in Dacca was Michael Sarkies. Later, however, the David baling firm was bought up by Messrs George Henderson and Company, and Sarkies by James Finlay and Company of Calcutta.[76]

Of the many European private traders active in Dacca in the late eighteenth century, only the Greeks, who had settled in the city, continued in active trade in the early nineteenth century.[77] However, with the passing of the Charter Acts which abolished the East India Company's monopoly of trade with India and China, and lifted most of the restrictions on private traders, the number of European private traders in Bengal notably increased. Their trade in cotton piece-goods, opium, indigo and jute flourished;[78] while the abolition of government customs and town duties further facilitated their commercial activities.

A steady flow to Dacca of individual Europeans, mainly British, began after the passing of the Charter Act of 1813; they came as indigo planters or their assistants, and established indigo factories in various parts of the district. The two indigo factories of 1801[79] had by 1829 risen to over twenty[80] and by 1838 to thirty-three.[81] In 1838 nearly 100,000 *bighas* of land were cultivated with indigo in Dacca district. The 2,500 maunds of indigo annually produced in the district were shipped through Dacca, where many of the planters lived, to Calcutta, and some at least of the financing of this trade was by Dacca's Indian capitalists. The production of indigo in Dacca remained at this level until planting was more or less abandoned in the 1860s. Two of the principal indigo planters, namely Josiah Patrick Wise and George Lamb, who lived in the city, participated in many aspects of Dacca's life and made considerable contributions especially to its educational and municipal development. In course of time they came to own almost all the indigo factories in Dacca, and also bought large zamindaris. Wise ultimately became one of the biggest and most powerful landowners in East Bengal, possessing zamindaris in Dacca, Mymensingh, Faridpur and Barisal, and owning houses and other properties in Dacca city. His property was valued at forty lakhs of rupees in 1873.[82]

Other Britons who came to Dacca in the 1840s engaged solely in commercial activities. Principal among them were William Foley, T.F. Rickets and J.J. Bett who traded in rice, pulses, indigo, safflower, oil-seeds, jute and other country produce, exporting them not only to Calcutta but to other parts of India.[83] One or two even ventured to organize industries in the Western style, the most remarkable example in Dacca being the sugar mill which was founded some time in the 1840s[84] and run by a joint stock company known as the Dacca Sugar Works Company. The mill however did not flourish and was closed in the early 1850s. In 1856 or thereabouts the building was purchased by William Foley who converted it into part house and part warehouse.[85] (The building still exists.) During the Sepoy Mutiny, the British sailors who arrived from Calcutta to quell the rebels used it as temporary barracks, and hence it came to be known as Mill Barracks and the neighbourhood as the Mill Barrack area. Foley was himself a successful trader—probably Dacca's first British jute merchant—and he also founded a commission agency and a flour mill. He was referred to at a distinguished gathering of Europeans as 'one who has done more than most of us to increase the wealth of Dacca'.[86]

The outstanding individual, however, among this European business community was a Scotsman, Alexander Forbes, the father of modern journalism in Dacca. He came to Dacca in about 1844 as an assistant to Wise. Afterwards he became an indigo planter, a manager of zamindaris and a merchant of country produce.[87] Besides his various commercial activities, he was also the Dacca agent of the Medical Invalid and General Life Assurance Society of London and Calcutta, and was closely associated with the British Agency Houses of Calcutta. He was among the first 'Mofussil' members of the Bengal Chamber of Commerce when it was re-established in 1853:[88] the other members from Dacca were Messrs. Wise and Glass (indigo planters) and F. Probby (indigo planter and commission agent).[89] Forbes did not become a major business figure, though his commercial activities were not unsuccessful, but in 1856 turned to commercial journalism, publishing *The Dacca News*, a weekly English paper, the first of its kind in Dacca. The paper first appeared on 26 April 1856.[90] Although ostensibly established to provide commercial information for the European business community, the indigo planters in particular, it quickly rose above the level of a mere commercial bulletin or planters journal. Under Forbes' editorship the paper soon grew into a powerful organ of public opinion, a valuable source of information upon local, provincial and international events and a resourceful critic of the administration. Its circulation rose from 200 copies in 1856 to 600 in 1868, the readers including indigo planters, European businessmen and officials, and English-educated Indians and students of Dacca.

The Dacca News may well have helped to promote Dacca's trade and commerce; it certainly raised its status, and drew public and government attention to its needs and problems. The paper furnished information on the price and stock positions of important articles, on the movement of shipping and other transport, and upon bank and insurance rates and facilities. At the same time its advertisement columns helped to popularize many of Dacca's products and made widely known many of the city's Armenian, Basak and Saha shops and business firms.

Forbes was, moreover, the secretary of the Dacca Bank, the first modern bank in the city, and amidst his commercial and journalistic preoccupations found time to play a leading role in the Dacca Municipal Committee, of which he became secretary. He also took part in the activities of the various literary and cultural societies of Dacca, in seminars, debates, sport and drama, and made valuable contributions to each. The commercial and political traditions of *The Dacca News* were well kept up by E.C. Kemp, who bought the paper in 1871 and changed its name to *The Bengal Times*.[91]

The individual merchants who established themselves in the city in the 1840s and 1850s were followed by a number of European Companies. The first of these was the Borneo Jute Company, which established a jute-purchasing centre at Dacca some time before 1863.[92] This company was owned by George Henderson, one of the leading jute manufacturers and traders of Calcutta. Then came Field, Wilson & Co., Ralli Brothers & Co., W. S. Cox & Co., the Camperdown Trading & Pressing Co. Ltd. and James Finlay & Company. Ralli Brothers (of Calcutta and London) was a Greek firm which started business in Dacca in about 1875 and soon grew to be one of the biggest jute companies in Dacca. It and the other firms established purchasing stations at Dacca, Narayanganj and at other inland markets in the district, shipped the jute to Calcutta, and set up jute baling and pressing mills in Narayanganj and Dacca employing thousands of workers.[93]

The jute trade of Dacca handled by these companies and by individuals increased very sharply as the statistics of jute movements demonstrate (see Table 3).

Table 3. *Movements of Jute, 1876–82.*

Year	Export market	Through Dacca (in maunds)	Through Narayanganj (in maunds)	Value of Dacca and Narayanganj exports (in rupees)
1876–7	Calcutta and other places	266,700	1,594,300	5,581,200
1881–2	Calcutta only	740,727	1,8,60,400	11,705,072

Source: See note 94.

This trade was a major factor in making Dacca a thriving commercial town and the centre of all the trade of East Bengal.

In Mughal times, Dacca had been an important financial centre, with numbers of indigenous banking houses, including the house of Jagat Seth.[95] As late as 1794 there were in Dacca 464 poddars and mahajans, bankers and moneylenders.[96] By the early nineteenth century, most of the large indigenous banking houses had withdrawn their capital from Dacca and in 1830 there were only thirty-two small shroffs left in the city.[97] At this point the amount of capital available to finance Dacca's trade and commerce was probably quite small.

The poddars and mahajans who still carried on their business were apparently not large-scale bankers or money-lenders. In 1840 Taylor noted:

> The transactions of Poddars at present are confined to granting hoondees on Calcutta, Patna, Moorshedabad, Benaras, Sylhet and Mirzapore. They advance money to indigo planters on bills drawn on Calcutta, and loans to the inhabitants on mortgages of houses, and land, and on jewels, gold and silver articles, etc. left in pledge with them. Many of them import English thread from Calcutta and retail to the weavers.[98]

Nevertheless, it was one such poddar family which provided the biggest banking establishment in the city, and supplied the credit needs of all its leading merchants. The rise of the Das family of Farashganj from the humblest position to that of millionaire bankers was the most remarkable financial success story in Dacca during the nineteenth century. Interestingly, the family's business expanded most rapidly not when Dacca's economy was booming during the second half of the nineteenth century but during the period of stagnation in the first half.

Mathuranath Saha, the founder of the Farashganj Das family, hailed from Subhadya across the Buriganga. Subhadya was a Hindu-dominated village where most of the inhabitants were of the Saha trading caste. However, neither Mathuranath nor his family was in business; both were very poor. Mathuranath started his business as a money-changer, probably in the 1820s, with very small capital. Every morning he crossed the river to the city and began work in the open air, spreading a jute-sack near Bangla Bazar which was then the financial centre of the city where the shroffs, poddars and mahajans had their shops. His business was to supply the market-goers with small change for their purchases. It is said that for changing a rupee for smaller coins, he used to charge one pice or one-fourth of an anna. By virtue of this business he came to be called a poddar. After a few years of hard and astute work his business had so increased that he abandoned his pavement site for a small *Kothabari* (brick house) near Bangla Bazar. (The house is now the Naoroz Bookstall.) Then, forsaking money-changing, he started a money-lending business and also engaged in the issue of hundis and encashment of bills of exchange. He thus became a petty banker in the traditional manner. But it was the money-lending business which proved the key to his success.

These were the worst days of Dacca. There were many impoverished families, particularly Muslim families, who were forced to borrow, mortgaging their houses, lands, jewellery and other valuables. They went to Mathuranath because he charged the lowest rate of interest. But few could repay and Mathuranath duly profited from their helplessness. He built a spacious house in Farashganj to which he brought his family from Subhadya; it has survived as No. 6 Hemendra Das Road. His money-lending and banking activities now involved granting and cashing bills of exchange for large sums, advancing loans to the leading merchants and traders and insuring their merchandise. He also appears to have had large dealings with European indigo planters and businessmen: witness the testimony of *The Dacca News* in 1857 –

> There are no men more trustworthy than the native bankers ... We have done business of many lakhs with Mathoor Mohun Sooroop Chand Podars and Bulloram Oadhup Podars of this city, and would risk more upon the word of one of these firms, than on many a man's bond, even though written on stamp paper of the strongest quality.[99]

After Mathuranath's death his two sons, Swarup Chandra Das and Madhusudhan Das, carried on the family business, making the firm, Swarup Chandra Madhusudhan Poddar House, the biggest Indian banking house in the city. In 1862, however, the Bank of Bengal established a branch at Dacca. Unable to compete with this bank, which soon took up most of the business of remitting money and cashing and granting bank drafts and bills of exchange, the brothers ultimately gave up their hundi dealings and concentrated on money-lending. It is interesting to note that they also took advantage of the bank. They borrowed heavily from the bank at five to six per cent and then made loans at higher rates of interest to those unable to deal directly with the bank. It is said that Rs. 100 advanced by them often brought in interest of Rs. 570 per annum.

From the late 1860s the Das family began to invest their wealth in land, though whether because of the competition of western banking institutions or from a desire to enhance their social status, or because of the security land offered, it is impossible to say. Madhusudhan Das, the second son of Mathuranath, bought zamindaris first, out of his own share of the business. He and the other members of the family who followed his example did not thereupon give up money-lending but rather extended it among their tenants.

Swarup Chandra Das did not become a zamindar, but his sons Sanaton Das, Raghunath Das and Ruplal Das bought extensive landed properties. In course of time Ruplal Das and Raghunath Das rose to become the biggest Hindu zamindars of Dacca city. It was they who built the two magnificent houses in Victorian style which still survive in Farashganj, known as Raghunath House and Ruplal House, the latter constructed by Martin & Co. of Calcutta and elaborately decorated with beautiful Grecian statues along its parapets. With the Das family of Farashganj was associated much of the glamour of Dacca's social life during the late nineteenth century, the nautch parties, the musical soirées, the lavish dinner and wine parties to which the élite of the city, including the European officials and their wives, were invited, the great marriage ceremonies, the colourful puja festivals and the boat races.[100]

The story of European banking in Dacca, of which the Bank of Bengal mentioned above was an important part, began in 1846, when some of the European indigo planters, merchants and landholders, a few British officials and a number of zamindars organized a joint-stock enterprise called the Dacca Bank. This was the first modern bank in the city, and the first to rival the indigenous banking houses.[101] The projectors of the bank were George Lamb, the Superintending Surgeon of Dacca, Captain H.M. Nation, Assistant Superintendent for the supression of Thuggee, Dacca,

Khwaja Alimullah, J. P. Wise and Nundalal Dutt, a wealthy vakil. John Dunbar, the Commissioner of Dacca, Dr T. A. Wise, the Civil Surgeon of Dacca, and Khwaja Abdul Ghani were the trustees of the bank;[102] Alexander Forbes was the secretary. The bank, instituted under a 'Deed of Partnership' valid for ten years, was authorized to raise capital up to Rs. 500,000 divided into 1,000 shares of Rs. 500 each. However, the paid-up capital never exceeded Rs. 300,000 at Rs. 300 per share. The shares were purchased mainly by the indigo planters, zamindars and businessmen of Dacca, and British officials. The firm of Kissen Mongol and Manick Chand Bysack of Burra Bazar for some time acted as the Calcutta Agents of the Bank.[103]

In June 1856, the Dacca Bank was wound up in consequence of 'the wish of many of the shareholders residing at a distance, and unacquainted with Dacca, to realise their shares'. However, those shareholders who lived in Dacca decided to open a new bank, the directors of the old bank observing at the meeting in May 1856 that 'from the increasing trade of Eastern Bengal, an enlarged capital can be safely and profitably employed'.[104] Within two months 873 of the 1,000 shares of Rs. 500 (Rs. 300 paid-up) had been bought by inhabitants of Dacca.[105] The directors of the new Dacca Bank were Khwaja Abdul Ghani, J. P. Wise, R. G. Carnegie, J. G. N. Pogose, Babu Mirtunjoy Dutt, Babu Dinanath Ghosh, William Foley and Babu Madhusudhan Das.[106] Alexander Forbes was reappointed as Secretary, later to be replaced by G. M. Reilly. On 20 January 1857, six months after its formation, the directors called upon the shareholders to contribute another Rs. 100 per share, which was promptly paid, and declared a dividend of eleven per cent. Some time later shareholders paid in the other Rs. 100 per share to give the bank a paid-up capital of Rs. 500,000.

From 1860, however, the Bank of Bengal had begun a correspondence with the government about establishing a branch in Dacca,[107] and in February 1862 it bought out the Dacca Bank in entirety, the shareholders of the Dacca Bank receiving Bank of Bengal stock amounting to Rs. 290,999 in exchange for their shares. From 1862, moreover, the Bank of Bengal provided general treasury and banking facilities to the Government of Bengal, and hence the new Dacca branch acted as government treasurer for the whole of East Bengal, receiving revenues from the district treasuries, supplying them with money, and transferring government revenues to Calcutta. In 1884–5 it received Rs. 5,307,039 from the Calcutta Reserve Treasury and from the Bakerganj, Faridpur, Mymensingh, Tippera, Noakhali, Chittagong and Jalpaiguri district treasuries out of which it provided all the funds needed by the Dacca-Mymensingh State Railway which was then under construction. The presence of this bank in Dacca transformed the city into the financial centre of East Bengal.

The Bank of Bengal proved a real threat to the indigenous banking houses, as has been seen, but the small traders, manufacturers and ordinary people derived little benefit from it since they could rarely furnish the sort of collateral security which a European-style bank required. They therefore continued their monetary transactions with the local poddars and mahajans. Thus, in 1878, to provide financial assistance to this type of person and to free them from the hands of the money-lenders, certain educated and well-intentioned persons of Dacca established a joint-stock loan company. The moving spirits were Dr Kali Kumar Das, a Sub-Assistant Surgeon of Dacca, together with various teachers and pleaders. The loan office started with a small authorized capital of Rs. 10,000 divided into 1,000 shares of Rs. 10 each. But the loan office soon attracted many other investors and in 1880 it raised its authorized capital to Rs. 100,000 divided into 10,000 of Rs. 10 each. In that year it had a subscribed and paid-up capital of Rs. 73,660.[108] In the same year it also became a registered Joint Stock Company. In spite of its small capital it made good profits, and for two years from 1880 it paid a quarterly dividend of two rupees per cent per mensem to the shareholders. It accepted deposits from the public and lent money on the personal security of two respectable persons as well as on substantial security of moveable and immoveable property. With the further increase of business, the nominal capital of the Dacca loan office was raised to Rs. 200,000, and by 1885 the paid-up capital had reached Rs. 147,020. Its activities were not confined, however, to the people for whom it had originally been intended, but had been extended to include zimandars, pleaders, government officials and the like.[109]

The increased propsperity of Dacca encouraged some revival of traditional arts and handicrafts, though not to a very marked degree. The production of fine muslins, which had continued during the 1840s, declined as this period advanced, unable to stand the competition of Lancashire in materials for shirts, dhuties, saris and chaddars. But the handloom production of coarser cotton cloth survived, using British yarn on Indian looms, and did so even against the competition of the mill-products of Bombay which entered the market in the 1870s.[110] The specialist embroidered cottons survived, too, the Kassidas continuing to find a market in the Middle East, in 1858 to some Rs. 600,000.[111] That proved, however, to be a peak figure, for war sharply reduced the offtake of the Turkish market. In January 1877, the *Bengal Times* commented on the starving condition of the Kassida weavers owing to a depression in the Turkish market that year; and in March 1878 the same paper reported, 'Owing to the Turkish War, the last two years have been years of contraction and stagnation in the Casseadah cloth trade of Dacca . . .'[112] A reduced trade did survive, however, until the end of the nineteenth century.

The production of the expensive Jamdani or fine flowered muslins tended in this period rather to increase than to decline, reflecting the appearance of new classes to replace the old Mughal and Hindu nobility as purchasers who like their predecessors thus became patrons of luxurious indigenous products.[113] The embroidery in this style was done in the process of weaving with bamboo needles, according to a paper pattern. A special feature of the Jamdani sari was the ornamental border of gold and silver thread with large, bold corners. Jamdaninagar in the city was the weavers' quarter. The manufacture of specially fine gold and silver thread for the weavers and embroiderers became a speciality of Dacca. Such thread was used not only in making Kassidas and Jamdani saris but also for the embroidery of caps.[114] In 1887, Jamdani muslins worth Rs. 287,000 were exported from Dacca.[115] The same social and economic trends which supported the revival of these traditional luxury handicrafts also encouraged goldsmiths and silversmiths, who produced both for local and export markets. Like embroidery this was basically a family or domestic handicraft industry, largely located in the Kamarnagar, Bangaon, and Amligola mahallas of the city. The industry was so profitable that it induced many Basak weavers[116] and also the Kuttis to take up goldsmithing. James Wise reported in the 1890s that the Kuttis 'have become expert goldsmiths, competing on equal terms with the Hindu in the finest filigree work'.[117] Dacca goldsmiths were particularly famous for their ability 'to make ornaments with small quantity of gold and make them light'.[118] The most famous among them were the houses of Luckman Karmakar and Jagannath Karmakar whose customers included the 'Rajas and Maharajas' of Bengal. Silversmiths acquired a similar fame, though their specialities were the *singhasans* (thrones of deities) and *taktanamas* (bedsteads) used for marriage and religious processions, besides more usual household articles such as betel and pan boxes, and scent bottles. Hriday Nath Majumdar, a good local writer, claims that the European ladies even preferred the beautifully ornamented bracelets, rings, brooches, safety-pins and flowers of gold and silver of Dacca to those prepared by the Calcutta firms.[119]

Another industry which remained totally in the hands of its traditional manufacturers and which also expanded during the second half of the nineteenth century was the conch-shell industry. The Shankaris themselves controlled the production of and trade in shell ornaments completely. They remained fairly settled in Shankari Bazar where they had lived since their first settlement in the city. Shell manufacture remained a cottage industry. The houses of the Shankaris were multi-storied buildings. Usually the front room of the ground floor was the shop, and the back rooms were convertd into production centres. The conch shells which were cut into slices and converted into ornaments were imported from the Maldives, Ceylon and South India via Calcutta. Some of the wealthy Shankaris of Dacca themselves imported the raw shells and then retailed them.

That the industry never declined to any great extent and that it further expanded with the revival of Dacca's commerce was due to the assured marketability of the *shankas* or shell-bracelets. 'Every Hindu female of Bengal puts on these *Shakas* which are indispensable to her so long as her husband is alive. *Shakha* is indispensably a necessity for a Hindu *Sadhava* (lady having a living husband), she breaks it off when her husband dies.'[120] It was this demand from almost all over Bengal that had kept the industry alive. Besides these shankas the Shankaris of Dacca also manufactured beautiful and artistically designed rings, bangles and necklaces. Unexpectedly, the jute-induced prosperity of East Bengal in the latter half of the nineteenth century led to a fall in the demand for shell ornaments other than shankas: women now wanted more valuable ornaments of gold and silver.[121]

The revival of trade and commerce also led to a renewal of

another traditional industry, boat-building. From the late 1850s the need for country-boats for shipping goods to Calcutta and other places steadily increased. The expansion of jute exports further augmented the demand until the growth of railways and appearance of river steamers in East Bengal slowed down their production.[122]

And when the demand for specialist carpenters in the boatyards slackened, general carpentry took over as prosperity and population returned to the city. The Saha businessmen of Farashganj turned their attention to trade in timber and wooden furniture as the demand increased. They established timber-yards, kept large supplies of *sal* and teak, and employed carpenters to saw the *taktas* (planks) and make various articles of furniture to supply the orders of the town and the mofussil.[123] Trade in timber became a flourishing business in Dacca, and Farashganj, once the site of the French East India Company's Factory at Dacca, grew up as the new furniture centre of Dacca. The example of the Saha merchants was later followed by other capitalists: carpentry ceased to be a completely cottage industry and the woodwork industry began developing along factory lines. While the timber business and furniture manufacture flourished, supplying the need of Daccaites and the people in neighbouring districts, construction work increased rapidly in Dacca in the second half of the century.[124] Individuals built brick houses, businessmen mills and presses. Government offices and the railway colony sprang up. This building activity generated new economic activities within the city creating opportunities for contractors and suppliers and new jobs for the labouring classes.

We conclude that the manufacturing industries of Dacca, which had been the basis of its importance in the Mughal period, had been reduced by the mid-nineteenth century to a secondary role. Some of the old industries like ivory working declined rapidly because their market disappeared, while others collapsed in the face of competition from machine-made articles, mostly from England, such as paper, dye, perfumes, gunny-bags, bell-metal-works, buttons and needles.[125] But later in the century the new wealth brought to the city by the trade in agricultural products, most notably jute, and to a lesser extent by the growth of the city as an administrative and educational centre, permitted the revival of some older handicrafts and provided alternative employment—as in the jute presses of Dacca and Narayanganj or in the railways—for old jobs that had been destroyed. Many of these new industries and the shipment of agricultural goods were moreover very labour-intensive. The transport revolution also created jobs for hundreds of coachmen and their assistants. Similarly, the increase in the number of Europeans—official and non-official—and of Indian bureaucrats and professionals stimulated the demand for domestic servants, guards and cooks. The ostentatious mode of living of some of the richest zamindars, merchants and bankers of Dacca also generated new jobs of this kind while increasing the demand for consumer goods and the patronage of cultural activities in the city. Lavish spending by almost all the merchants and traders on religious ceremonies[126] provided direct or indirect employment to many people. Most of the musicians, dancers and singers of Dacca were patronized by the rich zamindars and businessmen,[127] and this support eventually led in turn to the development of a modest manufacturing industry of musical instruments like the *tabla* (drum), sitar, *israj* and violins.[128] It should be added, however, that it was not until the twentieth century that any large-scale investment in modern factory-based industries began in Dacca.

We cannot be certain about the impact of the economic recovery on the people of Dacca. Detailed analysis of the economic life of the whole population of Dacca, involving a breakdown of income, wage structure, occupation and consumption, is rendered impossible by the absence of relevant source material. Occupationally the city's population could be broadly divided into five categories, viz. (1) zamindars and property owners; (2) traders, merchants and bankers; (3) service people and professionals; (4) manufacturers and artisans; (5) labourers and other wage earners. Dacca had a sizeable number of zamindars and property owners who derived their income from rural estates and urban properties. Following the steady extension of cultivation and economic growth in the latter half of the nineteenth century their rent income from land and urban property increased significantly. This class was thus on the whole a well-off group. Some of them were indeed very rich, and as we have seen led a lordly life. With the revival of trade and commerce, the profit of traders, merchants and bankers also rose steadily, and some of them were among the wealthiest people in Dacca. Among service people and professionals, government officials, school teachers, professors and some of the Nawabi staff were paid fixed salaries. Lawyers and doctors were said to have earned good incomes: Ananda Chandra Roy, the leading lawyer of Dacca, eventually bought the estate of the Armenian zamindar Lucas, in Barisal.[129] The incomes of the lower classes, however, were in marked contrast. Whereas, for example, senior civil servants received substantial salaries, clerks were poorly paid, and menials received just the bare minimum. In 1867 the European District Magistrate earned around Rs. 2,000 per month, the Indian Deputy Magistrates and Collectors between Rs. 400 and 500, the clerks between Rs. 10 and 80, and orderlies, peons and sweepers Rs 4 and 5.[130] And the income of lower-grade clerks and menials was very much the same as that of artisans, labourers, small shopkeepers and traders and other manufacturing classes who formed the bulk of the population. In 1862, for example, the monthly earnings of a carpenter totalled Rs. 9; of a mason Rs. 5; of a domestic servant Rs. 5; of a coolie Rs. 6; and of a horse-keeper Rs. 5. From the available information it appears beyond doubt that the great numbers of artisans, small traders, labourers, and other wage-earners lived almost at subsistence level. The economic recovery of the city in the latter half of the nineteenth century of course increased the demand for labour, and even pushed up earnings. But in real terms there was no improvement, because staple prices also showed an upward trend.[131] Moreover, the remarkable growth of population in the second half of the nineteenth century led to an ever-increasing supply of cheap labour which effectively barred any significant increase in wages. Henry Beveridge, the future author of a history of Bakerganj, remarked in 1873 that whatever prosperity the country had gained through agricultural expansion and the jute boom would soon be cut short, and 'the Malthusian doctrine will eventually be found to be the chief specific for the evils of Bengal.' He hoped 'that if native communes and municipalities are ever established in the mofussil, they will be allowed to impose taxes on early marriages and on the possession of more than one or two children'.[132]

NOTES TO CHAPTER IV

1 *Imperial Gazetteer of India—Eastern Bengal and Assam*, 312.
2 For details on the role of these bankers and moneylenders in the country's trade and commerce, see K.M. Mohsin, *A Bengal District in Transition—Murshidabad*, 1765–1793, ch. V.
3 For details see Karim, *Dacca*, ch. IV; also N.K. Sinha, *The Economic History of Bengal*, 1793–1848, III, 4; also Taylor, *Dacca*, chs. VI and XII.
4 For details on the impact of this monopolistic policy upon the country's trade and commerce in general, see J.C. Sinha, *Economic Annals of Bengal;* also N.K. Sinha, *The Economic History of Bengal*, vol. I.
5 Abdul Karim, *Dhakai Muslin*, (The Muslin of Dacca); 108; see also Sinha, *Economic History*, III, 41; C.E. Treveleyan, *A Report Upon the Inland Customs and Town-Duties of the Bengal Presidency;* C. D'Oyly and H.M. Parker, *Observations Upon the Transit and Town-Duty System of the Bengal Presidency;* Nirmal Gupta, *Dhakar Katha*, 54. The burden imposed by these internal duties may be weighed by the revival of cotton piece goods as an item of trade. In 1834–5, the last year in which duties were levied, the value of piece-goods exported through the Dacca Custom House was Rs. 387,000. In 1842–3 it was Rs. 936,000.
6 Taylor, *Dacca*, 365. In 1787 the total export of Dacca textiles was Rs. 5,000,000, see J. Wise, *Notes*, 385.
7 Board of Customs to the Governor-General-in-Council, 14 August 1828, Board of Revenue Proceedings (Customs) ,CIV, 6, 15 August 1828, 128–31; see also Collector of Customs, Dacca to Board of Customs, 18 April 1822, BOCSOP, CIII, 33, 7 June 1822, 47.
8 For details on the currency reform see C.N. Cooke, *The Rise, Progress and Present Condition of Banking in India*, 58–61.
9 Magistrate of Dacca to GB, BCJC, CXLVII, 55, 8 July 1802, 33.
10 Taylor, *Dacca*, 184–5.
11 In 1840, there were twelve bazars in the city.
12 C.J.C. Davidson, 'Dacca in 1840', BPP, XLII, p. 38; also J.H. Stocquelor, *The Handbook, of India*, 487.
13 *DP*, 16 Magh 1270 (January 1864).
14 See Ch. V for details.
15 Clay, *Leaves from a Diary*, 129.
16 Bishop R. Heber, *Narratives of a Journey*, II, 342.
17 Advertisement in *The Dacca News*, 21 February 1857.
18 *New Calcutta Directory*, 1862, see Mofussil Directory; also advertisements in *Dhaka Prokash*, 25 Asarh 1273 (8 July 1866); 6 Aswin 1280 (21 September 1873).
19 Yatindra Mohan Roy, *Dhakar Itihasa* 175.
20 Div. Comm. to the Board of Revenue, 2 May 1844, *Sadr Board of Revenue Proceedings*, LXXXVI, 15, 4 June 1844.
21 Taifoor, *Glimpses of Old Dhacca*, 352.

22 RSC, for 1868, II, 102.
23 Majumdar, *The Reminiscences*, 78.
24 Ibid, 79.
25 Rizvi, *Dacca District Gazetteer*, 239.
26 Commissioner Dunbar to Board of Revenue, Sadr Board of Revenue Proceedings, LXXXVI, 15, 4 June 1844, 2; also 'Trade of Dacca', Halifax Papers, MSS. Eur. F.78, 44.
27 Evidence of Josiah Patrick Wise before the Select Committee, House of Commons, May 1858, 'Second Report from the Select Committee on Colonisation and Settlement..., June 1858', *Parliamentary Papers*.
28 Dacca Commissioner's Report, 2 May 1844, Sadr Board of Revenue Proceedings, LXXXVI, 15, 4 June 1844, 2.
29 *The Dacca News*, 10 May 1856.
30 P. Addy, 'Politics and Society in Bengal', in *Explosion in a Subcontinent*, 101–2.
31 *The Dacca News*, 27 December 1856.
32 Ascoli, *Final Report*, 17.
33 Rizvi, *Dacca District Gazetteer*, 230.
34 Benoy Chowdhury, *Growth of Commercial Agriculture in Bengal*, I, 196–7.
35 Report of E. Currie, 8 February 1853, Bengal Public Consultation, XIV, 27, 14 April 1853, 17; also D.R. Gadgil, *The Industrial Evolution of India in Recent Times, 1860–1939*, 57, 149, *et passim*.
36 Geoffrey Tyson, *Bengal Chamber of Commerce and Industry*, 66, *et passim*.
37 Magistrate's Report in Divisional Commissioner's Administration Report for 1876–7, Proceedings of the Lieutenant-Governor in the General Department (Miscellaneous Branch), 21 September 1877, 135–6.
38 For details on the rise of Calcutta as the new commercial and trading centre of eastern India, see P. Banerjee, *Calcutta and its Hinterland—A Study in the Economic History of India, 1833–1910;* also R. Basu, *Urban Society in Bengal, 1850–1872, with Special Reference to Calcutta.*
39 Banerjee, *Calcutta and its Hinterland*, 7.
40 Clay, *Principal Heads*, 47.
41 *The Dacca News*, 10 May 1856.
42 It was at this time that Narayanganj, situated on a larger and more reliable river, the Sitalakhsya, began to grow into one of the major ports of Bengal, serving Dacca very much as the Shah Bandar had done in Mughal days.
43 Majumdar, *The Reminiscences*, 60; BAR, for 1881–2, 255.
44 The eight-and-a-half-mile road from Dacca to Narayanganj was remade and metalled in the 1860s to cope with the increased volume of commercial exchange.
45 As reported in *The Bengal Times*, 7 January 1885.
46 *Report on the Internal Trade of Bengal*, for 1876–7, ch. IV. Although for government's statistical purposes the trade passing through Narayanganj was recorded separately, the two centres were in fact halves of a single whole, for much of the trade at Narayanganj was owned, managed and financed by the merchants, bankers, agents and insurance companies of Dacca.
47 For details of this import-export trade with Calcutta, see *Report on the Internal Trade of Bengal*, 1878–9.

48 *Annual Report of the Sanitary Commissioner for Bengal, for 1877*, Appendix VI, p. LXVIII.
49 *Report on the Internal Trade of Bengal, for 1881–2.*
50 Kedar Nath Majumdar, *Dhakar Bibaran*, 34–5; Y.M. Roy, *Dhakar Itihasa*, 175.
51 Report on the Class, Caste and Charateristics of the Population of Dacca, 1871–2, Bengal Revenue Proceedings, 233, August 1872, appendix A, 69
52 J. Wise, *Notes*, 374.
53 *Dacca District Census Report, 1891*, 11.
54 Interview with Dr Arun Kumar Basak—a scion of the family of Madan Mohan Basak, Dacca, June 1976.
55 Taylor, *Dacca*, 186.
56 For details see Banerjee, *Calcutta*, ch. V.
57 Taylor, *Dacca*, 186.
58 Walters, 'Census of the City of Dacca', *Asiatic Researches*, XVII (1832), Statement 2.
59 Ibid.
60 *The Bengal Times*, March 1878, 189.
61 When some leading Hindu businessmen of Dacca and Narayanganj formed a joint-stock company in 1877, they clearly laid down that in no circumstances would the Company ever engage in the hide business; see the prospectus of the *East Bengal Mercantile Company Ltd.* (India Office Vernacular Tract).
62 Majumdar, *The Reminiscences*, 79.
63 Allen, *Dacca District Gazetteer*, 65. Dacca Muslims participated only as paikars and beparis.
64 Walters, 'Census of Dacca', *Asiatic Researches*, XVII, 548.
65 Advertisement in *The Dacca News*, 1 November 1856.
66 For details of this business see the advertisement in *The Dacca News*, 20 March 1858.
67 Clay, *Principal Heads*, 65.
68 *DP*, 12 Ashwin 1281 (August 1874).
69 C. N. Cooke, *The Rise, Progress and Present Condition of Banking in India*, 234–5.
70 J. Mesrov B. Seth, *History of the Armenians in India*, 574.
71 Names taken from *Thacker's Directory for Bengal*, 1864–84; *Thacker's Indian Directory*, 1885–7.
72 *BT*, 7 December 1878; see the article on Narayanganj, 764.
73 Statement of M. David, in H. C. Kerr, *Report on the Cultivation of, and Trade in, Jute in Bengal*, appendix B, Statement No. 3, also Seth, *Armenians in India*, 575–6.
74 See S. Osmany, *Chittagang Port: a Study of its Fortunes, 1895–1915.*
75 *BT*, 7 December 1878.
76 Seth, *Armenians in India*, 573–5.
77 D'Oyly, *Antiquities of Dacca*, 5.
78 Banerjee, *Calcutta and its Hinterland*, 2.
79 Taylor, *Dacca*, 136.
80 Magistrate of Dacca to GB, 30 September 1829, BCJC, CXXXIX, 5 1 June 1830, 76.

81 The Europeans who owned or worked in indigo factories in the district between 1810 and 1829 were George Lamb, J.P. Wise, J. Alexander, J. MacKay, A. Lamb, Arthur Donnelly, F. Leslibondois, N. Tutin, John Carter, A. Guerinsue (?), Nathaniel Law, F.F. Camberson, T. Bird, and G. Lamb. Of these five were Scots, four English, two Irish and three French; see also John Smith, *Experience of a Landholder and Indigo Planter in Eastern Bengal*.

82 Commissioner's Report, 1873, Proceedings of the General Department, September 1873.

83 *The Dacca News*, 8 May 1858.

84 An artist's sketch of this mill can be seen in the *Panorama of Dacca*.

85 *The Dacca News*, 29 August 1857.

86 Ibid., 14 November 1857.

87 Forbes' evidence before the Select Committee on Colonization and Settlement in India, 7 March 1859, *Parliamentary Papers, 1859*, vol. 18, 141.

88 The Bengal Chamber was originally established in 1834, see D.H. Buchanan, *The Development of Capitalistic Enterprise in India*, 174.

89 G. Tyson, *Bengal Chamber of Commerce and Industry*, 185–6.

90 It has been until now held that *Dhaka Prokash*, the Bengali weekly published in March 1861, was the first newspaper of Dacca whether English or vernacular; see K.N. Majumdar, *Dhakar Bibarana*, 74.

91 For a history of these two newspapers, see the article published in *The Madras Times* in 1874 entitled 'The Newspaper Press of India'; some extracts from this article were reprinted in *The Bengal Times*, 4 August 1877.

92 *Report on the Internal Trade of Bengal*, for 1876–7, 6.

93 In 1888 there were six such mills in Dacca and its neighbourhood. See *Bengal Statistical Proceedings*, 3177, April 1888, 20.

94 Figures taken from the *Report on the Internal Trade of Bengal*, for 1876–7 and 1881–2.

95 For details see Karim, *Dacca*, ch. V; Taylor, *Dacca*, 186–7; and Mohsin, *Murshidabad*, ch. V. There were fourteen such banking houses in Dacca during the eighteenth century, see Rizvi, *Dacca*, 224.

96 See appendix A to the letter from the Magistrate of Dacca to GB, 6 February 1794, BCJC, CXXVIII, 9, 14 February 1794, 12.

97 Walters, 'Census of the City of Dacca', *Asiatic Researches*, XVII, see the statements.

98 Taylor, *Dacca*, 187.

99 Editorial note, *The Dacca News*, 24 January 1857.

100 This history of the Das family is based on Satyen Sen's *Saharer Itikatha* and my interview with Babu Brojo Gopal Das, a direct descendant of Swarup Chandra Das, in Dacca in June 1976.

101 For details on the subject of the early European banks in India, see N.K. Sinha, *The Economic History of Bengal, 1793–1848*, III, ch. IV.

102 C.N. Cooke, *The Rise, Progress and Present Condition of Banking in India*, 234–5.

103 *The Bengal Directory and Annual Register*, for 1855, see Dacca in the mofussil section.

104 *The Dacca News*, 3 May 1856.

105 Ibid, 28 June 1856.
106 Ibid, 5 July 1856.
107 G.P. Symes-Scutt, *The History of the Bank of Bengal*, 158.
108 *DP*, 18 Aghrayan 1289 (3 December 1882).
109 Annual Administration Report of the Dacca Division, for 1884–5, Proceedings of the Lieutenant-Governor, Misc. Branch, 5 December 1885, file 31.
110 N.N. Banerjee, *Monograph on the Cotton Fabrics of Bengal*, 3–4, *et passim*.
111 *The Dacca News*, 12 June 1858.
112 *BT*, 20 January 1877.
113 N.K. Chattapadhya, *Dhaka Zelar Bhugal Ebong Shankhep Aitihasik Bibaran*, 13; Dina Nath Sen, *Bangla Desher Lt. Governor O Assamer, Chief Commissioner Adhinashhta Pradesh Samuher Bibaran*, 45–6.
114 For further details see Hakim Habibur Rahman, *Asudgan-i-Dhaka*; Khan M. Siddiq, 'Life in Old Dacca', in *Pakistan Quarterly*, IX (Summer 1959), 20–7.
115 K.N. Majumdar, *Dhakar Bibaran*, 111.
116 Taifoor, *Dhaka*, 73.
117 Wise, *Notes*, 73.
118 Majumdar, *The Reminiscences*, 76; see also Hakim Habibur Rahman, *Dhaka Pachas Sal Pahle*.
119 Majumdar, *The Reminiscences*, 78.
120 S.C. Mitter, *The Conch-Shell Industry in Bengal*, 5.
121 S.C. Mookherjee, *Travels and Voyages Between Calcutta and Independent Tipperah*, 14–15.
122 Annual General Administration Report for the Dacca Division, for 1884–5, Proceedings of the Lieutenant-Governor in the General Department (Misc. Branch), December 1885, file 31 (3–5).
123 Majumdar, *The Reminiscences*, 5; also *DP*, 4 Aghrayan, 1289 (19 November 1882), see report on indigenous industries of Dacca, p. 376.
124 For details see chapter V.
125 Taifoor, *Dhaka*, 73–7.
126 Wise, *Notes*.
127 Majumdar, *The Reminiscences*, 64–6; Taifoor, *Dhaka*, 324, *et passim*.
128 Majumdar, *The Reminiscences*, 80–1.
129 Taifoor, *Dhaka*, 352.
130 See Clay, *Principal Heads*, see the statistical section.
131 Compared with 1862, the monthly income of a carpenter, a mason, a servant, a coolie and a horsekeeper in 1850, for example, was seven rupees and eight annas, four rupees, three rupees and eight annas, three rupees and twelve annas and four rupees respectively. But in 1850 rice was sold at ninety-two pounds and nine ounces per rupee, whereas in 1862 it was sold at seventy-seven pounds and two ounces per rupee. See the 'Return of Prices of Articles of Consumption and Wages of Labouring Classes in Dacca between 1823 and 1862', Bengal Revenue Consultation, LXVI, 48, October 1863, Nos. 101–2.
132 'Administration Report of the Dacca Division for 1872–73', Proceedings of the Lieutenant-Governor of Bengal in the General Department, Miscellaneous Branch, September 1873, file 1, 52–4.

1. Nawab Khwaja Abdul Ghani

2. Nawab Khwaja Ahsanuulah

3. Dacca College

4. Dacca Madrasah

5. Dacca Waterworks

6. Ishrat Manjil, the garden house of the Nawab family of Dacca at Shahbag

7. Chauk Bazar, the city's principal market

8. Mitford Hospital

CHAPTER V

DEMOGRAPHIC AND PHYSICAL CHANGES

The revival of Dacca as an important centre of administration, education, trade and commerce eventually led to a growth in population and in physical structure. Neither development was spectacular, though both were significant.

The extent of Dacca's growth can be judged by comparing the approximate population figures for 1838 and beyond with those of 1801. In 1801 the figure given was about 200,000;[1] in Walters' 1830 census about 75,000[2] and in 1838, 68,610.[3] An estimate made during a revenue survey in 1859 put the population of Dacca as low as 51,636,[4] which seems very low, though it was repeated, in the absence of any fresh census, by the Acting Magistrate Arthur Lloyd Clay, in 1867.[5] In 1868 George Bellett, the municipal vice-chairman, gave the city at least 60,000 inhabitants.[6]

In 1872 the first official census was carried out which recorded the population of Dacca as 69,212—a total even higher than George Bellett had earlier estimated. Thereafter the population increased steadily.[7] In 1878 the Divisional Commissioner, Frederick Barnes Peacock, estimated that the city then had a population of over 75,000.[8]

An increase in the population of Dacca was certainly reflected in the 1881 census of the city, which returned the figure of 79,076 (by another figure 80,210)[9], a growth of over 14 per cent in the decade.

Following a complaint from the people living in the more distant suburbs,[10] the municipal commissioners of Dacca in 1882 agreed to revise the boundaries of the Dacca Municipality so as to exclude eight small mahallas widely scattered over a jungle area on the extreme north-western side of the city.[11] After the exclusion of these areas, the municipal limits of Dacca in 1883 contained a population of about 77,661.[12] The next census, of 1891, placed the population of Dacca within the new municipal limits as 83,633—a growth of more than seven per cent.[13]

Though in the thirty years 1855–85, the city population may have grown from under 60,000 to over 80,000, a 25 per cent increase, Dacca's growth was clearly quite modest. It resulted both from natural increase and from immigration. Unfortunately, lack of materials prevents any close analysis of the component factors. From about 1870, however, the recorded death rate from cholera, small-pox, fever and other diseases was dropping, though not greatly, an indication perhaps that improved sanitaton, a pure water supply, vaccination and other public measures were having a favourable effect.[14]

The employment opportunities available in Dacca were still limited, and no factory-based industrialization took place that might have required a large army of workpeople. Trade and commerce did require extra labour to handle goods and despatch jute, grain, oil, oil-seeds, and rice, the establishment of a few jute baling and pressing mills particularly leading to a demand for labour. But because the jute trade was a seasonal activity, whatever additional labour was needed was largely obtained from the city itself, especially from the manufacturing classes whose traditional products were gradually being ousted from the market by the influx of imported machine-made goods. Moreover, a large number of people came to work in the city as day-labourers, shop and business assistants and even as ministerial and menial staff of various offices, drawn from the villages situated on the south bank of the river Buriganga. They spent the day working in the city and went back to their homes in the evening. Rural Dacca was mostly happy and contented[15] in the pursuit of increasingly prosperous agriculture.

There was however a substantial growth in the immigrant labour force in Dacca. To this growth an important contribution was made by Hindustani and Urdu speaking Hindu and Muslim immigrants from Bihar and the UP. Employers generally preferred these up-country men because of their physical strength and supposed courage as coolies and guards. Many of them were also employed by the government as policemen, *barkandazes* (guards) and peons.[16]

The rate of immigration cannot be measured simply by the growth in Dacca's population, for despite improvements in the city's health and sanitation, the death-rate exceeded the birth-rate throughout this period. In 1875 the excess of deaths over births per thousand of population was 1.34; in 1881 9.05; in 1882 8.70; in 1883 3.33; and in 1884 12.45.[17] Like many cities in India and Britain, the population of Dacca long grew by importing people, to make good a higher urban death-rate.[18] Thus the census of 1891 revealed that a total of 25,639 people from other districts of Bengal and even other provinces were then living in Dacca. Of this total 10,448 came from contiguous districts, 1,690 from other districts of Bengal, 7,010 from Bihar, 107 from Orissa, 25 from Chota Nagpur and 6,359 from other provinces and countries.[19] The census also revealed the characteristic urban imbalance between males and females among the immigrants; thus the male-female ratio among immigrants from contiguous districts was 10:1; from other Bengal districts 2:1; from Bihar 6:1; from the North-Western Provinces 5:1; and from other provinces 9:1.[20] These typical immigrant worker patterns meant that much of the labour force was not reproducing itself in Dacca. They also meant that in addition to exporting wages by remittance, which were thus lost to the local landlords, shopkeepers and so on, the immigrant workers intensified social problems—prostitution, drinking and gambling.[21]

Qualitatively the most significant immigration was of the new English-educated class, most of whom eventually settled in the city. They came to join the local Bar, to become teachers or journalists, to practise as physicians and to take up employment in government and private offices, in banking and other commercial organizations. Most of these newcomers came from the district of Dacca itself, particularly from Vikrampur. Indeed the educated Vikrampuris formed one of the most impressive groups within the city. In 1871 they formed an association called the Vikrampur Hitasadhini Sabha or the Society for the Promotion of the Well-being of Vikrampur and its People. In the society's first year, over one hundred members subscribed among whom were high government officials, pleaders, professors, doctors and journalists.[22]

This new English-educated class soon carved out a prominent place in the society of Dacca: a contemporary thus declared, 'the educated Bengalis hailing mostly from villages [of Dacca] and other Districts form the gentry or the élite of the town.'[23] These Western-educated outsiders transformed Dacca, making it the intellectual and political capital of East Bengal. It was this group which, in conjunction with a small section of enlightened local people, established many of the reformist organizations and societies of the city, the most articulate manifestation of the progressive mind of these people being the establishment in 1861 by the Brahmos of the vernacular newspaper, the *Dhaka Prokash*. This newspaper at once sealed the status of Dacca as the seat of modernization in East Bengal. In similar fashion the foundation of the Dacca People's Association in 1873 as the first political association in the city marked the city's emergence as the centre of political activity in East Bengal.

One other feature of the growth in Dacca's population is of such importance as to require comment—changes in its communal composition. It is believed that in the seventeenth and eighteenth centuries the Muslims formed a majority of the inhabitants of Dacca. Even as late as 1801, a police report found that the Muslims outnumbered the Hindu householders of Dacca, '14$^1/_2$ to 13'.[24] In 1830 the Muslim inhabitants in Dacca according to Walters numbered 35,238 (exclusive of uncounted purdah females) and the Hindus 31,429 (also exclusive of such females),[25] and in 1838 according to Taylor the number of Muslims within the city, excluding the suburbs, was 32,463 and that of Hindus 28,154.[26] But thereafter the Muslim-Hindu ratio seems to have changed gradually until it became markedly different. Thus the first official census of 1872 gave the city 34,433 Hindus as against 34,275 Muslims.[27]

Too much cannot be made of small shifts in the numbers recorded thereafter, given the uncertain accuracy of these early figures, but it is clear that Muslim numbers rose more slowly than Hindu. In 1881 the figures were Muslims 38, 913, Hindus 39, 658; in 1891, 40,183 and 41,566; and in 1901, 41,728 and 51,247. By the twentieth century, therefore, Hindus were predominant. The growth of the Hindu population was partly due to immigration. The arrival of labourers from Upper India and Bihar, of the English-educated Bengalis, and of traders, artisans and labourers from the rural areas of the district of Dacca gradually raised the Hindu population above the Muslim.

The leadership of the Hindu community was shared between the Western-educated intelligentsia and the leading bankers, traders and merchants who, with another stratum of zamindars, largely controlled the economy of the city. Backed by increasing numbers of wealthy Hindus, this new élite was able to bid for a controlling influence over the administration of the city, even as early as the first municipal election in 1885.[28]

The decline and revival of the population of Dacca which have just been traced were matched by a contraction and subsequent expansion of the physical structure of the city. Between 1801 and 1840 many localities close to the city, such as Narinda, Faridabad, Wari, and Alamganj to the east and the north-east, which had been densely populated,[29] were largely abandoned, while Phulbaria, Diwan Bazar and Manohar Khan Bazar in the north, and Dhakeswari, Azimpur and Enayatganj to the north-west and west, still partly inhabited in 1801, became totally desolate. In March 1839, the Rev. William Robinson of Dacca Baptist Mission passed by elephant through the wild northern outskirts of Ramna to visit the Catholic Church in Tejgaon. To his colleagues in Calcutta he wrote:

> Tejga is a village (the glorious village as you will see its name imparts) about six miles from Dacca. It was once a populous place, but it is now almost a desolation... the way to it from Dacca lies through a dense jungle, once the site of numerous pleasure gardens: the walls of which in many places still remain. This jungle is beautiful in appearance, but it is not passed without danger, it being the habitation of tigers.[30]

Nor were the northern outskirts alone threatened. In 1818 Judge John Ahmutty of the Provincial Court had urged the eradication of the thick jungles on its outskirts which had been rapidly encroaching on the city, and 'which if not checked and cleared, threaten to render Dacca...as unhealthy as Moorshedabad, and equally surrounded with pernicious jungles.'[31] Twenty-two years later Col. Davidson found Ahmutty's prognostication fulfilled:

> The suburbs of Dhacca were formerly inhabited by thousands of families of weavers ... The majority of the weavers have long since deserted Dhacca to seek employment in agriculture... The consequence is that within half a mile of the city there exists one of the most pestilential jungles in India; nay the skirts of the city itself are beginning to bear the same appearance from the scantiness of its rapidly diminishing population.[32]

The jungle-beset city did decline further, for in 1859 when a topographical map was prepared, the main city was shown covering an area only a little over three miles and a quarter by one and a quarter.[33]

The 1850s, however, marked the end of decline and the start of physical renewal. Though the city limits did not alter much the internal physical structure of the town underwent vast changes. Medieval Dacca was finally transformed into a modern city with metalled roads, open spaces, street lights, and piped water-supply, the details of which will be related in the following chapters.

Here we are going to review the chief features of this renewed physical growth of Dacca. The pattern of that growth was set, however, during the years of decline. It was the new British administrators, looking to convenience and salubrity, and perhaps attempting to build in their adopted city[34] some features of that urban environment with which they were familiar at home, who turned their attention northwards to the higher ground which had been a favoured area under the Mughals. There in 1825 the Magistrate Charles Dawes had set about clearing the Ramna jungles and laying out a spacious green, opening out the choked northern outskirts of the city. The old road leading to the Ramna was renovated and widened, a large oval was cleared and enclosed with wooden railings, and round the perimeter a race-course was laid out. 'An eccentric civilian', Dawes had the course levelled and beautified with rare trees, such as casuarinas and mimosas. At the extreme north-west, half a mile from the winning post, he created a small hillock, known as 'Dawes Folly', thickly planted with superb fir-trees, crowned with a pavilion in the Gothic style.[35] Here he used to serve morning coffee to all visitors to the race-course. At a short distance from the Folly he also built his own bungalow.[36]

The whole area became a splendid open space, a favourite spot for outings, and the most 'pleasant drive' in the city, much used by Europeans and well-to-do Indians. Though the clearing of the Ramna area did not lead to any rush to build houses there, since the population was still declining and many city centre areas were still falling vacant, it did prove to be the key to later city expansion.

That expansion, however, was deferred for a decade. On the departure of Charles Dawes, and of his more illustrious successor Henry Walters, the greatest of improvers,[37] the city lapsed into total neglect. Much of the Ramna area was invaded again by scrub, and the work of Dawes undone. It was only with the arrival of yet another devoted civilian, Russell Moreland Skinner, as Magistrate of Dacca (1840–2) that the modern development of the city began.

In the 1840s there again started a slow but steady colonization of the Ramna area. Among the first families who bought land and built garden houses on the open ground west of the race-course were the Arathoons, a leading Armenian zamindar family of Dacca. They built their house just south of the Greek cemetery, where the Bangladesh Atomic Energy Centre now stands. A little further north Judge John Francis Griffith Cooke bought a large plot of land, on which he built a small bungalow. Upon his retirement, in 1844 or 1845, he sold this property to Khwaja Abdul Ghani. The Khwajas by this time had become one of the leading zamindar families of East Bengal and were anxious to demonstrate their status. Within a few years Khwaja Abdul Ghani had built a magnificent country house[38] with a complex of many fine buildings and audience halls, tastefully laid out in a beautiful garden. This garden, in the Mughal style, was named Shahbagh, [39] and soon the whole area came to be called by this name.

During the nineteenth century, the Khwaja's country house was the scene of balls to visiting dignitaries, of many glittering social gatherings for the city' s élite involving singing and nautch parties.[40] But its more lasting claim to fame is that it was in one of its audience halls that the Muslim League was founded in December 1906, during the time of Nawab Sir Salimullah, the grandson of Khwaja Abdul Ghani.[41]

Dawes, besides opening up the Ramna, had also cleared the area just beyond the Nawabpur and Thatari Bazar to the north-east of the city. To it was transferred the cantonment at Begun Bari in Tejgaon, a whole complex of sepoy barracks, officers' quarters and parade ground being created on the cleared ground. This area is still generally known as the Purana Paltan.[42] Dawes was both architect and builder for this new cantonment, though much of the work was carried out by his successor Walters and the Military Board.

Unfortunately, Dawes could not have chosen a worse place for the cantonment. It was situated on the bank of a branch of the old Pandu river, by then much silted up, and a breeding ground for mosquitoes. Malaria and other fevers soon struck sepoys and officers alike. Such was the unhealthiness of the place that the European officers declined to live in their quarters and had to be permitted to live in rented houses within the city.[43] The Indian Sepoys also showed their discontent. The unhealthiness of the Dacca cantonment acquired such notoriety that a transfer there was regarded as a punishment—one meted out, indeed, according to *The Dacca News*, to a sepoy regiment which had refused to cross the sea during the Second Burmese War.[44] The unhealthiness of Dacca cantonment even figured in Anglo-Indian fiction when the impassioned Marsden addressed his beloved Fanny in Sir G. O. Trevelyan's well-known sketch:

> You are a pucka angel. I would die for you. I would give up my accumulated arrears of privilege leave for you; for you I would do unpaid duty with the East Indian Regiment at Dacca.[45]

Finally, government had to abandon the area, and in 1853 the cantonment was moved once again, this time to a refurbished Lalbagh Fort. Four years later there took place in the fort the 'Battle of Dacca' in which British sailors and the European inhabitants of the city defeated the rebel sepoys of the 73rd Native Infantry in a skirmish. After the Mutiny the cantonment was finally removed to the Mill Barracks at the eastern end of the town. Thereafter the fort housed the Lalbagh police outpost and later became the headquarters of the Reserve Police Force.

Despite its unhealthiness, the old cantonment area had become a very beautiful place after years of constant care, one of the most picturesque in the town. The city authorities feared that with the abandonment of the cantonment the area would revert to jungle once more, and the money spent and all the gains to public health would be thrown away. The ground was therefore handed over to the Municipal Committee to be preserved as an open space. The Municipal Committee turned part of it into a garden called the Company's Baghicha; the rest was maintained as an open field which subsequently became the cricket ground for Dacca College, and a sporting centre where various athletic and wrestling competitions were annually held. It was also used by the sepoys as their parade ground, for target practice, and also for military exercises for reviews by visiting Lieutenant-Governors and Viceroys. Fittingly, this place has now been developed as the centre of sporting activities in Dacca, and here stands the city's only stadium.

Another development near Ramna occurred when the Brahmo Samaj in Dacca split in the late 1870s over the issue of Keshab Chandra Sen's marriage of his young daughter to the Maharaja of

Kuch Bihar in 1878. The followers of Keshab Chandra who became members of the New Dispensation moved their headquarters to Nimtali near Ramna in 1880. They occupied the old palace-residence of the Naib-Nazim with their families, building up a new mahalla called Bidhan Palli, the quarter of the New Dispensation Brahmos.[46]

No further expansion of the city on its northern side took place until 1885 when parts of Phulbaria were used as the site of Dacca's first railway station. About fifty acres of land were acquired for the station, staff quarters and railway workshop, round which a large railway colony soon developed. Further expansion in this direction did not take place until the city became capital of the new province of Eastern Bengal and Assam in October 1905.[47]

During the second half of the nineteenth century the city also expanded both towards the east and the west, particularly in the latter direction. The areas of Gandaria, Narinda and Alamganj in the east which earlier had been deserted were recolonized. These areas were largely occupied by the well-to-do people who wanted to move out from the crowded and unhealthy parts of the city centre and to build more spacious houses. Enayatganj, Hazaribagh and Nawabganj in the west also developed as extensions of the town, and more especially a new industrial area appeared on Nawabangj Char (island) in the Buriganga, where many jute pressing and baling factories and warehouses sprang up. It was well placed to receive jute, which was drawn mainly from north-west of the city, especially the Manikganj subdivision.

The growth of new areas was accompanied by a rebuilding of old residential areas. As early as 1865 the *Dhaka Prokash* noted a greater eagerness, whether from fear of fire or increase of wealth, to build brick-houses.[48] The trend continued. In 1881 *The Bengal Times* noted, 'Those who have not seen Dacca... for half a dozen years or so, would be surprised at the improvement and progress everywhere apparent. In Dacca old smoky huts are rapidly giving place to masonry buildings...'[49] Unfortunately, no figures for pucka and mud houses for the latter half of the nineteenth century are available after 1870 when it was found that out of a total number of 15,031 dwellings, 3,500 were pucka.[50] This shows a significant increase, however, when compared with the 1801 figure of 2,832 pucka houses out of a total of 42,949.[51]

Most of the building activity and expansion of the town took

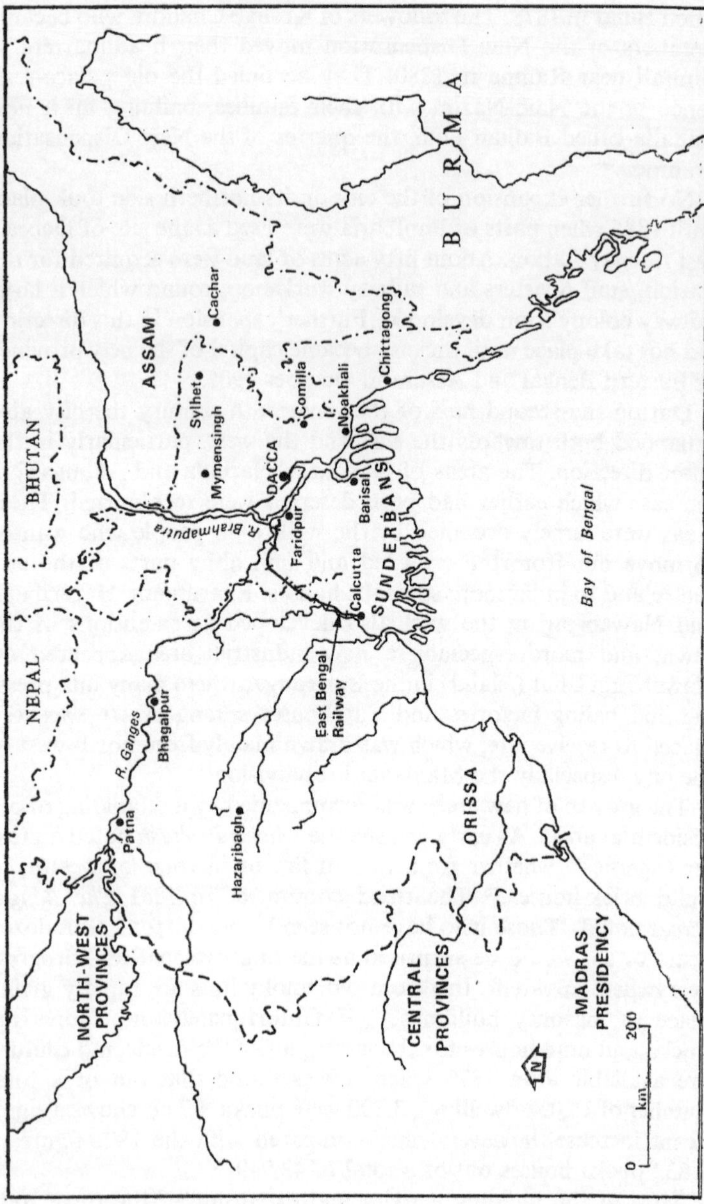

Map 1. *Dacca and its region* (adapted from A. L. Clay, *Leaves from a Diary in Lower Bengal*, London 1896)

place without any planning. However, the construction of any house, shop, garden, well or tank had to conform to the municipal bylaws; and these, though not always strictly enforced, generally prevented encroachment upon public lands and streets and some other abuses. As Dr William Henry Gregg, the Sanitary Commissioner for Bengal, after an inspection tour of Dacca, observed in 1889,

> Within recent years the town has been extended westwards, and the new houses and streets, which have been constructed according to nineteenth century ideas, stand out in striking contrast and to those of the old town which was built during the middle ages.[52]

Nevertheless, the only locality which was developed as a fully-planned residential area was the mahalla of Wari. The mouza of Wari was a khas mahal of about twenty-seven acres, south-east of the Thatari Bazar and north-west of the English cemetery. In 1839 the first agricultural settlement of the land was made, and the whole area was leased out on *jangalbari* (forest) tenure at an annual rent of two rupees per bigha of homestead and fruit-tree lands and four annas per bigha of lands used by the washermen for washing and bleaching muslins. The total revenue thus settled amounted to a little over ninety-one rupees. However, given the economic decline of Dacca, these rates proved too high and in 1841 a fresh settlement was made at something over fifty-nine rupees.[53] Even so, by 1876 five-sixths of the property had relapsed into jungle.

In 1876 the Municipality decided to buy and develop the Wari lands, but the offer of Rs. 1,475 for the whole plot was rejected by government as too low.[54] Finally in 1885, the government decided to manage the whole area itself, and the Collector of Dacca, Frederick Wyer, was entrusted with the improvement of the land. Wyer took a particular interest in developing the area. The jungle was cleared, the land levelled and broad roads with proper drains were constructed. The whole area was divided into a grid of spacious plots leased at an annual rent of six rupees per bigha, the lessee undertaking to build a pucka house of substantial character within three years. The plan of the house was to be approved by the Collector, and the construction of any additional buildings within the allotted plots was prohibited without his permission.

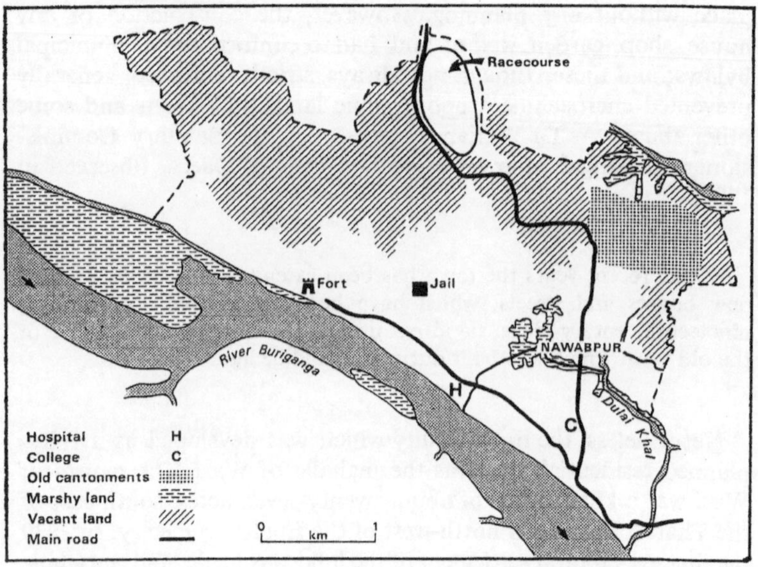

Map 2. *Dacca in 1859*

The plots were immediately taken up by senior government officials and professional people like doctors, lawyers and teachers, who built beautiful houses with gardens at front and rear. The houses were also supplied with electricity and piped water; with its broad metalled roads, well-lit and drained, Wari eventually became a quality, upper middle-class area—'the sanatorium of Dacca' as a contemporary described it.[55]

There was no expansion of the city south of the river, but the river front itself grew to be the most pleasing and beautiful part of the town. In Dacca there had always been a tendency to live near the river. As it was the principal means of communication with other parts of the country, river frontages were commercially valuable. The riverside was also very airy, offering a cool breeze which was a great comfort during the hot months from March to June, while the river itself was a major source of water supply. Only after the coming of the railway, a piped water supply and electricity for fans and coolers did the river front of Dacca lose its prime importance as a residential locality.

Prior to these developments, most of the rich inhabitants of the city had their residences here, and all the most elegant houses and buildings of Dacca fronted on the Buriganga. The magnificent houses of the zamindars, merchants and other richer people, the fine residences of the European officials, the remnants of the majestic Lalbagh fort, the old buildings of Bara Katra and Chota Katra, the domes and minarets of several beautiful mosques upon the edge of the river, gave to Dacca, as the traveller approached it, that look of a city rising from the sea which earned for it the title of 'the Venice of the East'.

The river was also however, a source of problems. It was tidal, so that at low tide, it exposed a foreshore which was muddy and noisome, causing great difficulties to those crossing the river or loading and unloading cargo.

In 1864, to protect the shore from flooding and erosion, to prevent the formation of great mud-flats at low tide and to facilitate the movement of passenger and cargo at the river ghats, the Commissioner of Dacca, C. T. Buckland, launched a scheme to construct an embankment along the southern front of the city.[56] He also planned a promenade behind the bund to beautify the waterfront and provide a pleasure walk.

Buckland was one of those British civilians who left lasting marks upon the country which they had been called on to administer.[57] At Dacca, the public had tremendous respect for him, and no one dared to incur his displeasure. He decided to construct the embankment by public subscription. Accordingly, he convened a meeting of influential residents, explained to them the benefits that would accrue from the embankment, told them that he wanted subscriptions for it. In Dacca not all the wealthy were charitable and open-handed; many among them could not see the benefits of the undertaking. However, Khwaja Abdul Ghani took the lead, donating Rs. 35,000, and a subscription of Rs. 20,000 also came from the zamindar of Bhawal, Kali Narain Roy.[58] Other subscriptions were slow to follow, and Buckland thereupon proceeded to use his official authority and influence to extract the necessary thousands of rupees. Many witty stories circulated among the British officials of Dacca about the tactics Buckland adopted to realize more money for the embankment from the reluctant donors of the city.[59] Eventually all the wealthy people of Dacca contributed, for no one dared to displease the '*Chotolat*' (the local Lieutenant Governor)!

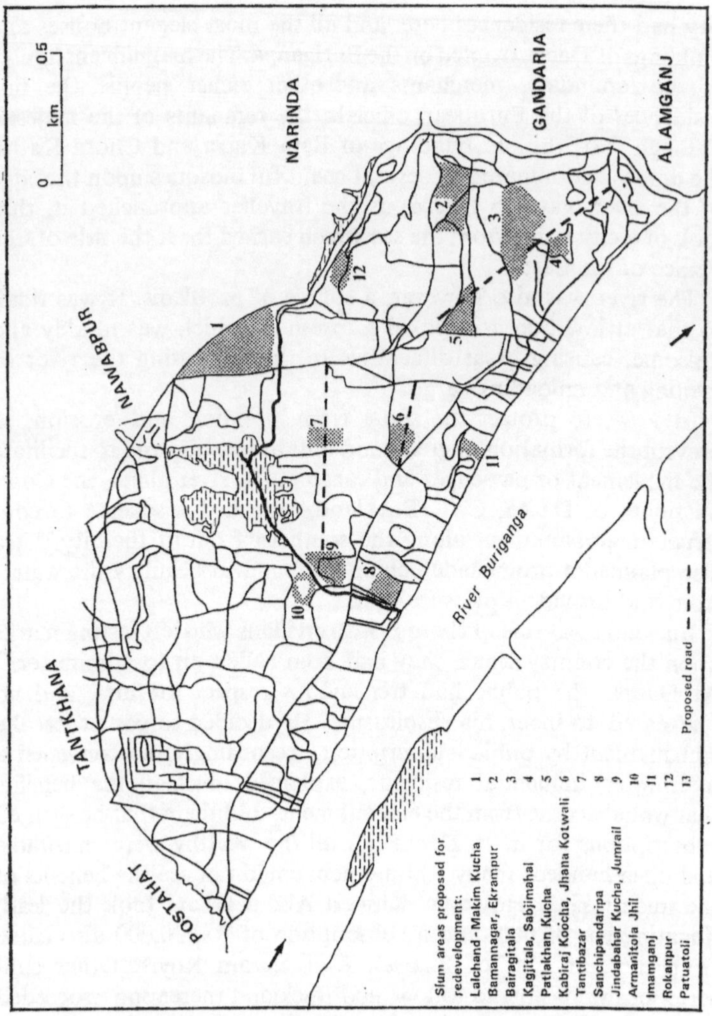

Map 3. *Dacca in 1869*

See also p. 190 (Ch. VII) for plans of city development

Even so, the subscriptions proved insufficient to realise the grand scheme of embanking the whole river front, though Buckland persuaded government to provide some funds. At first, therefore, embankment of that part of the river front which extended from near the present Northbrook Hall Ghat to Wise Ghat was undertaken, with further extensions both east and west deferred until more funds became available. The frontages of all the houses were obtained as 'voluntary' donations[60] and a raised strand was in time constructed. The embankment was faced with stone, and the top laid with bricks. Near the Sadar Ghat, part of the strand was left green, later being turned into a miniature park with a raised dais where visting dignitaries could be received on landing from their steamers and where the band of local regiment played in the afternoon for the pleasure of the crowd which assembled daily. The strand proved an ornament to the town and a boon—a spacious promenade overlooking the river with its busy traffic, where people could stroll in the afternoon and evening enjoying the cool breeze from the river. Since it was constructed under Buckland's inspiration it was appropriately named the Buckland Bund. No further development was then made until in the 1870s Khwaja Abdul Ghani undertook its extension westward from Wise Ghat to Badamtali Ghat, and in the 1880s Babus Ruplal Das and Raghunath Das carried it east from near the Northbrook Hall Ghat to their residence in Sabjimahal. The embankment, thus extended to about a mile in length, was later on handed over to the Municipality for maintenance.

Since the economic revival of the city greatly increased the value of land on the bank of the Buriganga, many of the vacant frontages were purchased and the low ground filled and built over. Among the public buildings that were constructed during this period the most important were the Mitford Hospital, the Waterworks, the Steamer Terminal and the Northbrook Hall. But the new buildings which added most to the lustre of the river front were the three magnificent mansions of Nawab Khwaja Abdul Ghani, Babu Ruplal Das and Babu Raghunath Das. Parts of the river front, especially those near the Sadar Ghat and the Steamer Terminal, also developed as wholesale markets where the rural population sold their vegetables, fruits, fish and other commodities to the traders of Dacca.

More fundamental changes, however, took place in the internal

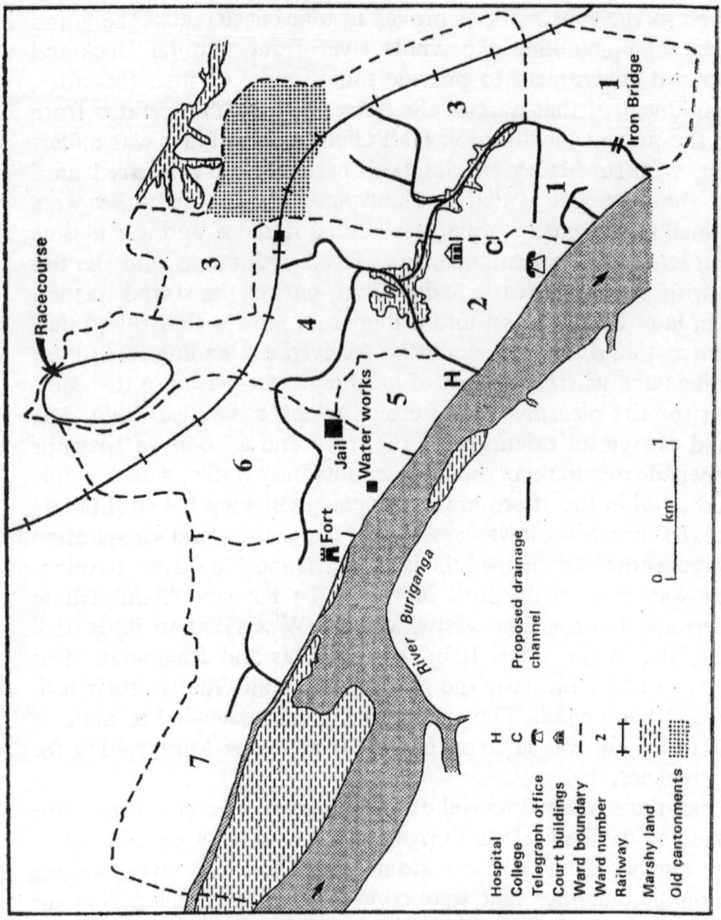

Map 4. *Dacca in 1889*

See p. 212 (Ch. VII) for drainage schemes.

character of the city. Until 1864, the public offices and the courts were all housed in rented buildings scattered about the town. When, on his visit to the city in 1862, Lieutenant-Governor Sir Cecil Beadon inspected these, he was at once struck by their unsuitability and by the inconvenience of their location. On returning to Calcutta he immediately ordered the construction of new buildings to house all the important offices and courts at Dacca on a single site.[61] Buckland chose 'a strip of land 100 yards in width on the west side of the public road leading north from the [St. Thomas] church and the college', some six acres in area—formerly the site of a ditch and lowland, but recently reclaimed and filled up by the municipal committee.[62] By 1866 the courts for the District Judge and his subordinate and the offices of the Magistrate and Collector had been built, and others followed.

The construction of these new offices and courts completed a fundamental change in the pattern of the town. During Mughal rule, the heart of the city had been the old fort round which were located all the central and provinical offices. This locality continued as the city centre during the years immediately after the establishment of British rule in Dacca. However, in the 1820s the Magistrate's and Collector's offices, the District courts, and other offices were gradually moved eastwards to the areas near the Sadar Ghat and Bangla Bazar—the localities which the British preferred, closer to their factory site, and near the river. Henceforth, the Sadar Ghat-Bangla Bazar area, and the localities north of it, grew up as the new city centre. The building of the new office blocks and courts completed this process. Thereafter the old fort areas receded into the background.

Other localities within the city also underwent radical changes from the late 1850s. When the population of Dacca began to rise substantially again, mostly by immigration, the newcomers settled down wherever accommodation was available. There were numbers of unoccupied houses in the city owned by the Armenians and Greeks, and by Muslim and Hindu zamindars and merchants. Many of these houses were brick-built. The Bengali officials and other professional people who came to Dacca rented such houses wherever they were found without being too discriminating about the locality. Thus they rented houses in areas formerly the quarters of weavers, carpenters, shell-cutters and silversmiths and goldsmiths. Likewise the coolies and other day labourers who came to

Dacca in search of jobs settled down in such areas as Goalnagar and Kamarnagar, the milkmen's and blacksmiths' quarters. Some of the lodging-houses of the school and college boys were situated very near to prostitutes' quarters. Even the Europeans—officials as well as non-officials—rented houses wherever they could be found, though they preferred to live in the better houses in the less crowded parts of the city. As it happened, they found accommodation mostly on the riverside near the Sadar Ghat and Bangla Bazar areas. This led to the development of what was sometimes loosely called the European quarter of Dacca, though in fact there was no positive segregation of residence of the Europeans in Dacca. Indeed the pattern of new settlement greatly altered the former exclusiveness of many localities, as when Tanti Bazar, the weavers' quarter was invaded by many other people, including the educated middle class.

At first, the merchants and bankers, who flourished with the revival of the city's trade and commerce, did not move out to the more spacious suburbs but built more commodious houses upon the sites of their old ones or in the near vicinity. Thus many fine buildings grew up along the narrow and tortuous lanes of the city. The Sahas who rose to be the most prosperous business community in the city built large houses in their ancestral locality of Bangla Bazar and nearby Farashganj during the second half of the nineteenth century. Madan Mohan Basak, who belonged to the weaving caste, built his magnificent house in the Nawabpur area amidst the poor huts of his less fortunate caste-brethren.

Later, when with the growth of population the central areas became overcrowded, there developed a move to the city's outskirts, more particularly among the rising educated middle class. Neither work nor caste-ties dictated their living huddled together like the shell-cutters, blacksmiths and weavers. The introduction of wheeled carriages and the extension of the piped water-supply facilitated this outward move and led to the growth of new residential quarters first in the immediate vicinity of the town where vacant lands were available or where lands had been recently reclaimed as in Tanti Bazar, Goalnagar, Lakshmi Bazar, Sutrapur and Armanitola, and then to the further suburban areas such as Wari, Narinda, Gandaria, Enayatganj and Chowdhury Bazar.

Changes also took place in the markets and business centres in the city. Although Chauk Bazar remained the main centre of the city's trade and commerce, Rai Shaheb Bazar near the new office buildings grew up as the principal market for the daily necessities of life. Farashganj, once the site of the French East India Company Factory and the French Settlement in Dacca, developed into a centre of the lime and timber trades; Nawabganj Char of the jute trade, and Hazaribagh, once a garden, became the centre of a trade in hides.

These shifts in use and the growth of population were not effected, however, without causing the most serious urban problems. These will be considered in the next two chapters.

NOTES TO CHAPTER V

1 HMS, vol. 456 (f), 287.
2 Walters, 'Census', *Asiatic Researches*, XVII, 538.
3 [James Taylor], *Cotton Manufactures of Dacca*, 4.
4 See the note to the revenue survey map of the city of Dacca, 1859.
5 Clay, *Principal Heads*, 130.
6 Bellet's Report in Div. Comm. to GB, 2 June, 1868, BJP, CCCCXXXIII, 27 October 1868, 134.
7 *DP*, 10 Bhadra 1285 (22 August 1878).
8 *DP*, 13 Jaishta 1285 (26 May 1878).
9 Census of 1881, III, 590, also *BT*, April 1881, 228.
10 They complained of being taxed without any return in public services—being beyond the reach of piped water, municipal roads and so on.
11 Proceedings of the Municipal Commissioners of Dacca, 17 June 1882, also Bengal Municipal Proceedings, 1838, September 1882, Collection 16 (44–51).
12 Administration Report of the Dacca Municipality, for 1882–3, DMRR Coll. 1.
13 *Census of 1881. The Provincial Tables*, 17; see Atiqullah, M. and Khan F. Karim, *Growth of Dacca City—Population and Area, 1608–1981.*
14 For details see chapter VII.
15 Skrine's 'Memorandum on the Material Condition of the Lower Orders in Bengal', as quoted in D.H. Buchanan, *The Development of Capitalist Enterprise in India*, 358.
16 *Dacca District Census Report, 1891*, 3.
17 Figures quoted from the *Annual Reports of the Sanitary Commissioner for Bengal.*
18 For further illustration on this point see Ellen M. Gumperz, 'City Hinterland Relations and the Development of a Regional Elite in Nineteenth Century Bombay', *Journal of Asian Studies*, XXXIII, 4, 1974, 581; also D.J. Bogue and K.C. Zachariah, 'Urbanisation and Migration in India', in R. Turner (ed.), *India's Urban Future*, 27–54.
19 *Census of 1891, Provincial Tables*, 134. Unfortunately, the census of 1891 does not give any breakdown of immigrant figures by community.
20 Ibid.
21 In 1830 there were about 234 prostitutes in Dacca, by 1870 the number had increased to 783; see Walters, 'Census of Dacca', and Municipal Proc., 25 March 1879.
22 India Office Library Vernacular Tract, vol. 1851.
23 Majumdar, *The Reminiscences*, 49.
24 HMS, 456 (f), 287.
25 Walters 'Census', *Asiatic Researches*, 548.
26 Taylor, *Dacca*, 222.

27 It is said that many aristocratic Muslim families who held zamindaris left Dacca early in the nineteenth century for their rural homes, as they found continued residence in the city unprofitable, see Dani, *Dacca*, 96; also Abuz Zoha Nur, *Unish Sataker Dhakar Samaj Jiban*, 12.

28 See chapter VII.

29 See the report of the Magistrate of Dacca dated 5 June 1793, BCJC, CXXVIII, 2, 14 June, 1793, 4.

30 Robinson to Calcutta Baptist Mission Society, 3 April 1839; Robinson Papers.

31 Ahmutty to GB, 13 October 1818, BCJC, CXXXIII, 58, 22 April 1819, 24.

32 Davidson, 'Dacca in 1840', *BPP*, XLII, 43.

33 See the Revenue Survey Map of 1859.

34 For this aspect of changes and development in Indian cities under British rule see Anthony D. King, *Colonial Urban Development—Culture, Social Power and Environment*.

35 'Dacca, the Ancient Capital of Bengal', *Friend of India*, 4 March 1876, 197.

36 Davidson, 'Dacca in 1840', 42.

37 For details see chapter VI.

38 This house was called 'Eshrut-Munzil'.

39 'Dacca, the Ancient Capital'.

40 Taifoor, *Dhaka*. Many Viceroys and Lt.-Governors while visiting Dacca were also entertained by the Nawabs in this house; see *DP*, 11 Bhadra, 1295 (26 August 1888).

41 Dani, *Dacca*, 130–1. Apart from this audience hall, the rest of the buildings have been demolished to make way for the new Arts Building of Dacca University.

42 A. Haider, *Dacca: History and Romance in Place Names*, 48–9.

43 Davidson, 'Dacca in 1840'.

44 The Regiment was the 38th of the Native Infantry. The editorial of 28 June 1856 declares, '. . .a finer set of men we never saw. In a few months fever had done its work. They were sufficiently punished. . . In three months the whole regiment passed three times through the hospital and at last when their young adjutant died, a firing party could scarcely be mustered from the whole of the companies to do the last honour to their officer. . .'

45 Quoted in a despath from the correspondent of *The Times* on 'The Rehabilitation of Dacca', *The Times*, 24 May 1909.

46 Majumdar, *Reminiscences*, 3–4.

47 For details see Dani, *Dacca*, 125–8.

48 *DP*, 8 Magh 1271 (20 January 1865).

49 *BT*, 30 March 1881.

50 Magistrates Report, 26 February 1870, BJP, CCCCXXXIII, 33, April 1870, 107.

51 HMS, 456 (f), 287.

52 *RSC* for 1889, appendix IV, LXXIX.

53 Deputy Collector of Dacca to Div. Comm., 7 October 1841, Letters Sent, No. 112.

54 Bengal Revenue Proceedings (Wards' Attached and Government Estates Branch) vol. 902, December 1876, collection 10, Nos. 41–2; also BRP, col. 2803, August 1886, collection No. 10, 8.
55 Majumdar, *Reminiscences*, 58.
56 'Dacca Forty Years Ago', *The Dacca Review*, VI, No. 2 (May 1916), 67–8.
57 Buckland in a private letter to Sir Richard Temple dated 23 June 1876, himself proudly spoke of his various public services in Dacca, see Temple Papers, vol. 144.
58 Nabin Chandra Bhadra, *Bhawaler Itihasa.*
59 Clay, *Leaves from a Diary*, 131; also [Graham] *Life in the Mofussil*, 11, 96–8.
60 Sen, *Saharer Itikatha*, 134.
61 Letter from GB to Div. Comm., 28 November 1862, Bengal Public Works Department Proceedings (General), XVI, 59, November 1862, 293.
62 Div. Comm. to GB, 1 November 1862, Ibid., 292.

CHAPTER VI

THE STRUGGLE FOR URBAN RENEWAL

Dacca's declining fortunes had reduced it by the 1830s to a noble ruin,[1] with its overgrown Mughal palaces, gateways, bridges,[2] tombs and mosques. Even Bibi Pari's[3] mausoleum in the Lalbagh Fort, one of the finest specimens of Mughal architecture, was near collapse for want of repairs, while the famous Dhakeswari Temple to the north-west was decaying amidst the encroaching jungle. And as people deserted the town, numbers of houses were unoccupied and decaying, becoming health hazards. In about forty years the city's housing stock had fallen from 44,000 houses[4] in use in 1801 to 16,279 in 1830[5] and 10,830 in 1838.[6] Ironically as the population declined, the main parts of the city grew overcrowded as people moved from the suburbs to the inner parts, building their '*choppers and chubbtras*', make-shift houses on the sides of the main roads. Later as the town revived and population grew again, the overcrowding became much worse.[7]

Dacca had also become very unhealthy and insanitary, a condition accentuated by its physical layout and uncivic habits of its inhabitants. Like most Indian towns, it was built haphazard, its houses, pucka or kutcha, closely packed and laid in narrow, crooked streets and lanes.[8] There were only two main roads, one running from west to east, the other south to north, meeting almost at right angles near the Sadar Ghat. From these a labyrinth of lanes branched off into the mahallas. The houses in the mahallas were usually arranged in *chauks* or blocks separated from each other by narrow footpaths, patches of jungle and the deep pits or *gor* from which earth had been dug for building purposes.[9]

Only the houses on the river front, owned or occupied by the Europeans and wealthy Indians, were built to a plan. Most of these had terraced gardens, their walls washed by the river in the rains.[10] Being generally two to four stories in height, they gave an air to the town. One visitor wrote in 1840, 'The houses appear white, shining and colonnaded like palaces; and the observer is prepared for splendour and magnificence, to be subsequently disappointed by ruinous decay.'[11]

The interior of the city revealed an equally grim picture. It was full of stagnant pools, ditches and marshes, and disused tanks and wells, while the Dulai Khal which pierced almost through the heart of the city had degenerated into a pestilential channel. These were the breeding ground of mosquitoes, and when used for drinking, a general source of disease. Most of the public thoroughfares had deteriorated, becoming extremely worn and dusty in the dry season, and muddy and almost impassable during the rains. Drains had become choked with mud and decaying vegetation.

In general the people were indifferent to matters of sanitation and public health. Most houses lacked a drainage system for the proper discharge of sewage. Privies were connected to burrow pits which were never cleared, the filth only being washed away by the rains. Certain houses had well-privies which were cleared once or twice a year, but were generally situated so close to the drinking-water wells as to pollute them by percolation through the sub-soil. The waste from such trades as shell-cutting was not removed, while hides were cleaned in public tanks and water courses. People drank therefore from dangerously contaminated water supplies in river, khal, tanks and wells. Only the well-to-do families sent their servants or engaged *bhisties* (water-carriers) to fetch water from the distant river Sitalakhya which was famous for its purity,[12] or constructed cisterns to store the rain water from their roofs.

Although the city had its complement of rich men, the bulk of the population was very poor. There was even considerable unemployment.[13] The poverty of the people meant that their diet was often poor and their housing bad. It is not, therefore, surprising that the people, ill-fed, ill-housed and inhabiting an extremely insanitary place, suffered from various diseases. Cholera, dysentery, typhoid, small-pox, malaria and the maladies of poverty took a heavy toll every year. From its first outbreak in epidemic form in 1817, cholera became an annual visitor carrying off large numbers of people. In 1825, 427 people died of the disease, and throughout the 1830s hundreds of cases of cholera were treated every year by the medical authorities—though medical facilities for the ordinary public were very inadequate.[14] The government had established a 'Native Hospital' as long ago as 1803, but it was, as Taylor noted, ill-ventilated and small, and capable of containing only forty patients.[15] The government provided an annual grant of Rs. 1,881, and the hospital had its own income of Rs. 1,000 per annum raised through public subscriptions, but these were insufficient.[16]

With poverty and decay had come apathy, and there was little indigenous leadership, no local institutions that could tackle the urban problems of Dacca. The various panchayats of the Muslims and Hindus were neither interested nor did they have any understanding of modern urban needs. Most of the old Indian towns were in a similar predicament, though in some cases, as in Ahmedabad, traditional institutions or leadership struggled to meet the civic needs of the townspeople. But in Dacca the earlier abolition of the office of the Kotwal had deprived the city of the one institution which oversaw its social welfare. In its absence, all the Magistrate of Dacca could do was to spend a paltry sum of Rs. 1,880, granted annually by the government to clean a city which in 1840 spread over nearly five square miles and whose population exceeded 68,000.

However, a new era in the history of Dacca's urban development dawned in 1840, when Magistrate Russell Moreland Skinner turned his attention to measures of urban improvement. As this period progressed, and Dacca's administrative importance grew and economic prosperity returned, more attention—both through government initiative and public pressure—was given to improving the unhappy state of Dacca.

In 1836 the Government of India had ordered inquiries into the 'state of municipal facilities' in the towns and cities of the Lower Provinces.[17] The move reflected a growing concern over deteriorating public health and the complete absence of sanitary measures in Indian towns. European officials regularly pressed government to provide adequate municipal facilities, and the civil surgeons, particularly those recently arrived, asked for measures to improve urban slums, water-supplies and public health comparable to those initiated in Britain.[18] In 1837 the Government of Bengal expressed its cautious willingness to ameliorate urban living conditions and passed a modified chaukidari act, Act XV of 1837, permitting a portion of the chaukidari tax to be devoted 'to the purpose of cleansing and repairing the towns in which the tax is levied.'[19] It was this modest opening which Skinner seized upon. He proved himself in time to be one of the greatest developers of Dacca in the nineteenth century. He was appalled at the state of the city, and using magisterial authority put in motion measures to redeem the situation. He first turned his attention to the reclamation of the Ramna area, and using the prisoners of the Dacca Jail, cleared the area and kept it in tip-top condition. With the success at the Ramna, he also began the rescue of other neglected areas, clearing jungles, repairing roads, filling the ditches and introducing general sanitary measures.

He soon judged, very correctly, that any long-term improvement of the city would require the attention of a more permanent institution, like a municipal committee, that could implement a comprehensive plan over a period of time. He appreciated the impossibility of a magistrate, often stationed for a short period, undertaking work of such a scale single-handed. Act XV of 1837 provided just the opportunity to set up such an institution and Skinner moved promptly. He therefore put the matter to such local dignitaries as Khwaja Alimullah, Nandalal Dutt, J. C. Sarkies and J. P. Wise. However, if Skinner is to be believed, they did not at first show much enthusiasm. Thus he reported to the government that he had taken great pains to persuade 'the most respectable natives to form themselves into a local committee to aid and assist the Magistrate in suggesting and carrying into effect plans for cleansing and improvement of the city. . .'[20] But whatever the initial response, leading officials and residents of Dacca met on 17 July 1840 and agreed to form such a committee, to meet at least once a month, with the Rev. H. R. Shepherd, the station chaplain, as their honorary secretary and chief executive. Those present at the meeting consisted of Armenian, European and Indian officials, merchants, vakils and zamindars.

As its first act the Committee requested the government to hand over the surpluses from the Dacca chaukidari tax, the rent of the Committeeganj,[21] and whatever sums might be available from the Dacca Ferry Fund, for urban development.[22] The Governor-General, Lord Auckland, expressed his delight at their initiative and immediately approved the formation of the municipal committee. He also authorized the grant of all the existing and future surpluses from the chaukidari tax plus the future proceeds of the Committeeganj, though not the other funds applied for, arguing that the funds handed over 'would be sufficiently large to enable them to make many improvements.' Skinner accordingly handed over Rs. 8,786 and also transferred the scavenger establishment of twelve sweepers and six cartmen with six carts and six pair of bullocks besides offering the use of the convicts in Dacca for street cleaning in the town.

The Municipal Committee formally came into being in August 1840 and soon it began formulating its own rules and procedures. During its existence it achieved some significant successes, both in organization and development of the city. It began by discussing the various urban problems of Dacca that it saw as stemming from economic decline and also from social malpractices which it resolved to tackle. It first turned its attention to improving the sanitation and communications of the city, very much as Dawes and Walters had done a generation earlier. For the purposes of 'cleaning and improving the city' it divided the whole town into five wards based on natural physical divisions, entrusting each ward to the care of three to four members living nearby. These members were given responsibility for supervising the conservation of roads, drains, wells and tanks and for general cleanliness, and were instructed to report any encroachment upon public thoroughfares to the secretary. A few sweepers were also allotted to each ward with dirt-carts, baskets and bullocks.

Almost all the roads of Dacca were in disrepair, and although the two main roads, namely the Nawabpur Bazar Road running north from Sadar Ghat to Thatari Bazar, and the Bazar Street, running westward from the Dulai Khal near Narinda to Lalbagh, had recently been partially widened and paved, the other roads required similar attention. The Committee, therefore, resolved to pave and widen the important thoroughfares, particularly to ensure the free circulation of air considered essential for public health.[23] Indeed it succeeded in repairing and paving most of the roads, and also widened the Purab Darwaza, Tanti Bazar, Sultanganj and Bazar Street, metalling the two main roads in their entirety. The roads were paved with bricks which were manufactured under contract; old and dilapidated buildings were also purchased to provide road ballast. Most of the work connected with the roads was done by the convicts, although occasionally hired labour was also employed.

Another major project undertaken by the Committee was the construction of a *bund* or embankment road across the Armanitola *jheel* or marsh, the dead end of a branch of the Dulai Khal. During the rains this marsh was full enough for neighbouring villagers to bring their boats to the city through it. But during the dry season it turned into a stagnant pool, a receptacle of filth and rubbish. Upon the suggestion of the Civil Surgeon, the Committee in 1853 decided to reclaim the jheel and its surrounds by constructing a road across it and filling the hollow lands, the road linking up with the main Chauk and Nawabpur roads. Within a year Nayasarak Road was completed and the depression filled, thus greatly improving the salubrity of the Armanitola neighbourhood and the communications between Armanitola and the south-eastern parts of the city. The Committee ran into legal difficulties, however, in acquiring the road frontages required for road widening and in fixing compensation for huts and houses compulsorily purchased.

Bridges too received attention; two new bridges were constructed of wood on the Nayasarak Road, and most of the old bridges of the city, particularly those over the Dulai Khal, were extensively repaired. The Committee also restored the drains along the principal streets, opening up and deepening them.

With a view to improving the health of the city, the Committee cleared many derelict houses and cut down jungles in and around the city. In this connection, it also considered the redeeming of the Dulai. It wanted to make the Dulai a free-flowing channel by deepening its bed and by diverting water from the Buriganga to purify the khal and to provide round-the-year water communications within the city and a safe harbour for boats.[24] The scheme was an ambitious one and proved beyond the Committee's financial capacity. Though on several occasions it did excavate and deepen parts of the Dulai chiefly with the help of the convict labour. The Dulai, however, remained 'liable to silt up in the middle, the current at both ends being affected by the tide'.[25]

The Committee also restored many of the disused public wells, and cleared and deepened several of the large public tanks for use as reservoirs for the dry season and for fighting the fires that frequently broke out in the city.[26] Among those so reclaimed, the most important were the Lalbagh and Armanitola tanks.

Perhaps the most significant work successfully carried out by the Committee was the reclamation of the Lalbagh Fort. The fort, a 'palace fortress', had been begun in 1678 by Prince Muhammad Azam, then the Viceroy of the province, but left incomplete by his successor, Nawab Shaista Khan, 'the fact that his daughter, Bibi Pari, died while it was in the process of construction leading him to consider it unlucky.'[27] Nevertheless the ground taken for the fort was very extensive. Within its huge walls and gateways there still survived the mausoleum of Pari Bibi, a mosque, an audience hall, a *hammam* or Turkish bath and a large tank with flights of stone steps on its banks. But by the 1840s the walls, gateways and interior buildings were overgrown and crumbling, the tank a stagnant and stinking pool. Indeed the whole neighbourhood had become overgrown with jungle 'where sickness and mortality prevailed to a great extent.'

In 1842 the Committee decided to renovate the Lalbagh fort and to render the space on which it stood 'a public ornament of the city', and to convert part of the ground within the fort into a public garden and a place of recreation. The scheme was perhaps more to European than Indian taste, an example, as Anthony D. King notes, of the way in which the 'colonial community' inspired by the 'metropolitan culture' created institutions to serve its own social and recreational ends.[28] The government provided a special grant, and convict labour was used to repair the walls and buildings. The site was soon cleared, and after the many poor people who had built huts within the walls of the fort had been compensated and moved,[29] a large flower garden was laid out. Much of this work had been done under the supervision of Skinner, the Rev. H. R. Shepherd and Dr Taylor. By 1847, after five years' labour, the transformation of the area was complete; a major architectural complex had been saved from ruin and as the Committee reported, the salubrity of the quarter had been greatly improved.[30]

The Committee also took what care it could of the sick and indigent of the city, providing the 'Native Hospital' with funds for maintenance and repair. It also decided, 'upon Christian motives' that the coolies employed by it should be given a day off every week on Sundays though they would be paid for seven days' work.[31] In July 1842, the Deputy-Governor of Bengal publicy expressed his deep satisfaction with the beneficial activities of the Committee and his hope that other towns would follow its 'good and praiseworthy example.'[32] Between 1840 and 1856 the Committee spent some 70,000 rupees[33] upon the municipal administration and urban development of Dacca, in addition to the free labour of the convicts.

Though the Committee did help ameliorate conditions in Dacca, it failed to solve some of the city's major problems. One of these related to Muslim burial grounds. The Muslim inhabitants of Dacca, especially the poorer section, followed the very dangerous custom of burying their dead in any vacant place, even within the enclosures of their houses. Given the high level of the water-table, the presence of decomposed bodies close to wells and tanks was a serious health hazard of which the people were completely unaware. The custom, it was said, owed its origin 'to the absence of any public cemetery, and to the fees which were levied by the owners of land appropriated for this purpose.'[34] The Committee decided, therefore, to lay out proper burial grounds in the city and five were chosen in Narinda, Aga Sadiq Maidan, Phoenix park, Lalbagh and Nawabganj.[35] The grounds were quickly cleared of jungle, cleaned and properly fenced with the labour of the convicts, and by March 1842 the first burial ground was ready on the Aga Sadiq Maidan. But hopes that the people generally would use it remained unrealized and most of the Muslim inhabitants continued to bury their dead in the old manner. An important source of Dacca's insalubrity thus remained.

The Committee's failure to solve the Muslim burial problem was matched by its general inability to obtain public co-operation in maintaining the civic welfare of the city. And when appeals for public hygiene did not elicit the appropriate civic response and the Committee attempted to bring compulsion to bear, it found itself faced with a series of lawsuits alleging violation of individual rights. In addition, as the Committee was not a corporate body, the lawsuits were directed against the members as private individuals. This was an unexpected development and discouraged the members from being too zealous about promoting change.

These failures underlined the limits within which a committee, instituted by a colonial power, had to operate. Fundamental changes in municipal government often necessitated, as the case of Muslim burial grounds showed only too clearly, the need for at least a measure of social reform without which there could be no change in deep-rooted public attitudes. The Dacca Municipal

Committee was not established under any municipal law but was appointed by the Governor-General as chief executive of the province. Such committees were also instituted in other towns like Hooghly and Chinsurah. Although the Government of Bengal was aware of the need for municipal improvement, it was not yet ready for the compulsory establishment of municipalities in the mofussil towns, being unwilling to impose the necessary taxes in the face of public apathy. No municipality was established in Dacca until 1864.

The consequent lack of power and authority of the Municipal Committee—unless its acts were carried out for it by the Magistrate—hampered its operations. Ironically the presence of the Committee even contributed to urban neglect. Although constitutionally the Magistrate was still in charge, the occupiers of this office with few exceptions came to regard the city's civic problems as the responsibility of the Committee[36] and consequently took little interest in them.[37] The government too had the same notion.[38] Thus there arose an anomalous situation, a sort of dual authority within the city, one body vested with responsibility and no power, the other given power without responsibility. The result was the serious neglect of health, sanitation and general conservation works, especially in the 1850s,[39] and it was this irregular situation which lay behind the Committee's dissolution in 1863.

Coupled with lack of power, the problem of funds grew more acute because of the reductions in the chaukidari tax. The tax was originally introduced in Dacca in 1813 for the maintenance of chaukidars. But it met with considerable opposition from the inhabitants. Regulation XIII of 1813, under which the tax was first introduced in Dacca, Murshidabad and Patna, gave legal effect to what had been a voluntary community practice in certain north Indian towns. It recognized its voluntary nature by leaving the rate assessments (upon houses and properties), tax collection and the appointment and management of chaukidars to the care of the community, through mahalla-panchayats. However, though the regulation contained the elementary principles of municipal and local self-government, the chaukidari body was designed primarily 'to aid the official police as a subsidiary organ with its roots in the community'.[40]

The Regulation could not have had a more inauspicious beginning in Dacca. A great number of inhabitants opposed its implementation, for policing the city in any form had never been a community practice but solely the concern of the government, so that the new tax appeared to be an imposition, the more burdensome because it came at a time of economic depression. The city grew tense over the issue, with some people supporting it, especially the up-country businessmen and bankers, while others resolved to defy the government. This only increased the determination of the authorities to implement it. The Acting Magistrate, John Bardoe Elliot, had to call in the army to quell a violent demonstration in front of the cutcherry; and was obliged to play a greater role in introducing the regulation, appointing to the mahalla-panchayats government supporters rather than true leaders.

The chaukidari force of 759 men when finally recruited was too large for the allotted money, and distinguished neither for character nor motivation, as Elliot admitted. He saw however, the advantage of providing for potential criminals, for, with a maximum wage of three rupees per month permitted by regulation, many of the recruits might naturally 'be supposed to have been either formerly rogues, or to have maintained a precarious livelihood by that mixture of alternate labour, indolence and dishonesty, so common among the lower classes of natives.'[41] But equally Elliot was aware of the danger of letting loose on the community such a body of men except under strict control—which indeed he and his successors were too overburdened to provide. This fundamental defect flawed the chaukidari system in Dacca as in many other towns, although Elliot did appoint a few *dafadars* (supervisors). The force was divided into three sections, one to guard the various outlets of the city, and the other two to patrol turn and turn about, along well-defined routes. About 500 in all were on night duty and initially Elliot reported a dramatic fall in crime in the city. Against this gain, however, had to be set much harassment and extortion, and the disaffection caused by the inequal distribution of the tax.

In 1816 moreover, under Regulation XXII, which extended the system, day-to-day management was provided for with the appointment of a chaukidari Sadr-Bakhshi (chief pay master), while assessment for the tax, up to a maximum of two annas per proprietor per month, was left with the panchayat.[42] The Magistrate in Dacca seldom intervened thereafter.[43] The system became oppressive, and respectable citizens kept aloof.

The chaukidari system nonetheless lasted for a long time, partly because the levy came to be the only major tax paid by townspeople, as transit and town-duties increasingly fell into disfavour as obstacles to trade and commerce, being finally abolished in 1835. Indeed Act XV of 1837 provided that a portion of the chaukidari tax should be appropriated for the purposes of sanitation, road repair, street lighting and general improvement. This Act also raised the maximum level of the tax upon any householder or proprietor from two annas to two rupees per month, though the average monthly collection from all the householders and proprietors was still not allowed to exceed two annas per month. It was thus the first Act to authorize the raising of a local tax for municipal purposes, and the first to recognize 'the necessity of sanitation in towns'.[44] The system did not, however, become less oppressive thereby. The inhabitants of Dacca repeatedly complained and even petitioned the Governor-General to modify or abolish the tax, and as late as 1854, Alexander Forbes, the secretary to the Municipal Committee, remarked,

> The corruption of the Panchayats, the venality and extortion of the Duffadars, the carelessness by which the tax has been allowed to fall into arrears and the rigour with which those arrears have been afterwards collected when almost forgotten by those who owed them, all these are deep causes of discontent...[45]

Where, to return to our main theme, did this leave the Municipal Committee? They had early noted the complaints against the tax, and in 1841 persuaded the Magistrate, and the government too, to allow them to investigate its administration. But their intervention went no further than a re-examination of the assessment schedules prepared by the panchayats, and that intermittently; the actual collection was still left entirely to the Sadr-Bakhshi and his staff and the panchayats, so that complaints continued. Government then intervened directly and, without much thought or enquiry, decided to lower the tax. The change was prompted by William Dampier, the Superintendent of Police, who visited Dacca in August 1843 and was told about the burden of the chaukidari tax upon 'the lower classes of people already impoverished by the decline of the trade in the city', and that in order to avoid the tax many families had left for the *char* (island) opposite the city—a site very 'unhealthy and inconvenient'. Dampier had reacted by instructing the Magistrate to revise the tax, 'relieving the poorer classes from any payment and others from over-assessment'.[46] In 1844 he ordered a further reduction so as to leave a surplus of no more than 200 rupees per month after paying the chaukidari establishment.[47]

The consequence was a sharp contraction in the income of the Municipal Committee, formerly more than 3,000 rupees a year, from the chaukidari tax surplus.[48] As a result, in 1846 they were forced to discharge the overseer of roads[49] and some of the road coolies. They represented to government the utter inadequacy of 'rupees 200 a month to meet the expenses of the conservancy department', and asked for an increase so as to leave a monthly surplus of 300 rupees. This was allowed, but was already inadequate, for in 1845 government had inflicted another grievous blow by passing a prison regulation which required convict labour to be employed inside the prisons only to such work as the making of jute-sacking and blankets which could be sold to pay for the maintenance of the prisoners. The Magistrate of Dacca had pointed out the great dependence of the Committee's activities upon convict labour,[50] but the government insisted and thus brought to a halt much of the conservancy and improvement work hitherto done by convict labour in Dacca and other towns.

Without adequate resources, legal powers or the labour of the prisoners, the Municipal Committee could do very little beyond keeping the main streets clean and carrying out a few essential works. Its tiny establishment in 1850 consisted of one English writer, one *sarkar* (accountant), three dafadars, one *chaprasi* (orderly), one gardener, one carpenter, one bricklayer, one guard, twelve sweepers, eight cartmen, eight carts and sixteen bullocks. The Committee members understandably lost interest and with the departure of Skinner, Taylor and the Rev. H. R. Shepherd, the Municipal Committee lapsed into inertia.

Dacca again degenerated into insanitariness, and not surprisingly a series of epidemics broke out in the 1850s: fevers, especially smallpox, which committed great ravages in 1850; cholera in severe form in 1851, 1853, 1855, 1856 and 1857. The medical authorities in Dacca ascribed the pestilential character and great virulence of the prevailing sickness to the extreme filthiness of the city and the complete absence of every sanitary provision in the shape of drainage, sewerage and removal of rubbish.[51]

Meanwhile, the Committee had been considering alternative measures to secure funds and authority. Eventually they sought to introduce Act XXVI of 1850 in Dacca. This was the latest of a series of acts intended to permit the establishment of municipalities in British India. In the 1840s the Government of India had determined that municipal charges should not be met out of general revenues, and the Bengal Government added that there should be no assistance for the improvement of towns unless the inhabitants came forward with reasonable contributions. This self-help principle was first incorporated in Bengal Act X of 1842 which enabled the inhabitants of towns to establish municipalities and to impose taxes for town development and public health purposes. When the Dacca Municipal Committee at government's invitation had sought to use this permissive legislation they could secure no public support. Act XXVI of 1850 to which the Committee now turned, though permissive as before, offered hope because the taxation for which it provided was indirect.

At the initiative of Alexander Forbes and Dr W. A. Green, the Civil Surgeon, the Municipal Committee in May 1852 submitted a petition to the government, signed by many influential residents, asking to introduce the Act in Dacca. It was pointed out that the main purpose in seeking the introduction of the Act was not to raise taxes but to appoint a municipal committee invested with legal powers and authority to carry out civic reforms.[52]

As the consent of a wider public was needed, a meeting was called for 21 May 1852 in the Dacca College compound, to explain the provisions of the Act, its usefulness and benefits, and the need to introduce it. On the appointed day a large crowd gathered to participate in what was the first public meeting of Dacca. Forbes and Dr Green adressed the audience, reiterating the Committee's main object in seeking the enforcement of the Act. Thus far the meeting went on smoothly but at this juncture, as Dr Green, who wrote the first history of the Municipal Committee in 1857, recorded, the Magistrate allowed a 'clerk' to address the audience. The clerk, whose name Dr Green did not mention, gave an emotional speech denouncing the Act and declaring againts its introduction in Dacca. The speech resulted in a tumult, the majority of the audience noisily demonstrated their objection to the Act, and left the meeting abruptly. The supporters of the Act afterwards angrily protested that the Magistrate's intervention was untimely and injudicious. But, as Dr Green admitted, 'the general feeling among the native part of the meeting was hostile to the introduction of the Act, that is to say disturbance of their present community from interference.'[53]

The meeting had been aimed only at preparing public opinion in favour of the Act. However, it was clear from the mood of the people attending the meeting that there was little chance of introducing the Act in Dacca, and when in July the inhabitants were asked to sign their names for or against the Act 'on the public list' in the cutcherry, all the signatures were against its introduction.

Both Forbes and Dr Green made sharp remarks about the outcome, and Forbes blamed it upon the opposition of some of the wealthier inhabitants (without naming them) whose 'pet nuisances the Committee had been endeavouring to do away with', adding also that these men had 'spread most ridiculous and unfounded reports concerning the intentions of the Committee especially with regard to an increase of taxation stating that not only the wheeled carriages but also large chattas [umbrellas] were to be taxed'.[54] They also accused the officials of Dacca of not seriously exerting their authority and influence upon the people. Their reaction was understandable for both men felt a personal sense of defeat and disappointment. But well before the final date of signing, a considerable number of inhabitants, over 500 in all, both Hindu and Muslim, had petitioned the Governor-General to withold his assent. For lack of information it cannot be said clearly as to how these counter-petitions were organized. In one petition (in English) it was argued that despite the committee members' assurances, it was probable that the people would be forced to pay new taxes, since without them the Municipal Committee could not carry out all the sanitary reforms which they had in view. And how quickly a new levy could degenerate without proper supervision into an engine of oppression was not difficult to imagine when one looked into the existing system of chaukidari taxation.

In addition to this fear of extra taxation and its oppressive operation, however, the petitioners also showed a lack of appreciation of the need for environmental improvement, though this was put to the authorities with considerable practical shrewdness. Thus in one Bengali petition the memorialists admitted that many streets in Dacca did need repairing, widening and lighting and that if this were done they would look more beautiful. But, they remarked, such improvements would only benefit the owners of carriages and horses and not the ordinary man. To the general public, impoverished and struggling to stave off the pangs of hunger, street lights would be a mockery, an eyesore. Those whom poverty prevented from lighting their own houses, were indifferent to the need for street lights. In another petition, the memorialists observed that the advocates of the Act had argued that if applied to Dacca it would help to reduce sickness. But these advocates, who were even making public speeches, were mostly outsiders, temporary residents for business or service. Why should the Daccaites listen to these outsiders on how to keep their city clean and healthy, to people who would not have to bear the permanent burden of taxes and other obligations if the Act was introduced? And as to the view expressed by some learned men that if a city were kept clean and tidy its inhabitants would be free from diseases, that, they remarked, was just unproved opinion. For they had long noted that in the Dacca cantonment, where at least 300 prisoners and labourers at one time had daily worked at great expense to uproot the weeds and clean the drains and ditches, many soldiers had nevertheless died of various illness. If the views of these learned men were correct, the petitioners asked, why in London, 'the splendid Capital of the British Empire', were hundreds of people every year dying from various diseases?[55] The Act was an innovation of man but the diseases were creations of God. What chance had a man-made law, they asked, against the Will of the Almighty?[56]

The petitioners were obviously referring to the efforts of Dr Green and Forbes. The attack on the reforming party, Dr Green and Forbes particularly, might be taken as another example of blinkered opposition that, roused by local apathy or prejudice, thwarted 'the heroic efforts of individual sanitary reformers', of which Gillion writes in his account of Ahmedabad's nineteenth-century municipal history.[57] But if there was narrow-mindedness at work there was also a realistic appreciation of the fact that the rewards of reform were often as unequally distributed as the tax burden, and that the scientific understanding of the causes of disease was still very incomplete, as the ill-health of the troops in their sanitized cantonments demonstrated. In any case, justified or not, the petitioners' opposition was enough to prevent the implementation of the Act in Dacca. Indeed opposition in Bengal as a whole prevented the Act being introduced anywhere, except Uttarpara in Hoogly District.

In August 1854, Sir Frederick James Halliday, the first Lieutenant-Governor of Bengal, paid a visit to Dacca. Taking advantage of his visit, the Municipal Committee approached him about the municipal problems of the city. They asked him in particular to allow the use of convicts once again, without whose labour the city had become steadily filthier and considerably more unhealthy, or else to give them a special grant for hiring labourers. They also asked for the tolls on the Buriganga ferries within the city boundaries, currently credited to the Provincial Ferry Fund. But more importantly they requested him to make the Municipal Committee 'a public body with the power of suing and being sued through the Secretary'.

At a meeting with Forbes, Halliday promised quick action. He argued that towns like Dacca ought to be compulsorily taxed for municipal purposes, which would require a new law, but this he assured Forbes would soon be introduced in the Legislative Council.

However, the Lieutenant-Governor's attention was even more pointedly drawn to the question of the chaukidari tax. The leading inhabitants of the city as well as the officials and the Municipal Committee all declared that the chaukidari system was not working properly. Halliday met similar complaints in other towns during his summer tour of 1854 and he decided that the Chaukidari Act had to be modified on the grounds that the taxation was 'pressing too hard upon the poor while the rich do not pay nearly enough', and that it was anomalous for the monies collected to pay for chaukidars to be in part expended on general items of municipal administration. Such items, Halliday argued, should be financed from a separate tax. As a temporary measure he ordered that the chaukidari tax then collected at Dacca should be reduced from Rs. 12,000 per annum to Rs. 5,000, of which Rs. 3,500 was to be laid aside for an efficient body of chaukidars. The balance of Rs. 1,500 would be handed over to the Municipal Committee, but since such a sum would be quite inadequate he promised them the receipts from the tolls on the Buriganga ferries and the surplus from the Dacca Jail Manufactures Fund, together with a government grant to make good the loss of convict labour in the conservancy work of the town.

On reaching Calcutta, Halliday took up in earnest the task of modifying the existing Chaukidari Act and preparing a new Municipal Act. He failed however to honour his promises to provide new financial resources for the Committee. So while the Municipal Act was under consideration, the public health of Dacca continued to deteriorate, and a dreadful cholera epidemic broke out in August 1855. Under pressure from the medical authorities,[58] the Committee made a plea to government for convict labour to help, and the Sessions Judge of Dacca, taking emergency action, allowed the use of 300 prisoners to clean the city, pending government approval. The use of the convict labour was sanctioned, though only for a two-month period, but Halliday sent a sharp reprimand to the people of Dacca, declaring that a town, the native inhabitants of which would do nothing for themselves, had no right to expect special treatment from the government.[59]

In the following year, the Government of Bengal passed a new Chaukidari Act, Act XX of 1856. Under it the tax could be raised in two ways, through a house assessment or from rates. The Act also laid down that the Magistrate might at his discretion exempt or relieve from the tax any occupier on the grounds of poverty.

It also provided as before that all surplus funds after the payment of the chaukidari establishment were to be spent for municipal purposes. It came into immediate effect in Dacca. As before, assessment was adopted as the mode of taxation, though a fresh assessment was not made until 1858.

The introduction of the Act gradually improved the night policing of the town. Unfortunately, however, it did not improve the resources of the Municipal Committee. The authorities in Dacca knew that the tax had been a burden upon many of the poorer classes of householders and therefore exempted large numbers of them from paying it. In 1859 the tax was levied on 8,012 householders out of the total of 11,819. The total collection amounted to Rs. 18,111 only, of which Rs. 15,536 were spent upon the chaukidari establishment and Rs. 1,860 on collection, leaving a mere Rs. 1,861 for the use of the Municipal Committee. The provisions of the Act limiting the aggregate sum to be raised to an average of two annas per month per house, and the maximum charge upon any householder to four rupees per month, greatly weakened its productive powers, especially as the rich were once again exempted from paying in proportion to their wealth. These defects were soon discovered, and the government therefore resolved upon further action. Meanwhile, however, it expressed great satisfaction at the results of the Act which had produced in 1858 for Bengal more than two and a half lakhs of rupees for the purposes of local police and conservancy, and although the sum spent on conservancy in that year for the whole province amounted to Rs. 30,522 only, which was 'clearly insufficient for its objects', the government claimed credit that something had been done in the improvement of sanitation of the towns throughout the country.[60]

That 'something' in Dacca was quite inadequate, as the Divisional Commissioner, Charles Tierney Davidson forcefully explained in December 1859 to the new Lieutenant-Governor Sir James Grant.[61] Poor Sir James had visited Dacca in August and had been so haunted by the stink from its fetid drains and uncleaned privies that he had left the city in a great hurry. On reaching Calcutta, he sent a strongly-worded letter through the Secretary to the Commissioner asking him to report why there were no proper conservancy arrangements in the city.[62] The Commissioner's stiff reply was to be resoundingly echoed three years later by the Municipal Committee. They, too, had been showing signs of frustration over the failure to improve the civic life of the town. By 1862 many of the local members long connected with the Committee like N. P. Pogose, Khwaja Abdul Ghani, and Govinda Chandra Dutt had become completely disenchanted so that after the resignation of N. P. Pogose no one was found willing to take up the burdensome duties of the honorary secretary. Thereafter the Committee almost came to a halt so that the Divisional Commissioner, Buckland, characterized it as a useless body. However, the members themselves clearly realized that if the Committee were to be a meaningful organization it had to be properly constituted. Hence at a meeting held on 6 February 1863, the members resolved to resign in the hope that such a step would induce the government to reconstitute the Committee on a legal and constitutional basis.

Francis Bruce Simson, the officiating Commissioner of Dacca, forwarding the Committee's resolution to government on 2 April

1863, noted the serious consequences of its resignation 'in dust and general inconvenience'. The Committee, despite inadequate powers, had made good use over the years of their limited funds. But a permanent municipal body, legally constituted, was essential and he therefore asked that Act XXVI of 1850 be now introduced. He was aware that the public's consent was needed, but he was hopeful that public support could now be easily secured, though it might be necessary to make a declaration that the introduction of the Act would not lead to any new taxation.[63] In reply the Bengal Government, while agreeing to extend the Act to Dacca if the people would apply for it, declared that nothing in the Act empowered the government to apply it conditionally or partially. It would depend entirely on the commissioners appointed whether there should be any taxation or not, and of what kind and amount.[64]

As it turned out, Simson had thoroughly misjudged the mood of the people. The Daccaites again rejected the Act, although this time the opposition was divided. Some 450 people signed in favour. They were, according to the Magistrate, 'mostly persons of a higher and more respectable class. . .'[65] The *Dacca Prokash* also supported the Act, commenting on the need for its introduction. The paper, however, had one reservation. It declared that if a new municipal committee were appointed, the commissioners must include representatives from all classes of the inhabitants, including educated Indians of course, and not the Europeans, Armenians and a handful of wealthy Indian businessmen and zamindars only, as had hitherto been the case.[66] Opponents of the Act were numbered in their thousands, many of them ordinary people, particularly poor Muslims, but led by three very influential men—Khwaja Abdul Ghani, J. Stephen and Mitrajeet Singh. Why the three objected to the introduction of the Act is not known. Simson, however, ascribed rejection of the Act to the false propaganda of one or two interested proprietors (without however naming them) who alleged that the whole exercise was an attempt to raise taxation.[67] The Magistrate, H. J. Reynolds, more candidly confessed that this was a generally held view of the purpose of the Act, commenting wryly,

'The ignorant impatience of taxations', which was formerly stated to be the characteristic of Englishmen, is shown in these documents [petitions rejecting the Act] to be equally instinctive in the minds of the Bengallee. Most of the petitioners state that the people are very poor, and that they are already overburdened with the Chowkeedaree and Income Taxes, and are quite unable to pay anything more.[68]

Such determined opposition from the majority of the people foiled the introduction of the Act, and with this ended a chapter in Dacca's urban development in the nineteenth century.

NOTES TO CHAPTER VI

1 See Taylor, *Dacca*, 363–71, *et passim*.
2 Municipal Committee to Magistrate, 22 May 1841, BCJC, CXXXXI, 56, 13 July 1841, 44.
3 The mausoleum was built by Nawab Shaista Khan in about 1684 in memory of his daughter Bibi Pari, who died suddenly. See Sayid Aulad Hasan, *Notes on the Antiquities of Dacca*, 4; also Dani, *Dacca*, 185–7.
4 HMS, 456 f, 287.
5 Walters, H, 'Census of the city of Dacca', *Asiatic Researches*, XII, 537.
6 Ascoli, *Final Report*, app. XXII, pp. XLIII.
7 *DP*, 25 Jaishta, 1270 (4 June 1863).
8 For further details on this point see John E. Brush, 'The Morphology of Indian cities', in Roy Turner (ed.), *India's Urban Future*, 59.
9 [Taylor], *Cotton Manufactures of Dacca*, 4.
10 For illustrations of some of these houses see *Panorama of Dacca*.
11 Davidson, 'Dacca in 1840', *BPP*, 37.
12 *RSC* for 1868, II, 113.
13 Taylor, *Dacca*, 366–7.
14 *RSC* for 1868, II, 103–4.
15 Taylor, *Dacca*, 356, also BCJC, CXXXXI, 47, 25 August 1840, 42.
16 BCJC, CXXXXII, 27, 8 January 1844, 181–2.
17 BJP, CIVI, 4, 27 December 1836, 217.
18 For a survey of urban improvements in nineteenth-century Britain see Gordon, E. Cherry, *Urban Change and Planning—A History of Urban Development in Britain since 1790*, 34–9 *et passim*.
19 BCJC, CXXXI, 14, 6 July 1837, 14. This Act was the second major attempt to ameliorate urban living conditions, the first being the establishment in 1823 of the Town and City Improvement Committees which were finally abolished in 1829. See my article 'Urban Problems and Government Policies: A Case Study of the City of Dacca, 1810–1830', in K. A. Ballhatchet and J. B. Harrison (eds.), *The City in South Asia—Pre-Modern and Modern*, 129–165.
20 BCJC, CXXXXI, 42, 19 January 1841, 115.
21 Committeeganj was a market established by a former 'Committee for the Improvement of the City of Dacca' which was set up in 1823 but dissolved in 1829. In 1840 the market yielded an annual income of 300 rupees.
22 Magistrate to Governor of Bengal, 22 July 1840, BCJC, CXXXXI, 47, 4 August 1840, 37. In his forwarding letter Skinner pointed out that such funds had been so handed over for municipal improvement at Hoogly and Chinsurah.
23 The influence of European sanitary notions is clear, though the resources for executing improvements were much smaller in India than in Britain. For civic reform in Britain, see Cherry, *Urban Change*; also Asa Briggs, *Victorian Cities*.

24 *Report* for 1841–2, BCJC, CXLI, 66, 18 July 1802, 106.
25 Clay, *Principal Heads*, 33.
26 In 1846 the Committee unsuccessfully applied to government for sanction for the acquisition of a fire engine. They were told that such fire engines would be unsuitable for Dacca, that the climate would soon damage the leather hoses of the fire engines, and that native workmen would be unable to service the machines. See BCJC, CXLII, 48, 27 May 1846.
27 Sayid Aulad Hasan, 'Old Dacca', *Dacca Review*, IV, 155.
28 A. D. King, *Colonial Urban Development*, 220. Thus clubs, libraries, cricket grounds and racquet courts sprang up in all the towns and cities where there were British in any number. The Lalbagh fort was the subject of one of Sir Charles D'Oyly's lithographs published in his *Antiquities of Dacca* in 1812. D'Oyly was the Collector of Dacca.
29 As usual the records do not show where the evicted though compensated poor went to, nor the effect upon overcrowding elsewhere in the city. The Committee, however, obtained a perpetual lease of the Lalbagh fort site at an annual rent of sixty rupees from Mirza Manzur Ali Khan and Salema Khanam, the descendants of Nawab Shaista Khan who owned the land.
30 Dr W. A. Green, 'History of the Dacca Municipal Committee', 26 January 1857, BJC, CXLV, 74, 24 September 1857, 164.
31 Ibid.
32 BJC, CXLI, 66, 18 July 1842, 107.
33 Dr Green, 'History of the Dacca Municipal Committee', BJC, CXLV, 74, 24 September 1857, 164.
34 *Report* of Dr J. F. Wise, *RSC*, for 1868, II, 101.
35 *Report* for 1841–2, BCJC, CXLI, 66, 18 July 1842, 106.
36 See the letter from the Magistrate C. F. Harvey to the secretary to the Municipal Committee, 5 December 1859; Miscellaneous Papers of the Dacca Municipal Committee.
37 Petition of J. Stephen and others to Govt. of India, 28 November 1856, Home Department (Public) Proceedings, 23 January 1857, 70.
38 GB to J Stephen, 2 April 1857, BJC, CXLV, 57, 2 April 1857, 73.
39 Petitions of J. Stephen and others to GB, 16 October 1856 and April 1857, BJC, CXLV, 61, 2 April 1857, 67 and 72.
40 Misra, *Central Administration*, 364.
41 Magistrate to GB, 28 January 1814, BCJC, CXXXI, 32, 12 February 1814, 8.
42 Sections XV and XVI, Regulation XXII. The normal pay of a chaukidar was fixed at two rupees with a maximum of three rupees per month, raised in 1817 to four rupees.
43 Secretary to the Municipal Committee to Commissioner of Dacca, 7 November 1854, BJC, CXXXXV, 40, 5 June 1856, 53.
44 Argal, R, *Municipal Government in India*, 4.
45 BCJC, CXLIV, 60, 16 November 1854, 209.
46 Dampier to GB, BCJC, CXLII, 6, 11 September, 1843, 79.
47 Dr Green, 'History of the Muncipal Committee', BJC, CXLV, 74, 24 September 8157, 164.
48 Ibid.
49 Ibid.

50 Magistrate to GB, 19 December 1845, BJC, CXLII, 44, 18 February 1846, 164.
51 Div. Comm. to GB, 2 April 1863, BJP, CXLVI, 60, May 1863, 159; also Secretary to the Municipal Committee to the Magistrate of Dacca, 11 September 1855, BJC, CXLV, 21, 18 October 1855, 96.
52 BJC, CXLV, 23, 15 May 1852, 94.
53 Dr Green, 'History of the Municipal Committee', BJC, CXLV, 74, 24 September 1857, 164; see the proceedings for 1852.
54 Forbes to E. Currie, 13 January 1853, Bengal Public Consultations, XIV, 27 April 1853, 29.
55 For an account of London in the nineteenth century, see D. J. Kirwan, *Palace and Hovel, or Phases of London Life;* also G. Kinsey, *The Growth of London.*
56 Petitions of the inhabitants of Dacca, June-July 1852 (freely translated), BJC, CXLIV, 23, 24 June 1852, 97 and BJC, CXLIV, 29, 30 September 1852, 90.
57 Gillion, *Ahmedabad.*
58 Dr Green to the Municipal Committee, 10 September 1855, BJC, CXLV, 21, 18 October 1855, 96.
59 GB to Sessions Judge of Dacca, BJC, CXLV, 2, 18 October 1855, 99.
60 Resolution of the Government, 28 November 1860, BJP, CXLV, 33, 28 November 1860, 383.
61 Div. Comm. to GB, 18 December 1859, BJP, CXLVI, 26 April 1860, 312.
62 Secretary to Div. Comm., 19 September 1859, BJP, CXLVI, 21, 22 September 1859, 210.
63 Div. Comm. to GB, BJP, CXLVI, 60, May 1863, 159.
64 GB to Div. Comm., 13 May 1863, BJP, CXLVI, 60, May 1863, 161.
65 Magistrate to Div. Comm. in Simson to GB, 24 August 1863, BJP, CXLVI, 65, October 1863, 327.
66 *DP*, 5 Asarh 1270 (18 June 1863).
67 Div. Comm. to GB, 24 August 1863, BJP, CXLVI, 65, October 1863, 327.
68 Magistrate to Div. Comm., Ibid.

CHAPTER VII

URBAN SOLUTIONS

The Bengal Act III of 1864 which led to the establishment of the Dacca Municipality was a landmark in the city's urban development. The institutional infrastructure of municipal administration was a direct product of governmental intervention. Several earlier Acts, as has been seen, had failed to achieve permanent results because they lacked teeth. Local public works and services had, therefore, of necessity been mainly government-financed, in Bengal by use of the surplus of the chaukidari taxes. However, the government's tight financial situation had allowed it to do very little.

The mutiny of 1857–8 had severely shaken the financial foundations of the Government of India. Post-mutiny financial embarrassment led to the imposition of local taxes for local purposes as the best means of relieving the central government. It was James Wilson, the new Finance Member of the Governor-General's Council, especially sent from Whitehall to bring 'Indian finances to equilibrium', who suggested the policy of financial decentralization.[1]

Soon afterwards the report in 1863 of the Army Sanitary Commission drew the attention of the Government of India to the generally unhealthy and insanitary conditions of most Indian towns and cities and urged the need for reform, further stimulating the central government's interest in local affairs.[2] In 1864 the need to relieve the central exchequer became even more acute when, at the instance of the European business community, the Government of India chose to abolish the income tax which had been introduced by Wilson as his immediate means of raising additional revenue. It was therefore resolved by the Government of India that 'the cost of town police forces must in future be directly borne by the townsfolk themselves.' In compensation, all towns laid under this burden were permitted to establish municipal institutions and authorized to raise, within the framework of government rules, the necessary revenues for urban needs. The manner in which these municipal institutions should be set up was left to the provincial authorities to determine.[3]

The resolution was quickly taken up by the Bengal Government. In March 1864, it passed the Municipal Improvement Act, Act III of 1864. The new Act did not repeal Act XXVI of 1850, but instead of 'demanding an application from the inhabitants of the town as an essential condition for the establishment of the municipality', it empowered the government to establish one anywhere it thought necessary without any prior application. Under the Act such municipalities were empowered to raise funds for 'improvement, education and other local objects' by levying rates upon houses, lands, animals, trades and other sources.[4]

The new Act was officially extended to Dacca on 1 August 1864. A government notification also defined the area over which the Dacca Municipality would exercise its jurisdiction. This area included the city proper and the few outlying suburbs like the mahallas of Jafarabad, Sultanganj and Dayaganj not shown in the 1859 map of Dacca prepared by the Revenue Surveyor.[5] A body of twenty-one commissioners was appointed by the government to run the municipal administration. They included three ex-officio members: the Divisional Commissioner, the District Magistrate and the Executive Engineer. Though, apparently by an oversight in the drafting of the Act, the Civil Surgeon did not appear as an ex-officio commissioner, in Dacca he was always appointed a commissioner. The seventeen ordinary members of the Municipality were A. D. Dunne, J. P. Wise, D. R. Lyall, G. Bellet, J. G. N. Pogose, M. David, Khwaja Ahsanullah, Jagannath Roy Chowdhury, Mitterjeet Singh, Govinda Chandra Dutt, Madhu Sudhan Das, Mirza Ghulam Pir, Muhammad Akmal Khan, Syed Abdul Mujeed and Ram Kumar Bose.[6] Of the total of twenty-one commissioners, eight were officials (six Europeans and two Indians) and thirteen non-officials. This ratio was roughly maintained throughout the period until the introduction of the elective system. By occupation eleven of the thirteen non-officials were big zamindars and the other two were a banker and a merchant. Many of these non-officials were also members of the former committee.

The first batch of ordinary commissioners was appointed by the government. Thereafter the Divisional Commissioner and District Magistrate nominated new members, choosing mostly from among persons whom they considered able and loyal to the government, though only after regular consultations with prominent members of the existing body. Indeed a letter from Magistrate Henry Beveridge suggests that in 1866 a number of the new members had been selected and nominated by the municipal commissioners themselves, Khwaja Abdul Ghani prominent among them.[7] The result was that the committee very soon became something of a clique, selected from among the commissioners' friends and supporters.

The chair of the municipality went ex-officio to Edward Drummond, the District Magistrate, who with the Divisional Commissioner selected a European landholder A. D. Dunne as his vice-chairman. He was succeeded, after a short interval by George Bellet, a professor of the Dacca College, who held the office twice before his transfer to the Presidency College, Calcutta.[8]

The first meeting of the municipality was held at the Divisional Commissioner's office on 11 August 1864, and was attended by six Europeans, three Armenians and seven Indians—a non-official majority. The proceedings began with a proposal from the chairman, Edward Drummond, that in view of the urgent need of funds for urban improvement, the rate of assessment upon houses and other landed properties in Dacca should be fixed for the year at the maximum limit permitted by the Act, namely seven and a half per cent of their annual rental value. Dr Alexander Simpson, the Civil Surgeon seconded this proposal. The motion led to considerable discussion and to counter proposals, J. G. N. Pogose, the Armenian zamindar, moving that the rate should be fixed at five per cent. In the end, however, the chairman's proposal was adopted by a majority of three. Next, the chairman proposed that the commissioners should empower the vice-chairman and himself to appoint a secretary at a monthly salary of 300 rupees. This also was seconded by Dr Simpson and was carried unanimously. Then Dr Simpson himself proposed a tax upon wheeled carriages, horses and elephants, Khwaja Abdul Ghani seconding the motion. However, Dr Simpson afterwards withdrew the proposal until the results of the collection of the tax on property were known. The chairman then proposed that a house be rented and furnished as the Municipal Office. This was accepted unanimously. Finally it was unanimously resolved, on the proposition of the chairman, that the commissioners should act as assessors of rates for the different mahallas of the city.[9]

The proceedings of the first day, however, set the pattern of the future meetings; all the important proposals came from the chairman or the European members, the native commissioners taking a secondary role in the deliberations. There were various reasons for this Indian apathy. Clearly to many the pattern of executive action established in Mughal days was still seen as the norm. The Divisional Commissioner and District Magistrate, and the European secretary—only once did the Armenian S. J. Sarkies break the run of European secretaries—had inherited the Mughal mantle of initiative and authority, and no attempt was made to mobilize the Indian majority to oppose or influence them. Witness the contrast in Ahmedabad where the native commissioners often led by the Nagarseth and the Kazi—the two traditional guardians of the city—practically determined the pattern of municipal administration.[10] In Dacca, most of the native commissioners being landholders and merchants had businesses outside the city which prevented their regular attendance at meetings.[11] Finally it may well be surmised that few of the Indian members were anxious to be actively associated with a committee whose first concern was to impose a new burden of taxation upon the citizens of Dacca, many of whose uncivic practices springing from past licence were now curtailed.

The newly-established Dacca Municipality being vested with legal power and authority went about its tasks vigorously. A house near the cutcherry was rented to accommodate the Municipal Office, and a European secretary, M. King, was appointed with an appropriate staff. The secretary ran the office, and had general supervision of conservancy works. Fourten *tahsildars* (tax-collectors) were appointed, each at a monthly salary of fifteen rupees, and ten overseers to supervise the conservancy work and to enforce the municipal regulations. A number of sweepers, road-coolies, bricklayers, gardeners, carpenters and bhisties were also appointed.

Once the commissioners had been appointed the government handed over to them the surplus funds which had been allowed to the former Municipal Committee: Rs. 12,045 from the chaukidari collections and Rs. 2,382 from the Committeeganj fund, together with Rs. 10,440 from the Local Fund for the repairs of roads.[12] The Magistrate also handed over all the properties of the former Committee, including the Committeeganj market and the old cantonment lands, and in July 1865 made over all the public ferries and pounds situated within the limits of the Municipality, and the income accruing from them, as from 1 May 1865.[13]

The first major act of the Municipality, however, irritated many and injured others, reminding the Daccaites that a new regime had appeared on the scene which would not allow them to continue their traditional way of life. This was the levy of rates upon houses and lands which the commissioners had decided to assess themselves in order to save money on hired staff. Each commissioner was entrusted with the assessment of certain mahallas.[14] It was a novel experiment.

However, complaints and criticism soon followed that the commissioners were assessing rates unfairly, levying low rates upon their own or relatives' houses while imposing high rates upon others. The *Dhaka Prokash*, edited by Dina Nath Sen, the educationist and social reformer, and having a wide circulation among the English-educated and upper-class Indians throughout East Bengal, remarked with characteristic acidity,

> The way in which the commissioners have assessed the house tax will support our assertion [that they were mostly unfit to discharge municipal responsibilities properly], and the unfairness they have displayed is sufficient to excite pain, anger and laughter. We have heard that many of them fixed the tax while sitting in their own houses, and that others did the same from the road-side, assessing some of the houses at a much higher rate than was fair. In some instances the rate is low enough, but generally they have been very unmerciful, fixing, for instance, the value of a thatched house that would scarcely bring one hundred rupees at two hundred rupees per annum. Many of the proprietors have pleaded against this kind of assessment, and prayed the commissioners to sell their houses at that rate, or try to procure tenants to pay such a rent, but in vain. Is not this a specimen of the injustice and ignorance of the tax gatherers?[15]

Indeed many of the householders of Imamganj, Madarjhanda, Champatali and Nalgola petitioned the Municipality against the commissioner Madhu Sudhan Das, a leading banker and property owner, for fixing excessively high rates upon their houses and properties while assessing his own properties at lower rates.[16]

The commissioners appointed an assessment subcommittee to consider such petitions and to hear complaints from the taxpayers about any inequality in assessments. Although in some cases the assessment had been unfairly made, the problem was that it was sometimes quite difficult, if not impossible, to assess the true value of a house. There had been no previous assessment of this kind and there were no professional surveyors and valuers in Dacca whose assistance could be solicited. The former chaukidari tax had been assessed not on the value of a property but upon the wealth of its owner. It was, therefore, not very easy to assess the rates especially upon the poorer, thatched houses. However, after months of labour, the commissioners finally completed the assessment by 17 May 1865.[17] Under Act XX of 1858, 8,148 taxpayers in 1863–4 had paid rupees Rs. 19,860.[18] Under Act III of 1864, the number of tax-payers was raised to some 16,000 and the total tax to rupees Rs. 40,143. Appeals against the assessment were heard by the assessment subcommittee and finally disposed of at the general meetings of the commissioners, but only in 125 cases was the assessment fixed by individual commissioners actually reduced by the Municipality. The new District Magistrate, Arthur Levien, held that the valuation and assessment had generally been as fair as possible.[19] Complaints, however, persisted that many householders were being unfairly taxed.

Despite many individual appeals, and a strong general resentment against the imposition of the maximum permitted rate of tax, the commissioners maintained the seven and a half per cent fixed in 1865 for many years, though with adjustments which made assessments more equitable. They felt that the increasing economic prosperity of the city would render the tax less burdensome. More importantly, they realized that any reduction in the house-tax would seriously weaken the financial basis of the Municipality.[20] Indeed, in 1870, the Government of Bengal was to pass an Act especially for Dacca which allowed the commissioners to raise the rate to ten per cent. However, this permission was not fully used in view of the general public hostility towards direct taxes, a feeling shared by a majority of the commissioners.[21] The local press was also not slow to point out the burden on the poor, and there was no dearth of petitions to government against any further enhancement of the house-tax.

However, in 1874, the commissioners resolved to 'revise the assessments in several parts of the town which [in their view] were notoriously under-assessed'. The revision was made by the commissioners in person and resulted in a net increase of Rs. 2,000. This result convinced the commissioners that the whole assessment required revision, the more so since, as the Administration Report of the Municipality for the year noted, 'The town had taken a great stride in prosperity since the tax was first assessed in 1864–5, and even apart from the inequalities of assessment, the general rise in the rents of houses would give a large increase.'[22] Though the reassessment was postponed—a new municipal act, Act V of 1876, was about to come into force in Dacca—the commissioners did increase the rate of house-tax in 1877 from seven and a half per cent to eight per cent to meet the dire need of the Mitford Hospital.[23] This enhancement plus subsequement revisions in the assessments eventually increased the income from the house-tax by more than Rs. 10,000. However, the rate was not increased beyond eight per cent during the period under review.

Besides the rates on houses and lands, the Municipality imposed further taxes. These were levied not only to increase normal tax revenues but selectively to secure compensation for costs incurred on the city's general development. Thus in August 1865, they levied a tax on wheeled carriages in Dacca, and on horses and elephants to meet road repair costs. Later a licence fee was imposed upon the hackney-carriages that plied for hire within the city limits, together with fees on bullock-carts, bullocks, and religious processions. In 1869, they imposed similar charges on those engaged in such trades and manufactures as brick-making, lime-burning, tile-making, the manufacture of earthen pottery, on soap-boiling and upon owners of dyeing houses and slaughter houses, and wood, straw and coal depots, all of which caused pollution and were health hazards.[24] A fee was also collected for the removal of rubbish accumulated in the course of trades or manufactures. In 1878, a privy-tax, better known as the House Service Fee, was also introduced for the removal of sewage from private latrines. Fines were also imposed for the breach of municipal regulations. All these taxes, fees and fines were resented by the public. However the income of the Municipality rose steadily from Rs. 53,469 in 1865–6 to Rs. 142,098 in 1884–5.

As soon as the commissioners had secured the necessary tax revenues in 1864, they set about organizing both the development and conservancy of the city, putting much emphasis upon sanitary improvement. Very soon the two main streets, Nawabpur and

Bazaar Street, had been remetalled, many mud roads and lanes repaired, and some metalled, and a few of the narrower streets widened, improving communications within the town. Many of the clogged drains were cleared, and new drains along the principal thoroughfares constructed. A great deal of heavy jungle was cut back, notably in the north, and hollows and ditches, the receptacles of stagnant water and filth, were filled in. Some of the derelict houses were cleared, and several tiled houses were also built at the Committeeganj market.

The commissioners also considered the problem of the town sewage. At a meeting held on 1 February 1867, the vice-chairman, George Bellet, drew attention to the filthy condition of many private privies and 'to the unsatisfactory and noxious manner in which the excrementitious matter of the town is disposed of'.[25] Since one of the problems was that there were not enough sweepers to man any improved sewage disposal system, the commissioners wrote to the authorities in Patna and Hazaribagh asking them to recruit mehtars and send them to Dacca.[26] (By June 1868, however, they had had no response from either district.) They also built a public latrine to serve Rai Saheb Bazar and set funds aside for others.

The problems of providing the Muslim community of Dacca with a proper burial ground was also dealt with. The principal Muslim graveyard at the Aga Sadiq Maidan, constructed by the former Municipal Committee, having been covered by encroaching jungle, was soon cleared and chaukidars were appointed to see that every corpse was buried at a depth of six feet.[27]

While the commissioners were pushing ahead with such schemes, a subcommittee duly drew up a comprehensive body of by-laws, modelled on the Bengal Government's draft code, prohibiting the use of thatch near public highways and the digging of tanks and wells in private compounds without the Municipality's sanction, requiring the closure of private urinals and privies on public streets, and so on. To many of these, particularly the prohibition against raising thatched houses and the digging of wells, the public at once objected, petitioning government to modify rules which would cause 'great hardship and inconvenience to the inhabitants'.[28] The commissioners were prepared to bend, but on the advice of Buckland, the Divisional Commissioner, who thought modification would destroy the by-laws' usefulness, the Bengal Government imposed them as they stood.[29] Amid considerable public resentment[30] the by-laws were formally introduced in February 1867, the commissioners sitting from 1868 as Honorary Magistrates to deal with offences against them and against the Municipal Act.

Despite this activity and the expenditure in 1867–8 of Rs. 27,078, or over forty-eight per cent of their total income, upon conservancy and development, the commissioners soon came under attack for their failure to solve all the city's problems. Early in 1866, Dr James Fownes Norton Wise, the Civil Surgeon of Dacca, in his annual sanitary report had complained that the Municipality had failed to adopt any comprehensive scheme for improving the health of the town, and had even gone so far as to question the advantages of municipal institutions in the country, recommending that they should be replaced by Public Health Officers armed with absolute power.[31]

This report of Dr Wise was only one of many such reports submitted for towns and cities in India by Civil Surgeons and Sanitary Commissioners. They signalled the appearance of a body of professional men quick to set themselves up as guardians of public health. Armed with medical and scientific knowledge and familiar with sanitary reforms in England, they lashed out at the way amateur civil servants and municipal commissioners were dealing with the sanitary and public health problems of Indian towns. But they also identified the sources of evil and suggested scientific remedies with an authority governments could not deny. This process began with the setting up of the Royal Commission on sanitation in India in 1861 and the subsequent appointment of Sanitary Commissioners for Bengal and to the Government of India. The Sanitary Commissioners now looked to the Civil Surgeons to act as instruments of change, as many local authority doctors came to act in England. This led to the intervention of the Civil Surgeons in local public health affairs and to the production of the voluminous reports to the Sanitary Commission.

Thus, in his report of 1868, Dr Wise returned to the attack describing Dacca as extremely filthy, and denouncing the commissioners for taking no measures to remove the town sewage. 'As no steps were taken to remove the filth from the city, it is year by year accumulating in the midst of the people and poisoning the atmosphere on all sides.' The most objectionable practice of digging kutcha-wells or pits into which all the excreta and rubbish of the house was discharged was almost universally adopted in Dacca, the municipality having failed to stop these insanitary practices. In general, he continued, the compounds and houses of the poorer classes were dirty, and the people did not carry out even the minimum of sanitary requirements.

He complained of the absence of a proper drainage system, and deplored the lack of pure drinking water in the city. He also called attention to the disgusting modes of cremation and interment of the dead, the latter proving so injurious that the soil in the town was dangerously contaminated by the decomposing bodies of the dead. Even the air could not circulate freely because of the encroaching jungles to the north, and the labyrinth of narrow, crooked lanes found in much of the city. No wonder, he concluded, that sickness carried off so many, for all the diseases which were most prevalent among the native community, he pointed out, were the consequences of bad food, foul air and impure water.[32]

The picture drawn could scarcely have been more gloomy but with what justice the commissioners were blamed is less certain. The *Dhaka Prokash* in 1865, for example, had been quick to complain of their unsuitability. A leader proclaimed,

> True, many of them have been here from their childhood, and display good qualities in their other duties to such a degree that they have won a good name; but not knowing how to work out the public good, they have been unable to display their wisdom and usefulness. It is not to be wondered, under the circumstances, that their works appear careless and faulty.[33]

But the District Magistrate, Arthur Levien, thought their work quite satisfactory.[34] Perhaps Divisional Commissioner Simson held the balance most fairly when in 1868 he claimed for the Dacca Municipality 'credit for having fairly employed the small income at their disposal in the best manner they could for the benefit of the city in matters of conservancy and public convenience'.[35]

In part the failures of the Municipality may be traced to institutional faults. The appointment of the District Magistrate as chairman, the key figure, put its affairs in the hands of an often over-worked official, not always committed to city reform, and always liable to be moved: four different magistrates held the chairmanship in the municipality's first four years. There were also many continuing legal problems. The closure of the many private, often unauthorized burial grounds in Dacca required special permission from government in Calcutta, and the commissioners had no power to require people to clean their house-compounds or to close their well-privies. The non-official commissioners were unwilling to exercise to the full what powers they had to end insanitary practices when these did not offend against customary beliefs and practices. Many Indian commissioners must have been constantly torn between the wish to secure official approval and patronage and the need as local leaders not to offend the feelings and beliefs of their followers.

Nevertheless, so bad was the condition of the city in these early years of the Municipality that in March 1868, the Rev. A. Mackenna, a Baptist clergyman of Dacca, took an extraordinary step. Bypassing the local authorities, he used a short visit to Calcutta to seek an interview with the Lieutenant-Governor, Sir William Grey, to report to him directly the condition of Dacca. Although he was not granted an interview, a petition from Mackenna was accepted.

Echoing Dr Wise, the Rev. Mr Mackenna in his petition declared that during his seventeen years' residence in India he had hardly come across a city more filthy and insanitary than Dacca. He lashed out at the Municipality, criticizing it for its failure to adopt more 'aggressive' measures to improve the situation. He even speculated about the causes of some of the diseases then affecting Dacca, commenting:

> If cholera be owing, as some physicians believe, who regard it as an extremely virulent type of fever, to malaria arising from jungle, then . . . there is amply sufficient jungle, in, near and about the city, fully to account for its presence. And if it be owing, as it is perhaps still more widely believed by others, to animal excrementa, tainting with their poisonous influences the air and water, then your petitioner is also of opinion, . . . that these causes abound in direful and needless profusion.

The Rev. Mr Mackenna, though aware that the Dacca Municipality possessed very limited funds relative to the size of the city was fully convinced that the conservancy of the town had been seriously neglected in the past. He therefore urged the Lieutenant-Governor to instruct the Civil Surgeon of Dacca immediately to report on the sanitary condition of the city, and to ensure that prompt measures were taken for its improvement.[36]

This unprecedented way of reporting local matters directly to the Lieutenant-Governor infuriated the officials at Dacca. The Divisional Commissioner Simson angrily protested that the Rev. Mr Mackenna had rendered no assistance to the commissioners at Dacca in dealing with evils discussed long before his arrival and in many cases actually tackled by the Municipality.[37] If the improvement was not more tangible, that was mainly due to lack of funds and to the un-cooperative or obstructive attitude of the native members of the Municipality. George Graham, the newly-arrived District Magistrate, also declined to acknowledge the truth and force of Mackenna's petition. However, he conceded that some of the observations were but plain realities. Inadequate funds were in part to blame, but the Municipal Act had not been enforced with sufficient firmness against individuals, partly from a disposition to leniency on the part of the commissioners and also from a want of energy in the native agency employed.[38] This rather one-sided view was also adopted by the Bengal Government, which noted 'a want of active co-operation on the part of the majority of Commissioners', but said less about the attitudes of the succession of District Magistrates. Government did, however, recognize that most of the evils complained of had arisen from want of funds rather than official inertia, and told Mackenna so.[39]

Mackenna's intervention was not entirely fruitless, for it roused the Municipality to greater and more vigorous effort. The new chairman, George Graham, notably did his best to rally the townspeople and the Indian commissioners to comprehensive action,[40] arguing that no piecemeal efforts would be effective. At his instigation, therefore, Dr Henry Charles Cutcliffe, the new Civil Surgeon of Dacca, a Fellow of the Royal College of Surgeons, prepared a very comprehensive scheme for the sanitary improvement and modernization of Dacca, to pay for which he suggested that a loan should be raised of two or three lakhs of rupees. Dr Cutcliffe's very important scheme incorporated his experience both as a Civil Surgeon and as an active sanitarian and town planner in the North-Western Provinces, and drew upon his reading about public health and sanitary reform measures in America and Europe, as well as in

Britain.[41] But the most significant aspect of his scheme was that it incorporated his understanding of Dacca's history. The city's recent past had been very unhappy, and many of its urban problems had originated from its economic decline. But Dacca's worst days were over, and the city could reasonably look forward to a brighter future. Any development plans, therefore, would have to take these factors into consideration.

Dr Cutcliffe's scheme was thorough and exhaustive. He began with measures for improving the ventilation of the city. Ground should be taken for two broad streets parallel to the river to run the entire length of the city, and for a considerable distance beyond the existing limits of the town to allow for future growth. Broad transverse streets should then be constructed dividing the city into rectangular blocks, of convenient size for conservancy purposes.

Each should have a public latrine, adapted for both sexes, in charge of a *jamadar—mehtar* (head sweeper) with a staff of male and female sweepers. These latrines should be worked on the dry-earth system, so successfully used by the Municipality of Cawnpore and also at the Alipore Jail, Calcutta, under the supervision of its medical adviser, Dr Fawcus. This would permit the closure of the existing obnoxious private privies until a full sewage system could be adopted. To dispose of the filth from the latrines, jungle land to the north should be purchased, part to be used as trenching ground and the rest by rotation kept under cultivation as a model farm. 'Cattle, poultry and other stock might be kept with profit to the farm and great advantage to the city and the station of Dacca'. In Cawnpore, he pointed out, sugarcane was grown on the trenched land, and at Alipore Jail, plantations had been found most profitable. At the same time a much larger conservancy establishment was required, with a band of reliable inspectors to enforce the conservancy by-laws. Since mehtars could not be procured in sufficient numbers in Dacca, he suggested that they be recruited from the North-Western Provinces, allotting them a separate mahalla of their own, and providing them with huts free of cost.

Dr Cutcliffe wished to plan for the future development of Dacca upon the green-belt system. He had a vision of an expanding Dacca, and to prevent haphazard growth or further overcrowding of the existing city, he suggested that the municipal area should be extended and mapped out ready for future use. The waste jungle to the north and north-west should be included within the munici-. pal limits, and beyond it a belt of evergreen trees should be planted. 'Space would then be procured for future extension of the suburbs for conservancy grounds, for cemeteries, and for a farm,... and irregularities in squatting be prevented,' while within the town 'one or two open spaces of ground... should be left unbuilt upon. They should be laid out as open grass plots, or as flower gardens, with ornamental trees.' Such open grass plots in the midst of the city would do much to secure a proper supply of pure air for the inhabitants.[42]

He also suggested a dispersal of population from the crowded localities. Part of the proposed loan should be invested in reclaiming waste lands as building sites where quality housing should be built to yield good rents. Slum areas should likewise be bought for clearance and redevelopment at higher rentals, the new houses catering for various categories of tenants. He also proposed 'to lay out with regularity and due reference to sanitary requirements, new streets in and around the city.'

Next, he recommended the opening of new and the immediat- closure of old burial grounds within the city. (The old cemeteriee should be left as clean open grass plots.) He also urged the modernis zation of the city's markets and the construction of better, carefully located slaughter houses, with neat rows of iron-roofed sheds with paved floors and shallow drains.

He suggested improved lighting of the streets, though using kerosene rather than gas on the Cawnpore model. Most important of all, he identified the supply of pure drinking water as the prime want of the city, a *sine qua non* of any sanitary scheme for Dacca. Water, he suggested, could be brought from the river Sitalakhya, ten miles to the east, which was famous for its purity, pumped by steam power through iron pipes, and if necessary filtered in Dacca. With improved water supplies would go a more efficient drainage system; the 'old deep drains should be everywhere abolished, and shallow saucer drains universally laid down'. And since the Dulai Khal was 'a notorious nuisance', it should either be deepened to secure an ever-flowing channel, or filled in altogether. Elaborate plans were submitted for both measures. As an engineer would be required to advise on these schemes, government should be reques- ted to depute one to Dacca without delay. At the same time a plea should be made to allow the use of convict labour again for the improvement and conservancy of the city.

Finally, on a more purely medical note, Dr Cutcliffe urged that a regular system of registering births and deaths be at once instituted and that effective measures be taken for controlling venereal diseases. The fearful prevalence of syphilis in the city should be dealt with by imposing the measures already in force in the cities of Europe and in the military cantonments in India.[43]

Dr Cutcliffe's scheme was a splendid specimen of the town planning and sanitary reforms which nineteenth-century European experts advocated for the towns and cities of the Indian subcontinent. His model was obviously European, and in matters of sanitary reforms, many of the remedies which he suggested were indeed those which Edwin Chadwick had some years earlier prescribed for the then equally insanitary British towns and cities.[44] The driving of broad straight streets through the crowded confusion of the city quarters, a waterworks scheme and the new stone saucer-profiled drains represented the radical engineering approach to the problems of the city, with none of that feeling for organic growth and ameliorative change on which Patrick Geddes would later place so much emphasis.[45] He also displayed a rather optimistic vision of the financial burden which the city might be expected to bear. Dr Cutcliffe was not just prescribing the current remedies, however, as in some ways he was many years in advance of his time. The proposals for the creation of open spaces within the old city, for the forward planning of suburban development, and for municipal investment in building lands, both within and outside the city, so as to secure to the municipality the unearned profits of rising land values were not in the common idiom of contemporary town planning. In the subcontinent they would not be put into practice until the twentieth-century era of Improvement Trusts.

The scheme in general was much liked by the municipal commissioners and officials of Dacca, Khwaja Abdul Ghani declaring that if faithfully carried out, the Doctor's scheme would transform Dacca into 'an envied place for the habitation of men and would make a heaven of hell'. Although the scheme was not adopted in its entirety, all the later improvements of Dacca were essentially based upon it.

The scheme of this theoretician, scientist and dedicated health officer then came before the municipal commissioners who would have to fund it and secure public approval. They met on 28 April

1869, with Graham, J.G.N. Pogose, D. R. Lyall, the Assistant Magistrate, M. David, J. May, the Executive Engineer, A. MacBean, the manager of the Bank of Bengal, Dacca Branch, Mitterjeet Singh and Koylash Chandra Ghosh, Head-Master of the Dacca Government School, present. Many of the commissioners had already submitted written reports on the scheme. Lyall, for example, had suggested that instead of constructing two broad streets, one should be built along the southern bank of the Dulai Khal using material excavated from it. This would avoid the expense of pulling down many pucka city houses. Pogose had commented that although dry earth conservancy was undoubtedly excellent, getting the people to adopt it would be extremely difficult and if at once insisted on might produce much dissatisfaction. He was in favour, however, of the establishment of a lock hospital 'for women of the town' as a curb upon the curse of syphilis. Most of the commissioners concentrated on the cost of the scheme. However admirable the scheme, it was, they felt, much too ambitious and financially impracticable. Khwaja Abdul Ghani stressed this point: he had written,

> ...to raise money in any shape from the people of Dacca to enable us to carry into execution the sanitary improvements would be a thing next to impossibility. The people of this city are too poor to be able to make such large investments for sanitary purposes...[46]

Graham was, however, more hopeful and argued that the Municipality could raise money much more easily than was supposed. Indeed, he took the opportunity to criticize the commissioners, the Indian members more particularly, for their failure to provide constructive suggestions and for regarding 'the idea of extricating the town from its lamentable state of filth and unhealthiness as hopeless'. In a written memorandum he set down the priorities and the way of raising funds to finance them. His financial proposals included the doubling of the existing house-rate, doubling the tolls on the Buriganga ferries, and the introduction of a dog-tax. To double the house-rate might appear a startling measure, but the 16,132 taxpayers currently paid only Rs. 40,000 in rates, an average of less than two and a half rupees a year. 'To double this', Graham argued, and 'make it five rupees a year, cannot be considered oppressive, for as [a] rule the tax falls heaviest on those who can best bear it.' Increased ferry tolls should yield an additional Rs. 3,000 a year. The dog-tax he proposed was two rupees a year, animals without owners being destroyed. With an estimated ten thousand dogs in the town, the theoretical yield would be Rs. 20,000. This he accepted as improbably high, however, and he did not expect more than Rs. 7,000 from the dog-tax.

Graham estimated that his scheme would yield an additional income of about Rs. 50,000 per annum. Money should be borrowed on the security of these taxes to begin work on the town's three most urgent needs, namely, a supply of pure water, the regular removal of sewage, and improved ventilation. Two lakhs of rupees paying interest at four per cent per annum could easily be borrowed on the security of the additional taxes, especially since the rich commissioners of the Municipality might themselves subscribe to the loan 'without feeling any sensible pressure on their pecuniary resources'. He also proposed that the government be requested to hand over to the Municipality the tolls on the Dulai Khal, hitherto a source of provincial revenues. He therefore moved that the commissioners should ask the government to give them permission to levy the new taxes, and to borrow two lakhs of rupees on the strength of them and to provide the free services of an engineer to work out detailed estimates for the work proposed. Government, when informed of the Municipality's additional income, might itself provide another two lakhs of rupees at four per cent: if so then all Dr Cutcliffe's plan could easily be implemented.

He argued that much of the loan would be spent on remunerative works which in the long run would pay back the capital and interest. He wished particularly that much of it should be invested in purchasing waste lands in and about the city, to be reclaimed and sold as building sites at a profit. When some of the commissioners asked 'where are the wealthier people to come from?' to take up improved sites, he answered,

> Make your city attractive, and they will come. Many Zamindars of the surrounding districts would, I believe, have a house in Dacca if they could obtain a proper site, and were not afraid of their lives. At present the name of Dacca is a bugbear to all, and not undeservedly so.

Graham's bold plans created a stir among the commissioners. Most of them, however, opposed the doubling of the house-tax in which the people would not acquiesce. This was certainly the reaction of the press. The *Dhaka Prokash* accepted the merits of Cutcliffe's plans and the need for further taxation, but declared that the doubling of the house-tax was out of the question since it would inflict great hardships upon the poor of the city. Instead it suggested a number of indirect taxes, including a tax upon the theatrical and musical parties which visited Dacca during the pujas.[47] The *Hindu Hitoishini*, the mouthpiece of the orthodox Hindus of Dacca, made the same objection. It asked, 'But how then are the expenses to be met?', answering thus, 'Let the wheel tax be increased, for those who can afford a ride in carriage will certainly find it a small matter to pay a trifle more.'[48] This objection of the people against direct taxation for municipal needs was, however, a common phenomenon throughout the subcontinent.[49]

However, Graham's enthusiasm was not to be dampened, and on 10 May 1869, he pressed the commissioners to endorse his proposals. The other commissioners present at the meeting were MacBean, Platts, David, Lyall, Ahsanullah and Koylash Chandra Ghosh, who put forward various amendments. Graham lost patience and the commissioners, unwilling to oppose the District Magistrate further, accepted an amendment from Lyall that they should retain a power to exempt from the increase in house-tax those they believed unable through poverty to pay. With this amendment Graham's proposals were carried by eight to one, only Ghosh voting against them.[50]

The proposals now required government approval, since the Municipality had no power of independent financial action, and taxation would require new legislation. On 12 June 1869, Graham submitted his proposals to the Divisional Commissioner Simson, requesting him to move the government to authorize the Municipality to act. He acknowledged that the Municipal Commissioners' decision did not represnt the wishes of the general community, indeed he could well imagine a 'monster petition' against the taxation. But the taxation would not be really oppressive and the authorities must endeavour 'to benefit the community in spite of themselves.'[51]

Simson, if Graham's *Memoir* is to be believed, set his face against the whole plan, at first declining even to forward something which he dubbed 'chimerical'.[52] Graham records that he thereupon personally begged Simson 'to let it go up to the government and not to throw cold water on it, as the Dacca people would take their cue from him'.[53]

Simson did eventually forward the plan, and made amends for his initial doubts: he confirmed in great detail the insanitary state of Dacca and declared that he fully supported the municipal commissioners' comprehensive proposals, including the tax changes—except the dog-tax, which he thought impracticable—since government had distinctly announced that it would provide only limited funds for local improvements, leaving citizens themselves to 'purify their city and do so chiefly at their own cost'. Simson particularly stressed the key importance of the loan to all the proposals for 'the improvement of the health of this important city'.[54]

The Government of Bengal, always careful to avoid causing popular discontent, rejected the municipal commissioners' scheme outright. However, the Lieutenant-Governor Sir William Grey was willing 'to deal with the town of Dacca on special grounds, and to recommend such legislation as may be required', but only after preparation by the local Executive Engineer of a 'rough general estimate of the probable expenditure to be incurred in effecting the contemplated improvements'. This should show the outlay on permanent unproductive improvements and the annual charges of conservancy and police. The government would then be in a position to determine to what extent municipal taxes should be raised.[55] Graham's hope of seeing some of his projects being undertaken while he was still in Dacca was thus frustrated.

The impulse to improve however, was not destroyed, and the assurances of the Lieutenant-Governor provided hope. Dacca also gained a new and influential friend in Dr David Boyes Smith, the Sanitary Commissioner of Bengal, who visited the city at the request of Dr Cutcliffe and then himself submitted a scheme for its development.[56] Moreover, Dacca was fortunate in having Lyall as successor to Graham. Already as a municipal commissioner he had taken a keen interest in Dacca's problems. He was to prove one of the most able and successful official chairmen of the Municipality, during whose incumbency the city saw many lasting developments.[57] His achievements were also facilitated by a curious accident of history: that for almost eight consecutive years he was left in charge of the Dacca District, a phenomenon very rare in an era of frequent transfers.

Until new taxes could be introduced, Lyall and the local Executive Engineer[58] mapped out a more modest interim plan of action, in the following order: conservancy, ventilation, improvement of the Dulai Khal, surface drainage and pure water supply. Lyall estimated that for each of these works at least Rs. 50,000 would be required, except the water-supply which would need not less than a lakh. The extent to which these works could be carried out would therefore depend upon how large a loan could be secured.

Lyall showed that if government would allow a doubling of the Buriganga ferry tolls and grant Dacca the Dulai Khal tolls also, the Municipality could raise its annual savings from about Rs. 6,000 to Rs. 9,000 a year. This would be enough to service the interest charges of a loan of Rs. 150,000 at six per cent, and this he proposed to raise under Act III of 1864. This loan should be spent upon dealing with the first three items on his list. Hitherto 'conservancy' in Dacca had meant simply street-sweeping. Nothing was done to remove the sewage, for the existing municipal income would not allow. He therefore put forward a plan for establishing an efficient system capable of removing the entire sewage of the town. For this he proposed to divide the whole town into ten conservancy blocks. 'In each of these, there would be a public latrine and depot for carts, coolies etc, and to each would be assigned a certain number of privies.' He calculated that the daily removal of sewage from all the privies would require an establishment of 160 sweepers, 50 filth carts, 50 bullocks and 50 wheelbarrows or pails. To dispose of the sewage he selected the Segun Baghicha or old teak garden north of the town, which then belonged to the Municipality, as the trenching ground, and also proposed to purchase lands adjacent to it for cultivation with night-soil manure. To provide this equipment, staff and trenching grounds, the minimum basis for 'an efficient system of conservancy' would absorb the best part of 50,000 rupees.

For the further considerable recurrent expenditure on conservancy 'the people of the town must pay.' Hence he suggested a tax upon householders for cleaning their privies at the rate of eight annas per pucka privy and two annas per kutcha privy per month. This would fall lightly on the people, for in Dacca the well-to-do people already paid a *bhuimali* about two annas per month to clean their privies, while the poor who dug cess-pits got them emptied once in two years at a cost of two or three rupees. The new tax would thus simply divert private expenditure into municipal funds for a better and more satisfactory service.

The second task was to open up the most crowded and squalid mahallas. Lyall proposed the complete demolition of parts of them and the construction of new streets parallel to each other for ease of conservancy operations and proper ventilation, together with a systematic levelling and filling of the ground. Fifty thousand rupees should be spent in buying up land and houses, paying reasonable compensation, and improving the ground. The improved building sites so created could be resold at higher prices later on. If existing laws would not allow the Municipality thus to deal in land, legislation would be required, since otherwise the Municipality would simply improve the town for the benefit of private land-owners.

The third sum of Rs. 50,000 was to be spent on the improvement of the Dulai Khal. This should be profitable. He proposed to buy those lands on either bank which lay under water during the rains, to deepen the bed of the canal and by throwing the earth on the sides to form a road and a bazaar. This would be very popular, allowing boats to be moored close to the shops in a protected khal instead of in the open river. He was absolutely confident that the work would yield sufficient profits at least to pay the interest on that part of the loan spent on it, while simultaneously it would remove a source of unhealthiness in the city. If the first and third of these works proved profitable or at least paid their way, then a further lakh could afterwards be raised and applied to the fourth and fifth schemes. He made the point, however, that Rs. 150,000 was the largest loan which could be raised and serviced at any one time without unduly burdening the town.[59] His scheme when submitted to the municipal commissioners was approved by them.

Simson, in forwarding Lyall's scheme to the government, urged its adoption. He did remark, however, that rather than improving Dulai Khal, more should be spent on the clearance and redevelopment of the most crowded and filthy localities in the town, 'where innumerable families abide, surrounded by filth which cannot be got out or removed, and where diseases such as cholera, smallpox and the worst kind of fevers find easy access, and where accordingly deadly havoc and devastation are caused by their yearly attacks'.[60]

This time Sir William Grey approved of the whole scheme. He authorized the Dacca Municipality to raise the loan and to double the tolls on the Buriganga river, and also agreed to hand over to them the receipts from the Dulai Khal tolls. He also resolved that the Legislative Council should pass a special Act for Dacca authorizing the commissioners to impose a privy-tax and also to acquire lands for improvement and to dispose of them again at a profit. Even more important, he resolved that the new Act should empower the commissioners to raise the house-tax to ten per cent on the annual value. This would enable them to carry out all the essential works, though if the funds still proved inadequate they should first improve the conservancy and the slums of the town.[61]

A special 'Act for Improving the Sanitary Condition of the Town of Dacca', Act VII of 1870, was accordingly passed which, together with Act III of 1864, gave the Dacca Municipality a very wide range of fiscal, financial and civic powers. A number of inhabitants, however, petitioned the Governor-General to withhold his assent, but Lord Mayo declined to comply and so the Act came into force in November 1870.

Following the enactment of the Conservancy Act of 1870, Lyall made elaborate arrangements for town cleansing and sewage removal in anticipation of the additional funds to be secured on loan. He also launched a stricter civic administration. A Eurasian overseer was appointed to supervise the sweeping of the town and cleaning of public drains by the convicts and municipal workmen. *Domes* (sweepers) were appointed to remove the carcasses and unclaimed corpses from the city to places set apart for their burial. Voluntary supervision by the municipal commissioners of the conservancy of the mahallas having been found unsatisfactory, ten ward overseers were appointed who reported all cases of insanitary practices, encroachments, and obstructions to the vice-chairman or the secretary who thereupon took prompt action. The overseers were particularly instructed to see that private latrines were maintained properly and regularly cleaned. A revised code of by-laws required householders to keep their compounds clean, to fill up their cesspools and ditches, and to stop the dumping of household rubbish on the public streets except at specified collecting points. Particular attention was given to free the river Buriganga from pollution by stopping the people from throwing rubbish, excreta and carcasses into its waters. Violations of the municipal act or by-laws were strictly dealt with: notices were issued, summonses served, and the offenders fined upon conviction.

In 1871–2, 2,116 notices were issued, 1,309 summonses served and 214 people fined.

The increased acitivity of the Municipality, especially of the overseers, aroused much resentment, but certainly improved the cleanliness of the town.[62] Even the *Dhaka Prokash*, always critical of the municipal commissioners, in an editorial in December 1872, acknowledged their work.[63] Typically, however, the editor went on to the carping criticism that their enthusiasm had become oppressive. No Daccaite could escape the fear of being suddenly summoned for some slightest breach of the conservancy rules. The editor also warned the commissioners to watch the overseers, said to be harassing innocent people by falsely reporting against them and even extorting bribes by threatening to lodge complaints for alleged violations of the municipal laws.[64]

Lyall was anxious to see his scheme for sewage disposal get under way quickly and particularly the construction of public latrines. Earlier, in 1869, the Executive Engineer of Dacca, A. F. Baird, had stressed that the building of public latrines was indispensable as a basis for 'the compulsion of the use of *proper* private latrines by those who decline, or find it inconvenient to use the public ones, and to put a stop to the filthy habits of the people of Dacca...'[65] There were then in the city seven 'public' latrines privately owned by the mehtars who charged for their use but kept them in the most unsatisfactory manner. These needed to be closed and replaced. Already by 1870 the Municipality had constructed three new latrines, but more were needed, while to remove the sewage from these and from the private privies of the entire town, the planned conservancy system would have to be immediately implemented. Lyall therefore soon finalized all the necessary requirements. But then a series of crippling set-backs occurred.

In December 1870 he had induced the municipal commissioners to raise Rs. 50,000 on the open market by issuing debentures under the new Conservancy Act. The Bengal Government, however, advised the commissioners not to borrow on the open market, as the Government of India was about to provide loans at cheaper rates for local public works. The commissioners thereupon stopped the debenture issue, and on 21 April 1871, Lyall submitted proposals for borrowing Rs. 50,000 from the central government for a conservancy scheme, showing in great detail how the money would be spent. He suggested, however, that the Municipality should first borrow only half the amount, so as to start immediately a limited operation for sewage removal from the most filthy mahallas without imposing a privy-tax. He hoped that once the people had seen the practical benefits of the scheme they would afterwards more readily acquiesce in paying a privy-tax. He emphasized that even this partial scheme would greatly strain municipal resources unless government now handed over the promised Dulai Khal toll receipts. The ultimate cost of the conservancy establishment and the interest repayments on the full loan would require both the tolls income and a privy-tax. The Bengal Government readily recommended Dacca's application for a Government of India loan. It made no move, however, to hand over the receipts from the Dulai Khal tolls.[66] Lyall's truncated scheme was then threatened from a new quarter. In August 1871, the new Lieutenant-Governor Sir George Campbell visited Dacca, and was promptly lobbied by the inhabitants who objected to the proposed privy-tax on two grounds. They strongly opposed the new financial burden and also the municipal cleansing of private privies—not from any ignorance of the need for cleanliness but as a threat to the seclusion of their womenfolk. In Dacca most privies were situated inside the house compound, and inaccessible except through the courtyard. The admission of male sweepers into these inner courtyards would breach the rules of purdah, observed by Muslims and higher-caste Hindus alike. (Similar problems were faced by other municipalities, for example, Patna and Allahabad.) In Dacca both the old conservative élites of the city and representatives of the English-educated middle class took part in the appeal to Campbell, the latter exploiting the conservatism of the general public in order to establish their influence in the city. They even went to the unusual length, for this period, of sending a letter of congratulation to Campbell through their public organ, the newly-formed *Dacca People's Association*, when in June 1872 he suspended the imposition of the privy-tax in Dacca, though this brought upon them a sharp rebuke from the *Dhaka Prokash*.[67]

Immediately after his visit to Dacca, Campbell wrote to the municipal commissioners. He did not think that a loan could be justifiably used merely on such impermanent work as importing sweepers and purchasing filth-carts and bullocks. He therefore asked them to revise their proposals in favour of investment in works of a permanent nature. He did promise, however, to grant

Rs. 5,000 from the Provincial Fund for an assault on the town's accumulated filth. But since the proposed privy-tax appeared especially unpopular in Dacca, he suggested that it would be better to use their legal powers to enhance the house-tax rather than introduce a much-hated impost.[68]

Campbell's attitude finally destroyed any chance of implementing Lyall's original plan,[69] in which the establishment of an efficient conservancy system had been an essential element. Since Lyall was still determined to tackle the sewage problem, he took up Campbell's suggestion and raised the question of enhancing the house-tax with the municipal commissioners. But the others except for Khwaja Abdul Ghani and his son Khwaja Ahsanullah opposed this. They did agree, however, that a reduced privy-tax could be introduced at the rate of one anna per kutcha and four annas per pucka privy per month for the maintenance of the conservancy scheme.

Finally, in April 1872, a revised plan for a loan of Rs. 25,000 for permanent works was submitted to the Bengal Government, repayment to be a first charge on the house tax, with rupees 2,000 per annum set apart for interest payments and a capital sinking fund. In his forwarding letter, however, Lyall pointed out that under the orders of the government, which ruled out spending loan money on such impermanent works as purchasing filth-carts and importing mehtars, the conservancy scheme could not be implemented without a privy-tax.[70]

In June 1872, the Bengal Government authorized the Dacca Municipality to make a formal application for the loan under the Local Public Works Loan Act, Act XXIV of 1871. But government also pointed out that final orders thereon must await the outcome of the new Bengal Municipal Bill then under the Legislative Council's consideration.[71]

In July the municipal commissioners did make a formal application for a loan primarily on the security of the house-tax, though they assured the government that since they had no liabilities, repayment would not be difficult.[72] But their problems were not yet over, for the Government of India now asked them to submit a fresh application assigning their entire revenue from all sources as security, not merely the house-tax. This done, the Government of India on 25 October 1872 finally sanctioned the loan repayable over nineteen years by annual instalments of Rs. 2,000 including interest at four and a half per cent.[73] In November 1872, the Bengal Government sanctioned the grant of Rs. 5,000 which Campbell had earlier promised, while in December 1872 it also transferred the Dulai Khal to the Dacca Municipality, authorizing them to collect the tolls.[74]

With these much increased resources Lyall at last started to implement his elaborate conservancy scheme. By 1875 fifty mehtars and mehtranis had been recruited from Cawnpore and seven public latrines completed. These latrines were put under the charge of the municipal sweepers, who were provided with accommodation nearby. In 1876 the Municipality acquired 300 bighas of land at the Segun Baghicha for trenching grounds and for cultivation. A regular system for the removal of sewage from the public latrines and a few private ones, and for its disposal in the trenching grounds was put into operation from that same year.

But the regular cleaning of the thousands of private privies was left in abeyance after Campbell had suspended the imposition of a privy-tax in the face of public opposition. Lyall determined nevertheless to go ahead with his plan even without taxation. As the Municipality had enough men and equipment, he decided to service the private privies at least of a part of the town. Moreover, the drive to introduce the privy-tax was not given up, and the public gradually came to accept the idea. In June 1875, at Lyall's persuasion, the commissioners adopted a new set of by-laws which authorized them to close all well-privies and other ill-constructed privies, and to compel their owners to replace them by approved surface privies. They also empowered the Municipality to clean private privies upon one month's notice, wherever the householders failed to do so themselves. Where the cleaning was by municipal sweepers, owners were required to pay for the service.[75]

The Bengal Government approved of these by-laws which came into effect from July 1875. They caused some public disquiet but no overt opposition, perhaps because their legality being in doubt they were not rigidly enforced.[76] It is interesting to note that Dacca's attempt to deal with the problem of private privies through specially devised by-laws created an air of hope among other municipal authorities. For example, as soon as the Dacca by-laws were published, the Patna Municipality decided to follow Dacca's example.[77]

In July 1876, the new Municipal Act, Act V of 1876, came into force in Dacca. This Act repealed all previous municipal Acts including the Dacca Conservancy Act of 1870. But although Dacca now became a First Class Municipality, the Act made no such provision for the compulsory establishment of a conservancy system or the imposition of a privy-tax as Act VII of 1870 had done. The Municipality was therefore obliged to adopt some by-laws under the new Act similar to those of 1875.[78] With this renewed authority, the Municipality began the cleaning of private latrines, starting in the worst areas of Shankari Bazar and Sabzi Mahal.[79]

Meanwhile the Sanitary Commissioners had been drumming into government the cost in urban health of the lack of comprehensive sewage schemes in towns, which was mainly for lack of funds but also for want of legal powers. In 1878 the Bengal Government at last responded, passing Act VI of 1878 which made the establishment of a conservancy system and the imposition of a scavenging tax compulsory in all First Class Municipalities.

The Dacca Municipality quickly extended the Act to the city, and after correspondence with the Howrah Municipality about a scavenging fee resolved to impose a privy-tax. The Act came into force from 1 January 1879, a last success for Lyall as chairman of the Municipality. Unhappily there was confusion about the rate of tax. In October 1878, the commissioners resolved to exact the tax at half the house-rate of eight per cent but initially to start at two per cent or a quarter of the house-tax.[80] In March 1879, Lyall asked the government to sanction the tax which he reported had been fixed at two per cent, and it was this which on 20 March 1879 was accepted by government resolution.[81]

It soon became apparent that the cleaning of private privies by the Municipality would cost about Rs. 25,000 a year whereas the tax would only yield half that amount at two per cent. The new chairman Arthur Forbes pointed out that Lyall in fixing the rate (at two per cent) had completely overlooked 'the clear terms of the resolution passed by the Commissioners', and that the Municipality could not afford to provide a free service: people must pay for the sanitation. Personally he favoured the tax to be levied straightaway at half the rate of the house-tax.[82] But the commissioners resisted such ideas insisting that direct taxation in Dacca was already too high, and that any increase would be greatly resented. Finally, after much discussion, it was decided that the tax should remain at two per cent but that an annual premium ranging from eight annas to five rupees according to the annual house-rate should also be levied, no one, however, to pay less than one anna per month.[83] Accordingly, a schedule of House Service Fees was prepared which came into force in October 1879.

The conservancy scheme could not, however, be put into operation simultaneously throughout the town chiefly because of the difficulty in procuring sweepers. By June 1879, the Municipality had been able to recruit only 85 of the estimated 300 sweepers required. The band of sweepers ultimately secured from Cawnpore proved, moreover, to be a turbulent force. They were recruited under a system of contract, a few months' salary being paid in advance. Many of them, however, deserted, many frequently remained absent from work and spent much time in drinking. Moreover, they regularly demanded more wages—initially each was paid six rupees a month—and did not hesitate to go on strike to enforce their demands. More importantly, it was also soon discovered—to the consternation of all—that the conservancy scheme was still a loss maker, so that from 1880 certain outlying areas of the town, were excluded, though the householders were also exempted from the scavenging tax.[84]

The conservancy scheme, first put into operation in 1879 in Block 1, was however soon extended to the other six blocks by 1881. In the annual report for 1879–80, the vice-chairman Arthur Tute observed,

> [The] Privy tax was introduced this year—a great innovation... The result up to date has been an expenditure of rupees 10,801 ... against an income of rupees 3,378 ... showing a dead loss of rupees 7,523 ... This like all other new forms of taxation was and is very unpopular in Dacca. The hardship is more sentimental than real for out of 750 appeals tried by native members of the Committee, 23 cases only were recommended for modification or remission ... in some instances it was found impossible to work the privy tax under an anna a month at the very lowest, and the very lowest coolie in Dacca gets rupees 6–7–0 per month, and it is not excessive to demand one anna from him when compared with the inestimable benefits the cleaning of the town brings with it.

He added that since the introduction of the scheme, the winter months had been markedly free of the cholera which almost every year had caused great havoc in Dacca.[85] The conservancy scheme also enabled the Municipality gradually to close the well-privies which had so long been a primary source of disease in Dacca.[86]

As in the case of conservancy, Dacca also saw great improvements in many other aspects of its civic life during the post-1868 period both under the leadership of Lyall and of his successors. Particular attention was given to the maintenance and improvement of roads and streets, the Municipality spending an annual average of some Rs. 14,000 on these between 1870 and 1885. The task was a daunting one, there being some 300 roads and lanes covering about 115 miles in all to repair, widen, and metal. Most of these were narrow, crooked and unpaved. The narrow streets caused congestion of trafic while the unmetalled ones became impassable during the rains and extremely dusty in the dry season.

Following severe criticism of their performance during the late 1860s by the press and public, the municipal commissioners turned their attention more seriously to road improvement, allotting to this a large part of their revenue. They paid particular attention to widening the more important roads for the easy movement of pedestrians and of the ticca-garries, roadside houses and huts which obstructed the streets and formed bottlenecks being compulsorily purchased. Despite constant attempts, the Municipality succeeded only partially in widening the main thoroughfares, as the streets were generally hemmed in by pucka houses, the compulsory purchase of which for demolition proved beyond its financial capacity.

As the streets could not be greatly widened, the commissioners concentrated more on the repair of roads, an expensive process for most of the roads being made of mud needed annual repair after the rains. The heavy monsoon rainfall caused severe damage, holing the roads and carrying off much of the surface dressing. The metalling of roads was therefore adopted both to minimize recurring outlay and to improve the surface for traffic. Initially bricks were used for paving the roads. However, this caused other difficulties for the bricks wore badly and were quickly ground into dust by traffic. To overcome the problem, *jhamma* or vitrified bricks, and iron-slag or black laterite were later used. Even these did not prove very effective, and the roads had to be remetalled every two or three years at great cost.

Watering of the streets during the dry season was another expense of the Municipality. At one time this had been done through voluntary subscriptions but after the establishment of the Municipality, the commissioners themselves took over the duty. Bhistis using water-skins were employed for the purpose.

However, the watering of the streets was also not without problems. During the dry season, the tanks and ditches from where water was drawn themselves dried up, rendering the procurement of water for street-watering extremely difficult. Three reservoirs were therefore specially constructed in 1870 from which water could be drawn through Persian wheels. After the establishment of the Waterworks, the supply problem was more nearly solved, special stand-pipes being installed to fill the municipal water-carts.

One feature was, however, common to the work of widening, repairing and watering of the roads of Dacca by the Municipality—a clear-cut discrimination in the laying out of limited funds in favour of the wealthy and influential. After some 22 years, only 29 miles out of an estimated 115 miles of roads and lanes were metalled,[87] these being the thoroughfares serving the European and the richer Indian districts. The municipal hand was less visible in the lanes and by-lanes where the mass of people lived.[88] Thus the Nawabpur Bazar road through which the Europeans and the richer Daccaites drove was invariably kept repaired and watered.

The vernacular press protested at this injustice. Thus the *Hindu Hitoishini* of 1 March 1873, complaining of the disrepair of roads in the 'native' section of the town, commented scathingly, 'This is strange that while the Committee are sustained by our rice, they act so ungrateful a part, scarcely ever considering whether they ought to do anything for our welfare or not...'[89] Even the European press was moved to comment, as the *Bengal Times* did in 1881:

> Of what value is Native life, especially poor native life, in comparison to having the European thoroughfares of the town, streets over which roll the conveyances of the wealthy proprietors, and drains that might offend delicate olfactories, kept in order? Evidently, judged by the prescription of municipal committees, life in the lower grades of the Native Society has little or no value, and assuredly none as contrasted with the comfort of the well-to-do community.[90]

However, even a limited development of the road network of the city created the further problem of traffic control. In the old days, pedestrians, pack-bullocks and horses had used the roads at will. But the introduction of faster, wheeled carriages, especially ticca-garries plying for hire, often driven by mere boys, endangered all foot passengers, scarcely a week passing without serious accidents. And since there were no appointed ticca-garry stands, great congestion was caused in the most populous streets. In 1874 the *Dhaka Prokash* urged the Municipality to introduce a system of registration of hackney-carriages like the one then in force in Calcutta, as a means both of control and of increasing the Municipality's tax revenue.[91] The District Superintendent of Police also urged the Municipality to establish ticca-garry stands.[92] The Municipality eventually issued special orders to pedestrians to use the sides of the roads, earmarked special corners as ticca-garry stands, and passed new by-laws to regulate hackney-carriages.[93] The driving of ticca-garries by anyone below the age of fourteen was prohibited, the use of lights by wheeled vehicles at night was ordered, and the registration of all wheeled vehicles was introduced to control their movement, check the carrying of stolen goods, and also to raise the fee income of the Municipality.

The recommendations of Dr Cutcliffe and the demand from local residents and the press for street lighting were also eventually met, though belatedly, in 1878. It was public charity which came to the rescue. In 1877 the Committee formed to organize the celebration of Queen Victoria's proclamation as 'Empress of India', offered the Municipality a sum of Rs. 6,445 to provide lamps and lamp-posts for the town, the cost of their maintenance to be borne by the Municipality. After correspondence with the Calcutta Municipality about the cost of lamps and their maintenance, the commissioners agreed to accept the offer and to light one hundred lamps, neither the gift nor municipal resources being sufficient to operate the two hundred lamps needed to light all the streets and lanes of Dacca.[94] In 1878 the first sixty lamp-posts were put up in the most conspicuous parts of the city, starting with the main road running from the Municipality's Office near Wise Ghat to the Chauk Bazar.[95] By 1886–7 a total of 145 street-lamps had been put up along all the principal roads. The cost of their maintenance in that year was Rs. 4,117.[96] The lamps were fuelled by kerosene on the Cawnpore model. However, kerosene lamps were not ideal: any strong wind put them out so that the city was regularly plunged into darkness. In 1884 Babu Ruplal Das offered to bear all the expenses of electric lighting but the Municipality declined the offer, not having the funds to meet the cost of maintenance.[97]

Perhaps the most successful improvement in Dacca's urban life was the installation of a modern Waterworks, a product of public charity and municipal funding. 'The supply of pure drinking water,' remarked Dr Cutcliffe in 1868, 'is a *sine qua non* in any sanitary scheme for the improvement of the healthiness of Dacca', and in his plan he gave it top priority. Simson and Lyall, though admitting the need, suggested that it might come later, when more funds were available. Simson argued, moreover, that if the planned conservancy arrangements were carried out the river Buriganga would become purer, and the necessity for a supply of filtered water would be thus proportionately reduced. However, as hopes of improved conservancy were frustrated by government reluctance to allow the raising of a loan, and as most people obtained their drinking water not from the river but from such traditional sources within the city as wells, khals and tanks, the water of which was heavily contaminated with sewage, it was soon realized that the people must be supplied with pure drinking water if they were to be given freedom from disease, particularly cholera.

Dr Cutcliffe had suggested that water should be piped to the city, using steam power, from the river Sitalakhya and Lyall also supported that scheme. The favoured plan, however, was that of drawing water from the Buriganga. Although the river was highly polluted, it seemed evident that so deep and wide a river as the Buriganga could not be more impure than other rivers such as the Hughly which were used as sources of drinking water, and that if the external sources of pollution like dumping of rubbish into its waters could be checked it ought to be easy to render it harmless and safe for human consumption. The first plan to use the Buriganga, produced by Simson, was a simple one: to install a reservoir at Lalbagh, to pump up water from the Buriganga and after filtering it, to distribute it in three lines of surface aqueducts following the three levels of the city, which all ran parallel to the river.[98] It soon became clear, however, that even this simple plan would cost a larger amount than the Dacca Municipality could afford. It was at this point that private munificence came to the rescue. In 1871, Khwaja Abdul Ghani was awarded the title of C.S.I. by the Government of

India in recognition of his many charitable and philanthropic works in Dacca and elsewhere, and of his loyalty to the British Government. As an acknowledgement of this honour and as an 'expression of his gratitude to Providence for the recovery of His Royal Highness the Prince of Wales from a dreadful malady [typhoid]', Khwaja Abdul Ghani in December 1871 placed at the disposal of the government a sum of Rs. 50,000 for the permanent benefit of the city of Dacca.

A committee was appointed which resolved that a supply of pure drinking water would be the fittest and most lasting boon. Estimates were then made for installing a waterworks scheme but were found to exceed the amount of the gift. Khwaja Ahsanullah, the son of Abdul Ghani, who was a member of the committee, then himself made a further donation of Rs. 50,000.[99] Even then it soon became apparent that although the two munificent gifts would make possible the installation of a system there would be very little or nothing to spare for its subsequent maintenance. The matter was further complicated by the fact that Khwaja Abdul Ghani had specifically desired that the water should be free, no water-rate being charged to the inhabitants for water supplied from hydrants. The committee then put the matter to the municipal commissioners who replied that maintenance was beyond their financial capacity to undertake. The committee was thus forced to consider other charitable works. None found much favour with Khwaja Ahsanullah, who also particularly wished that the waterworks in Dacca should be associated with the name of none but his family. He therefore took up the matter with his father, who at once made another donation of Rs. 50,000. Here was the capital which suitably invested could form the necessary Water-Works Maintenance Fund.

The financial difficulties thus solved, the Municipality finally resolved upon a scheme of water supply from the Buriganga. On 9 August 1874, in a colourful ceremony, the foundation stone of the Dacca Water-Works was laid by Lord Northbrook, the first British Viceroy to visit the city. In his speech he thanked Khwaja Abdul Ghani and his son and promised personally to convey the news of the donation—singularly appropriate to the event which it commemorated—to the Prince of Wales. The new waterworks, he hoped, would contribute to check disease in Dacca as the introduction of pure water had done in Calcutta.[100]

The Public Works Department of the Bengal Government was

entrusted with construction, but such a slow pace was set that *The Bengal Times* launched a vigorous attack on the inefficiency and lethargy of the Engineer-in-charge. It soon became apparent, moreover, that a waterworks capable of supplying water throughout Dacca would require much more money than had been donated. The additional funds were provided, however, by the Bengal Government, its contribution to the final cost of Rs. 195,350 being Rs. 95,350, for which a system was developed capable of supplying 200,000 gallons of water daily.[101]

Finally, after nearly four years of waiting, the waterworks were formally opened for public use on 24 May 1878.[102] At a joyful ceremony, the people of Dacca expressed their gratitude to Khwaja now Nawab Abdul Ghani for his philanthropic work.[103] *The Bengal Times* sets the scene:

> We are glad to see on Thursday last, that the water was running freely through the town. The little native children appeared to revel in it. It appeared to us scarcely fit for drinking purposes, having an earthy taste, and being rather thick, but in time we have no doubt that this defect will be remedied and the munificence of our kind hearted Nawab be carried to a successful end. During the distressing hot weather of the last few days, a plentiful water supply has been a boon to the thirsty thousands of Dacca.[104]

At first water was supplied to a very limited area; the water-pipes being laid over about four miles, from the Engine House near Lalbagh through the main Bazaar Street as far as the Kotwali by the Chauk and Mitford Hospital. At Kotwali they branched off in two directions—one passed by the Narinda Road and the Iron Suspension Bridge and the other ran towards the Jail. Besides supplying water to the Mitford Hospital, the Lunatic Asylum, the Jail and the Chauk Bazar, the mains provided for all the people living along their routes through twenty-five hydrants. The daily supply of water at first amounted to about 35,000 gallons, much less than the actual requirements of the town or what the pumping engines could provide. But the supply of water could not be increased without an extension of the mains and for this there were no funds.[105]

The limited supply of filtered water naturally failed to achieve the main purpose of the waterworks, that of preventing people from drinking impure water and of closing down polluted wells, canals and the like. Although most people within reach of the hydrants readily used them, large numbers continued to obtain their drinking water from traditional sources.

The problem again was one of money, for the Municipality was unable to afford any further extension of the mains.[106] It was also now discovered that the defective siting of the reservoir meant that some areas of the city could not be served at all. Another unwelcome discovery in 1880 was that even though only a part of the city had been supplied, maintenance charges, at Rs. 7,500 per annum, were nearly double the interest accruing on the Water-Works Maintenance Fund. In order to meet the difference, the Municipality had either to increase existing taxes or raise new ones. In either case this would amount to an indirect water-rate and so would contravene the conditions imposed by Nawab Abdul Ghani.

One solution considered was to offer a piped supply to householders willing to pay for the amenity and thus to secure revenue, though this would require an extension of the mains to the more prosperous parts of the city. Discussion of this proposal was overtaken, however, by a malaria epidemic in 1880, with such heavy mortality in north-western areas and the suburbs of Nawabganj and Amligolah that a temporary hospital had to be opened in Lalbagh.[107] Most of the north-western mahallas were, however, fearfully unhealthy because of poor drainage and the pollution of canals and wells which were the sources of drinking water.[108] In a report specially called for by the Bengal Government, Dr John Gay French, the Civil Surgeon of Dacca, emphasized that if the health of these suburbs were to be improved, pure drinking water had to be made available.[109] The Bengal Government responded by instructing the local officials to extend the water supply to these areas.

On 19 December 1881, the municipal commissioners decided to draw Rs. 25,000 from the Water-Works Maintenance Fund to extend the water mains along the Chaudhuri Bazar, Nawabganj, Amligolah, Lalbagh Masjid, Bangshal, Bangla Bazar and Cemetery roads. The Divisional Commissioner F. H. Pellew rejected the proposal to raid the Maintenance Fund as illegal.[110] Unable to raise money from the Maintenance Fund, the commissioners then resolved to apply to the Government of India for a loan of one lakh of rupees under the Local Authorities Loan Act, Act XI of 1879, to be used not only to extend the water supply but also to construct additional reservoirs, to repair the existing ones and to modernize the waterworks. The capital and interest of the loan would be repaid from the savings on the municipal police—the cost of which was to be borne by the government itself from August 1882. The District Magistrate, Charles Cecil Stevens, while forwarding the above resolutions to government stressed the urgency of their case.[111]

The application for the loan led to a slow and vexatious correspondence such as had engulfed the earlier application for a loan. By now, however, the Government of India had veered right round in favour of borrowing for local improvements on the open market, and the application was accordingly turned down.[112] The Municipality thereafter decided to issue debentures on the open market. The issue was not a success however, and the commissioners turned again to the Maintenance Fund for their capital. In March 1883, they decided to borrow the entire Rs. 50,000 of the Fund, and submitted a definite proposal to the Government of India, which was sanctioned after much correspondence in February 1884.[113]

The money was urgently needed, for only when the water-mains served the whole town would it be possible to consider banning the use of traditional water supplies. But in 1882 there was an alarming discovery that during certain months of the year the hydrant water itself was likely to be contaminated. This was due to percolation of sub-soil water—which was diluted sewage in Dacca—into the filtered water reservoir. The bottom of the filtering beds was nine feet below ground level; therefore when the sub-soil water rose above this mark during the monsoon months of June to October, it passed into the filtering beds and polluted the water.

The Government Chemical Engineer who revealed this information reported to Dr Alexander Crombie, the Civil Surgeon of Dacca, that his analysis had also showed that the water of the large public wells much used by the people was heavily polluted, and thus totally unfit for consumption. When furnished with this information, Dr Crombie at once wrote to the municipal commissioners urging them not only to put the filtered water reservoir right but also to close all the cess-pools and wells, both public and private, beginning with the areas already supplied by the hydrants.[114]

The commissioners at once set about making the reservoir watertight, and closing the public wells that lay adjacent to cess-pits and near the existing water-main lines. To protect the hydrants they prohibited the construction of drains or cess-pits in their proximity and ordered householders with such items on their properties, either to close them immediately or to disclaim ownership so that the Municipality could fill them in. But although the European commissioners wanted to close private wells, too, along the hydrant line, the Indian members rejected these recommendations as likely to cause inconvenience, especially to women in purdah.[115] They also argued that the closure of cess-pits and other measures already taken would largely stop the contamination of the wells. Closure was therefore postponed until piped water could be offered to every household. Since this was a costly operation, the Municipality made no attempt to undertake it. A few wealthy households however obtained piped connections by providing all the costs themselves. The bulk of the population had to rely on an extension of the hydrant supply.

This supply was enlarged impressively. In 1878, 35,000 gallons of filtered water had been supplied; by 1883, that figure had increased to 95,000 gallons a day. The mains were extended to a total length of eight and a half miles and almost two-thirds of Dacca's inhabitants were provided with access to filtered water. With so much achieved the commissioners naturally wanted to provide for the other third of the population. The permission given to borrow the Rs. 50,000 of the Maintenance Fund made it possible to continue extension of the water supply from municipal funds. They were aided again by private benefactors. In 1884, Khwaja, now Nawab Ahsanullah offered to extend the mains complete with hydrants at his own cost from Nawabpur road through the thickly populated parts of Thatari Bazar as far as his private garden house at Dilkusha on condition that the extension should be called the Connaught Extension in commemoration of the visit to Calcutta of His Royal Highness the Duke of Connaught. The Municipality accepted the terms of the offer, and the Connaught Extension was handed over to the Municipality for public use on 24 October 1884.[116] The same year Madan Mohan Basak similarly offered to extend the mains along Cemetery Road to Jorepul, a scheme completed in 1886. Public and private effort combined by 1893 to extend the mains to a total of over sixteen miles with 129 hydrants and 14 stand-pipes for street-watering. The average daily supply of filtered water had risen to 360,000 gallons while

70,000 of the total population of about 84,000 had access to water, amounting to somewhat more than five gallons a day.[117] The city as a whole, however, was only supplied with pure water in the twentieth century.

What is true, nevertheless, was that the supply of filtered water provided Dacca with one of its primary wants and coincided with an impressive improvement in public health. As early as 1879, the vice-chairman, Khwaja Muhammed Asghar, noted in the annual report,

> It is the general belief of almost all classes of people in Dacca that the comparatively fewer cases of cholera and other epidemic diseases in several portions of the town during the year were mainly owing to the distribution of filtered water.[118]

In December 1880, the *Dhaka Prokash* commented,

> Since the supply of filtered water began, the health of the people living along the main roads along which the pipes were laid out, has not suffered at all. Cholera which was here so long creating havoc every year has now disappeared from the central parts of the town. Even the prevalence of fever, dysentry and so on has declined.[119]

While the gradual extension of water-supplies contributed greatly to the improvement of urban life, the Municipality also turned their attention to other problems. In Dacca, the overcrowded lodging-houses or messes rented by students attending schools and colleges were a health problem on which the medical authorities regularly pressed the Municipality.[120] The commissioners in the 1870s instructed lodging-house owners to keep their houses clean, and ordered the municipal overseers to ensure that this was done. The commissioners also contributed funds for the registration of births and deaths by the city police, and for the vaccination programme of the Civil Surgeon though this was limited by the strong religious opposition by Vaishnavite Hindus and Faraizi Muslims alike.[121] In this regard the experience of Dacca was not unique for opposition to vaccination was common in almost every town including places like Delhi.[122]

The municipal commissioners also took positive steps especially under the pressure of the Civil Surgeons for the carc of the sick and indigent, and gave succour to the needy. They made a free disrtibution of medicine on several occasions, and spent money to combat the serious cholera, smallpox and fever epidemics. Prior to their taking over the charge of the Mitford Hospital in 1882, they made regular contributions to its funds, especially during the financial crisis of the 1870s. After 1882, they bore all the expenses of the hospital, and also provided special wings for the treatment of venereal diseases.

The disposal of dead was also vigorously tackled. There were two traditional burning ghats for the cremation of Hindus, one at Dayaganj on the Dulai Khal in the east and another on the Bagchandka Char in the Buriganga to the west. But because of the high price of firewood and the exorbitant charges by the domes who arranged the funeral pyres, poorer Hindu families could not afford the price of a complete cremation. The semi-charred corpses were immersed in the river—'a bamboo stake is then driven through the belly into the bed of the stream'.[123]

The Municipality first concentrated on attempts on having corpses cremated thoroughly. But the two burning ghats were located at a considerable distance, and were difficult to reach in the rains. In 1869, therefore, District Magistrate Graham called a public meeting to solicit contributions from the Hindus of Dacca for two new pucka burning ghats nearer the city. Many leading Hindus, including the Basaks of Nawabpur, promised contributions.[124] However, the charitable and civic impulse proved evanescent, and the scheme was eventually dropped for lack of funds. It was not until 1874, therefore, that the Municipality constructed two ghats, one at Silbari in Postogola, the other at Kanuzis Char, the cost being largely borne by Babu Govinda Chandra Datta, a former municipal commissioner and a zamindar of Dacca. All burning ghats were kept under strict municipal surveillance and at the two new ghats contractors were appointed who supplied the wood and other materials for cremation at a fixed charge of three and a half rupees for adults and one rupee and two annas for children under the age of ten. Municipal domes were appointed to oversee cremations. High-caste Hindus, however, complained that at the municipal ghats all castes used the same facilities,[125] and many among them made private arrangements for cremation elsewhere. The lower and poorer castes on the other hand complained of the high fees charged. Nevertheless the improvements were considerable, and one health hazard had certainly been curbed.

In the same period arrangements for burial of the dead, haphazard for a long time, were also reformed. The three Christian cemeteries, for Europeans, Armenians and native converts were well kept, but Muslim graveyards within the city were overcrowded and the common practice of burying the dead within the house compound, or on vacant land between houses—'in the midst of the living', as an outraged Dr Wise put it in 1868—was clearly a major risk to public health. In 1867 the municipal commissioners renovated the public graveyard at Aga Sadiq Maidan but since the other graveyards in the city were not closed, few Muslims used it. In 1868, therefore, twelve old graveyards, both public and private, in the Champatali, Begam Bazar, Purab Darwaza and Aga Naqi Dewri mahallas were listed for closure. This was sanctioned by government in 1869[126] and strictly enforced by a subcommittee consisting of Graham, Dr Wise and Khwaja Ahsanullah. The commissioners also resolved rigidly to enforce the by-laws which forbade burials at places other than designated public cemeteries, while at the same time, a second burial ground was laid out at Purana Paltan to serve the population further to the north and east. Both the siting of the new graveyard and the closure of the old were accepted without protest by the Muslims of the city. Grave-digging in the municipal graveyards was done on contract and to rules laid down by the medical authorities, though with no methodical layout of plots. By 1882, Aga Sadiq Maidan cemetery, the nearer to the heart of the city, and therefore heavily used, had become 'dangerous to the health of the town and unfit for further use'. It was replaced by a large new site at Purana Nikas, northwest of the city.

The problem of the disposal of the dead was not, however, totally solved. Old habits and prejudices persisted; the Muslims continued to use private burial grounds, especially those at the eastern end of the town, where the Municipality had not provided any ground until a new graveyard was laid out at Gandria in 1889. And more unfortunate still, no complete stoppage could be made to the practice of interment within the enclosures of private dwellings.[127]

Efforts were also seriously made to reform the city's markets for these were least known for their cleanliness. As trade and commerce returned to the city and business ran at a brisk pace, especially during the latter half of the century, attention to reforming the markets was all the more urgently required. But before that the condition of the markets was really deplorable. Even the Chauk Bazar had so degenerated that Dr Cutcliffe in 1868 described it as 'discreditable in any town and conspicuously disgraceful in such a city as Dacca'. None of the city's twelve markets was properly swept and cleaned, while most lacked any effective drainage capable of coping with monsoon rain, or even with the water constantly used in the hot weather to keep fish and vegetables fresh. Again, though there were numbers of buchers' shops in these markets, and there was in Dacca a separate colony of butchers Kosaitoli, there were no proper slaughter-houses in the city.

There being no specific laws to deal with the public markets, the Municipality tried to improve them by enforcing the provisions of Act III of 1864 and the by-laws. However, the general insanitary condition of markets throughout the towns of Bengal drew repeated condemnation from the Sanitary Commission which in 1876 drove the Bengal Government to legislate for them. The new Municipal Act, Act V of 1876, therefore empowered the com missioners to establish new municipal markets and provide licences for private markets. Such licences, renewable annually, would be granted free of charge by the commissioners, but only upon their chairman's certificate that the land occupied by the bazaar 'is fit to be used as a market...' The commissioners would have the power to prohibit the use of uncertificated and unlicensed markets.[128]

The Bengal Government had suggested to the Dacca Municipality that it apply the sections relating to municipal markets, but it was met with the reply that there were no municipal markets in Dacca and no intention of establishing any.[129] Initially the commissioners had also been indifferent to using the new powers to improve the sanitary condition of private markets in Dacca. But under strong pressure from the Civil Surgeon the relevant sections of the Act were enforced in December 1876. Even then little use was made of the new powers, for in 1879 the Sanitary Commission had again to report that the private markets in Dacca were 'kept in a filthy condition.'[130] (That many of the markets were owned by the commissioners themselves or by their relatives and by other notables of Dacca, may well account for the inaction.) However, the repeated complaints of the Sanitary Commission made continued neglect difficult and the commissioners did gradually take stricter measures to improve market sanitation. On many occasions the Magistrate also issued notices against the sale of rotten fish or vegetables, and penalized the offenders for endangering the health of the city. However, such measures often backfired, for the ordinary and lower classes of people in Dacca in those days were extremely prone to go on strike in protest against what they described as official high-handedness. When in 1882 the fishmongers were penalized for selling bad fish, they struck at once, and the complete withdrawal of fish from the markets caused great distress to the fish-loving Daccaites.[131]

At much the same time, the commissioners were at last driven to act to clean up the city's slaughter-houses. Initially they had taken no major steps except banishing the slaughter-house for cattle to the Topkhana, half a mile beyond the northern limits of the city. The offal was thrown into the jungle to be devoured by crows, vultures, dogs and jackals, but there was no drainage system into which the blood and excrement could be sluiced away.

In 1875 the Commanding Officer of the Native Infantry at Dacca, objecting to the presence of the Topkhana slaughter-house so near his troops' camping site (Purana Paltan), compelled the Municipality to move it. At the new site (the exact location of which is not known), the Municipality built a large masonry platform and appointed a mehtar to keep it clean. But the Civil Surgeon, Dr H. B. Purves, in 1881 found the place 'sickening and revolting', and asked the Municipality to close it, and build a new one 'upon approved principles'.[132] The vice-chairman, Arthur Tute, immediately wrote to the Calcutta Municipality for plans of their model slaughter-house, and in 1882 the commissioners sanctioned Rs. 2,000 for one. Though none was built during the period under review, stricter measures were taken to clear offal and blood regularly from the existing slaughter-houses, and to cart these for burial in the municipal trenching grounds.[133] But until an effective drainage system had been created for the city as a whole, truly hygienic slaughter-houses were impossible to attain.

From the middle of the century all the British experts had emphasized that proper drainage systems for Indian towns were essential for healthy urban life. In Dacca, however, actual progress was minimal.

A comprehensive scheme was first evolved in the 1860s for a complete drainage system, with a network of surface drains carrying the city's entire fluid refuse into the Dulai Khal and thence to the Buriganga. The Dulai would thus have become the main drainage channel of Dacca—a task which it already performed to some extent. The scheme formed one of the items of Cutcliffe and Graham's multi-lakh project for the development of Dacca. Unfortunately, like some other schemes, this too was not implemented for lack of funds, or the willpower to procure them.

In the event, the Municipality spent very little money on the drainage of the city. It constructed a few masonry and kutcha surface drains along the main streets which were kept reasonably clean and open. Nothing was done, however, to provide for the congested localities; there most of the houses were without any drainage at all. Most people in Dacca, as the Sanitary Commissioner Dr W. H. Gregg reported as late as 1889, lived 'in the concentrated essence of filth of all descriptions as there is no proper drainage to carry it away.'

The municipal commissioners were not unaware of the problem. In 1882–3, their vice-chairman, Koylash Chandra Ghosh, identified the accumulation of liquid sewage and rain-water in house premises as a major cause of unhealthiness in Dacca,[134] a verdict repeated in the report for 1883–4,

> Proper drainage is a very pressing want of this municipality. The drainage is very defective in every respect and besides objectionable. All the main outlets fall into the [Dulai] Khal ... The pollution of the Khal is a serious matter and the only way in which this can be avoided or remedied is by carrying out a general drainage scheme on an extensive and therefore expensive scale. Unfortunately the Commissioners have not the means of doing anything in this direction.[135]

The problem of drainage remained unsolved. At different times in the 1870s and 1880s the levels of the town were measured as a preliminary step towards devising a better system of drainage but further action could not be taken for lack of funds.

Another aspect of Dacca's urban life which remained largely untouched was the hapless slums. Indeed the municipal authorities appeared insensitive to the need for slum clearance, their standard excuse being the leanness of their purse. Cosmetic changes on the periphery of these areas were carried out, such as new roadworks through compulsory purchases and demolitions, but the inhabitants were otherwise left to their own devices. Tables 4 and 5 show the income and expenditure distribution of the Dacca Municipality between 1865 and 1885.

The history of urban development of Dacca during this period was one of mixed success. The task faced by the municipal authorities had been daunting. However, both the Municipal Committee and Dacca Municipality went about them steadily. Whereas the former achieved little success owing to its lack of legal power, the latter's record was more impressive, though it too could not solve all the urban problems. This was largely due to lack of funds. While the people of Dacca were generally hostile to being directly taxed for their municipal needs, the municipal commissioners as a body also showed no readiness to brave the popular wrath by forcing taxes through. There was, however, considerable poverty, and no injection of substantial government funds. But more important, there was also a lack of awareness of the benefit of improved modes of urban living. In Dacca, the impulse to improvement came from the British officials with their mid-Victorian zeal

Table 4. *A statement showing the income (excluding the balance of previous Year) and expenditure of the Dacca Municipality in the 1860s, 1870s and 1880s*

Year	Income (in rupees)	Expenditure (in rupees)
1865–6	53,469	48,409
1870–1	47,730	47,646
1875–6	82,272	68,158
1880–1	111,476	89,510
1884–5	142,098	156,231

Source: Annual Administration Report of the Dacca Municipality, DMRR, Collection 1.

Table 5. *Expenditure distribution of the Dacca Municipality (in Rupees. Figures rounded off to nearest hundred)*

Year	Roads	Conservancy	Police	Public Health	Water Supply	Street Lighting	Education	Others	Total
1865–66	16,700 (34.50%)	9,000 (18.59%)	11,300 (23.34%)					11,400 (23.55%)	48,400
1870–71	8,600 (18.14%)	9,100 (19.07%)	16,500 (35.10%)	360 (0.75%)				13,140 (27.95%)	47,700
1875–76	11,200 (16.71%)	22,400 (33.43%)	15,300 (22.83%)	360 (0.53%)				17,740 (26.47%)	67,000
1880–81	12,600 (14.07%)	30,300 (33.85%)	17,000 (18.99%)	9,800 (10.94%)	4,100 (4.58%)	1,100 (1.22%)		14,600 (16.31%)	89,500
1884–85	30,100 (19.14%)	33,200 (21.11%)		24,600 (15.64%)	19,800 (12.59%)	4,200 (2.67%)	600 (0.38%)	44,700 (28.43%)	157,200

Source: Administration Reports of the Dacca Municipality.

for cleanliness and planned development. In contrast, in Ahmedabad, as Gillion records, the desire and drive often came from the local people helped by the city's indigenous institutions, the result being far more satisfactory than in Dacca.

Even so, by 1885, amenities unheard of previously, like a pure water-supply, conservancy system, and street-lights, were at every Daccaite's doorstep. The city could also take pride in having some important landmarks of modern urban life—metalled roads, improved markets, good transport, municipal gardens and a hospital, like its more prosperous counterparts Calcutta and Bombay or its older sister-city Delhi. With such amenities Dacca by the late nineteenth century had become a much better place to live in; a vast improvement on the decaying conurbation of the previous half-century. More important, its municipal progress was certainly far greater than that of many other Bengal towns. Detailed comparisons must await the completion of extensive urban studies. But for the moment, the *Bighyapani*, the Dacca Bengali weekly, a regular critic of the Dacca Municipality, provides a valuable testimony. In 1866 the paper along with its staff was moved to Mymensingh by its proprietor. Soon after this transfer, the editor penned a leader which must have pleased the city fathers. Struck by his new insanitary and polluted surroundings he confessed that looking 'at the disgracefully dirty condition of Mymensingh', he felt inclined to praise the Dacca Municipality for their laudable work.[136]

What is more, by 1884 the stage had been reached when the paternalist official domination of the civic body could be brought to an end and the choice of future patterns of development could be entrusted to the citizenry and their elected representatives.

NOTES TO CHAPTER VII

1 C. E. Buckland, *Bengal Under the Lieutenant-Governors*, I, 293–4.
2 Argal, *Municipal Government*, 7; also J. B. Harrison, 'Allahabad: A Sanitary History' in K. Ballhatchet and J. Harrison (eds.), *The City in South Asia*, 170–1.
3 For details see H. Tinker, *Local Self-Government in India, Pakistan and Burma*, ch. II, and B. B. Misra, *Administrative History of India.*
4 See Tinker, *Local Self-Government*, ch. II.
5 *Calcutta Gazette*, 27 July 1864.
6 Ibid.
7 Magistrate to Div. Comm. 4 September 1866 (discovered at DMRR).
8 B. C. Pal, *Memoirs of My Life and Times*, I, 167, 169, 181.
9 Proceedings of the municipal commissioners of Dacca, *DP*, 3 Bhadra 1271 (18 August 1864).
10 Gillion, *Ahmedabad*, 116–17, *et passim.*
11 Many Daccaites were to complain of the lack of a true city element in the membership of the municipality.
12 J. N. Sil and L. Johnson, 'A Brief History of the Dacca Municipality', DMRR, Coll. XXXII.
13 Municipal Proc., 15 September 1865.
14 Report of the vice-chairman G. Bellet, BJP, CCCCXXXIII, 24 October 1868, 134.
15 Editorial, *DP*, 1 Magh 1271 (13 January 1865).
16 *DP*, 7 Phalgun 1271 (17 February 1865).
17 Report of the vice-chairman, BJP, CCCCXXXIII, 134.
18 Ibid.
19 Administration Report of the Dacca Municipality for 1865–6. (Discovered at DMRR; now preserved with the other Administration Reports.)
20 Municipal Proc., 15 March 1867.
21 ARDM for 1875–6; DMRR, Coll. 1.
22 ARDM for 1874–5; DMRR, Coll. 1.
23 Sil and Johnson, 'Dacca Municipality'.
24 BJP, CXLVII, 11 October 1865, 250.
25 Municipal Proc., 1 February 1867.
26 Municipal Proc., 17 June 1867.
27 Clay, *Principal Heads*, 88.
28 BJP, CCCCXXXIII, 14 December 1866, 143.
29 Ibid., 14 December 1866, 144.
30 See editorial, *DP*, 23 Poush 1273 (6 January 1867).
31 Quoted in Magistrate to Div. Comm. 27 May 1868, BJP, CCCCXXXIII, 24 October 1868, 133.
32 *RSC* for 1868–9, part II, 97–129.
33 RNN, 21 January 1865.
34 ARDM for 1865–6, DMRR.

35 Div. Comm, to GB, 2 June 1868, BJP, CCCCXXXIII, 24 October 1868, 133 133.
36 Mackenna to the Lt-Governor of Bengal, 26 March 1868, BJP, CCCCXXXIII, 24 October 1868, 131.
37 Div. Comm. to GB, 2 June 1868, BJP, CCCCXXXIII, 24 October 1868, 133.
38 Magistrate to Div. Comm., 27 May 1868; Ibid.
39 GB to Div. Comm., 27 May 1868; Ibid.
40 [George Graham], *Life in the Mofussil*, II, 135–6.
41 He quoted from Mr Simon, the Sanitary Officer with the Privy Council, for example, on the causes of disease in British cities and their remedies.
42 Dr Cutcliffe had made similar plans for some of the towns in the Meerut Division.
43 Plan of Dr Cutcliffe, BJP, CCCCXXXIII, 30 September 1869, 28.
44 See Edwin Chadwick, *Report on the Sanitary Condition... of Great Britain.*
45 See. P Geddes, *Report on Town Planning, Dacca:* also P. Kitchen, *An Introduction to the Ideas and Life of Patrick Geddes...*, 256–7.
46 BJP, CCCCXXXIII, 33, March 1870, 2.
47 *DP*, 21 Baisakh 1276 (2 May 1869), 88–91.
48 RNN, 5 June 1869.
49 See Gillion, *Ahmedabad;* see also Narayani Gupta, *Delhi Between the Empires, 1803–1931, 229, et passim.*
50 Municipal Proc., 10 May 1869.
51 Graham to Simson 12 June 1869, BJP, CCCCXXXIII, 30 September 1869, 28. Graham admitted that he had failed to induce the wealthy of Dacca to subscribe to a loan.
52 Simson was a very experienced official; for nearly a decade he served the district and division of Dacca as Magistrate and Commissioner. He knew the problems of Dacca city and its people more intimately than any of his other contemporaries who held the charge of the city. He also knew very well the countryside. For an account of his sporting activites in Dacca see F. B. Simson, *Letters on Sport in Eastern Bengal.*
53 *Life in the Mofussil*, III, 136.
54 Simson to GB, 27 June 1869, BJP, CCCCXXXIII, 30 September 1869, 27.
55 GB to Div. Comm., 27 June 1869, BJP, CCCCXXXIII, 30 September 1869, 27.
56 Sanitary Commissioner to GB, 20 December 1869, BJP, CCCXXXIII, 33, March 1870, I.
57 In gratitude for his public service, the commissioners of the Municipality later named a street of Dacca after him. Lyall Street in old Dacca still bears his name.
58 Government had refused on financial grounds to depute one of its engineers.
59 Lyall to Div. Comm., 26 February 1870, BJP, CCCCXXXIII, 33, April 1870, 107.
60 Simson to GB, 23 March 1870, ibid., 106.
61 Resolution of the Lt-Governor, 14 April 1870, ibid., 108.
62 In February, the Bengal Government noted that in Dacca, where great efforts had been made of late to introduce improvement, the Municipality

was decidedly unpopular; see the *Annual Report on Municipal Taxation and Expenditure in the Lower Provinces of Bengal* for 1873–4, 7.

63 The *Prokash* never regarded the commissioners fit persons. It particularly resented the absence of English-educated Daccaites on the Municipal Committee. Hence it was always unwilling to give credit to the Municipality even when it did some notable works.

64 *DP*, 16 Poush 1279 (29 December 1872).

65 BJP, CCCCXXXIII, 33, March 1870, 2.

66 Government was still consulting the P. W. D., then in charge of the Dulai Khal, about the terms on which it might be handed over to the Municipality.

67 Leader article, *DP*, 31 Bhadra 1279 (15 September 1872).

68 GB to Div. Comm., 9 October 1871, BJP, 246, October 1871, 89.

69 It does not seem that any attempt was made to revive the plan for raising a loan on the open market.

70 Chairman to Div. Comm., 25 April 1872, BJP, 249, June 1872, 108.

71 GB to Div. Comm., 21 June 1872, BJP, 249, June 1872, 110.

72 Chairman to Div. Comm., 16 July 1872, BJP, 250 August 1872, 108.

73 GI to GB, BJP, 251, November 1872, 241–2.

74 GB to Div. Comm., BJP, 251, December 1872, 252.

75 BJP, 257, July 1875, 83A (4–5).

76 ARDM for 1875–6, DMRR, coll 1. A new Municipal Act was about to be enacted.

77 See R. L. Ross and J. G. Cumming, *Municipal Administration and Reform in Patna City;* see the chapter on 'The Conservancy of Latrines: the Difficulties, Practical and Financial,' 15. As in Dacca early hopes were also not fulfilled in Patna.

78 BJP, 923, September 1876, 150 (78–9).

79 Municipal Proc., 9 October 1877.

80 Municipal Proc., 24 October 1878.

81 Bengal Municipal Proceedings, 1327, March 1879, file 204 (1–3).

82 A. Forbes, 'A Note on the Increase of the Privy-Tax', dated 18 June 1879, DMRR, Coll. 28, file II.

83 Municipal Proc., 2 September 1879.

84 Later these areas were also excluded from the jurisdiction of the Municipality as the inhabitants from these places represented that since they received no municipal benefits they should be exempted from municipal taxes.

85 ARDM for 1879–80, DMRR, Coll. 1.

86 But in 1885 the Municipality could only clean 5,000 privies out of an estimated 12,000. This involved a labour force of 180 mehtars and 90 mehtranis, and 140 filth carts and 140 bullocks.

87 ARDM for 1886–7, DMRR, Coll. 1.

88 ARDM for 1883–4, DMRR, Coll. 1.

89 RNN, 8 March 1873; see also *DP*, 9 Asarh 1291 (22 June 1884).

90 Leader article, *BT*, 4 May 1881.

91 *DP*, 19 Ashwin 1281 (August 1874). Registration of hackney-carriages and palankeens was first introduced in Calcutta in 1864 under Act I of that year.

92 Ticca-Garry, DMRR, Coll. XXXII, file 20.
93 BMP, 923, September 1876, collection I5C (81).
94 Municipal Proc., 11 September 1877.
95 ARDM for 1878–9, DMRR, Coll. 1.
96 ARDM for 1886–7, DMRR, Coll. 1.
97 Electric lights were installed in Dacca in 1901.
98 Simson to GB, 14 April 1869, BJP, CCCCXXXIII, 28 May 1869, 1. The early water supply of Calcutta was carried in open aqueducts in this fashion See plate 8 facing page 181 in S. W. Goode's *Municipal Calcutta, its Institutions in their Origin and Growth.*
99 It has been wrongly stated by every writer on Dacca that this money was donated by Abdul Ghani rather than by his son, for example, see Dani, *Dacca;* for a brief history of the donation compiled by the chairman of the Municipality, A. W. Paul, in 1883, see Bengal Municipal Proceedings, 2028, November 1883, 16 (18–19)
100 *The Pioneer*, 15 August 1874.
101 Report on the Dacca Water-Works by Major Smyth, the Superintending Engineer, P. W. D., 4 December, 1879, BMP, 1479, January 1880, collection 16 (6–7).
102 It consisted of two vertical immersion boilers and two engines, with four settling tanks, two filter beds and one filtered-water reservoir.
103 *DP*, 13 Jaishta 1285 (26 May 1878); Khwaja Abdul Ghani, in 1875, was awarded the title of Nawab by the Government of India, see F. B. Bradley-Birt, *Twelve Men of Bengal in the Nineteenth Century*, 182.
104 *BT*, 15 June 1878.
105 Report of Major Smyth, BMP, 1479, January 1880, collection 16 (6–7).
106 In 1879 some small addition was made possible by another gift of Rs. 20,000 from the Nawab family to commemorate Queen Victoria's assumption of the title 'Empress of India', though use of the main was delayed because the hydrants had to be imported from England.
107 Altogether 740 people died of malaria in that year.
108 *RSC* for 1880, 69.
109 BMP, 1838, July 1882, collection 16 (29).
110 Ibid., collection 16 (31).
111 Ibid., collection 16 (33).
112 GB to Div. Comm., 23 June 1882, Ibid., collection 16 (37).
113 GB to Div. Comm., 13 February 1884, BMP (Misc Branch), 2242, March 1884, collection 16 (6).
114 BMP, 2029, December 1883, collection 1 (103).
115 Municipal Proc., 12 January 1883. The Indian members present at the meeting were the vice-chairman Koilash Chandra Ghosh; Govinda Chandra Das; Madan Mohan Basak; Dina Nath Dhar; Srinath Rai; Iswar Chandra Das; Brojendra Kumar Roy; Maulvie Obaidullah; Shakauddin Mahmud; and Syed Golam Mustafa.
116 Nawab Ahsanullah to the chairman, 1 February 1884, 'Water Works Extension Files,' DMRR, Coll. XXXI.
117 Report on the Dacca Water-Works by K. M. Asghar, DMRR, coll. XXXI.

118 ARDM for 1878–9, DMRR, Coll. 1.
119 *DP*, 21 Aghrayana 1287 (5 December 1880).
120 *RSC* for 1868, 11, 116.
121 *DP*, Aghrayana 1276 (21 November 1869); *RSC* for 1883.
122 N. Gupta, *Delhi*, 163.
123 *RSC* for 1868, II, 101.
124 Municipal Proc., 25 March 1869; also *DP*, 11 Jaishta 1276 (23 May 1869).
125 *Urdu Guide*, 20 February 1876, RNN, 4 March 1876, 6.
126 BJP, CCCCXXXIII, 28 April 1869, 144.
127 *RSC* for 1881, appendix V.
128 Sections 209–302. *The Acts of the Lieutenant-Governor of Bengal in Council* for 1876.
129 Chairman to Div. Comm., 9 September 1876, BMP, 923, October 1876, file 75 A (15).
130 *RSC* for 1880, see appendix IV to the report.
131 *DP*, 12 Ashwin 1289 (16 September 1882).
132 Civil Surgeon to the Municipality, August 1881, DMRR, coll. XXXII, file 20.
133 ARDM for 1883–4, DMRR, coll. 1.
134 ARDM for 1882–3, DMRR, Coll. 1.
135 ARDM for 1883–4, DMRR, Coll. 1.
136 RNN, week ending 30 June 1866.

CHAPTER VIII

GROWTH OF ELECTIVE LOCAL GOVERNMENT

The demand for truly representative local self-government, operated under an elective system, was made by middle-class liberals, both Indian and British, soon after the establishment of municipalities in India in the 1860s.[1] In response, after granting a measure of self-government to the three Presidency cities,[2] the central and provincial governments extended the privilege to the other towns by a series of Acts. Thus in Bengal the election of two-thirds of the members including the chairman and vice-chairman was first allowed under Act VI of 1868, on condition of prior application to government. But the elective principle was not automatically put into practice, and though Act II of 1873 authorized the ratepayers to elect their chairman where Act III of 1864 was already in force, by 1884 the Bengal government had applied Act II only to Serampore, Krishnagar and Burdwan.[3] It was Act III of 1884 which extended the elective system to all the important municipalities in the province, Dacca included.

A demand for an elected municipality had early been heard in Dacca among the English-educated middle class, and the long delay in granting the demand, even after Burdwan and Krishnagar had received the privilege in 1875, was particularly galling. The criticism of the unreformed system was, therefore, detailed and sweeping.

One major criticism was of the dominant role, the tutelage, of the District Magistrate, the *ex-officio* chairman of the municipality. When he lacked interest in municipal affairs, or when he was pre-occupied by other duties, the administration of the city suffered. When he was more involved, too often he used his prestige and authority to limit the freedom of discussion and action of the commissioners, the native members particularly. Critics also argued that he used his power to appoint commissioners with much partisanship, selecting Ji Huzoors and Ap Ke Wastes, or yes-men and toadies, thus making the municipality even more of a one-man show. A second issue was that while the ratepayers provided the money they had no say in the municipal administration and no control over the allotment of its funds. Most of the non-official native commissioners, big zamindars, merchants and bankers, selected from the same areas year after year, were quite ignorant of the true state of the city and the living conditions of its poorer classes. As a result municipal funds were unfairly spent upon the improvement of those parts where the Europeans, rich Indians or the commissioners themselves lived, to the neglect of the rest of the city. Many native members failed to attend municipal meetings, oppression of the ratepayers by municipal employees was ignored, and, while no action was taken against commissioners who broke municipal laws, ordinary ratepayers who did so were severely fined and punished.[4] The remedy for all these grievances and defects, it was argued, was to do away with control by officials, and with obstructive, self-seeking commissioners, by transforming the Dacca Municipality into a representative elected body.

The more articulate sections of the citizenry voiced their discontent in public meetings and through petitions to the government. They were strongly supported by the vernacular press, and the European papers too expressed disappointment at municipal failures and maladministration and demanded electoral reform.[5] There was however a measure of difference between the two in their criticism. The vernacular press attacked the composition of the municipality and called it a useless body, complained of the heavy burden of municipal taxes, and often unfairly ascribed all the city's ills to the commissioners' inefficiency. The European press on the other hand had more to say on the public-health problems, sanitation and cleanliness of the city. It poured scorn on the attitudes of rich Indians who would fritter away thousands of rupees on weddings and yet were loth to help pay for civic improvements. Following the bitterness created by the Ilbert Bill, the European press moreover took an unsympathetic view of the Indian demand for constitutional reform of the municipality.

There was much to criticize in the performance of the Dacca Municipality. But the general insanitary and neglected state of Dacca upon which the critics harped, certainly did not originate in any inefficiency or indifference of the municipal commissioners.[6] Nor were all the non-official commissioners mere 'yes men', any more than they were as a group ignorant and selfish, without interest in improvement. Even though the Magistrate kept a tight rein upon the administration, he allowed complete freedom of discussion to the commissioners, so that most policy decisions and administrative actions were taken upon majority votes. In course of time—perhaps partly in answer to criticism—many able, educated and public-spirited individuals had been appointed. Such men as Khwaja Muhammad Asghar,[7] the son-in-law of Nawab Abdul Ghani, Koilash Chandra Ghosh, the Headmaster of the Dacca Collegiate School, Dr Prosanna Kumar Roy, the Science Professor of the Dacca College, or Upendra Nath Mitra, the Law Lecturer of the Dacca College and the Government Pleader, represented a great improvement in the quality of the municipal commissioners. The only criticism of the Magistrates which is difficult to rebut is that they persisted for too long in requiring that the vice-chairman and the secretary should be European. Their assumption that Europeans would ensure greater administrative efficiency was itself unwarranted, while their regular appointment left the municipality open to attack as both an official and a European preserve.

However, the fundamental motive of the critics was to wrest control of the municipal administration from the hands of the officials and their chosen favourites. The setting up of municipalities in the country was a response to the need to introduce local taxes for municipal purposes when the government found itself unable to allot any substantial funds on this account. Such taxation was to be made palatable by involving local residents in municipal administration. The local officials who were asked to form such bodies invariably selected people who were not only influential and wealthy but loyal to government. Thus in Dacca the members of the Nawab family, leading bankers and businessmen, and native government officials were always selected as municipal commissioners and consulted at times on matters of state. This élite-oriented municipal body may not have failed in municipal administration, but it was resented by the newly-educated class and even by the non-official Europeans who wanted to bring more freedom and intelligence into local government.

It was none the less true that successful working of the municipality did depend too heavily on the initiative and energy of the Magistrate. Since the nominated commissioners were not answerable to constituents, it fell to the Magistrate to see that they took an active part. It was also mainly his responsibility to see that the municipal administration was conducted both efficiently and fairly. Yet the Magistrates as a rule were over-burdened with other official duties, while their frequent transfer further slowed the pace of municipal work.

The passing of Act II of 1873, which provided for the election of the commissioners, vice-chairman and chairman at the discretion of the government gave the critics their opportunity. Their instrument was the newly-formed Dacca People's Association which organized a petition to the Lieutenant-Governor of Bengal for the introduction of the elective system. The Association, one of many such political associations and pressure groups in Bengal,[8] aimed at acting as a bridge between the rulers and the ruled, to air native grievances and to voice their demands for various administrative, political, economic and social reforms.[9] It was founded by English-educated, mainly middle-class Hindus, urban idealists and 'patriots', as the *Dhaka Prokash* described them. Its membership included lawyers such as Ananda Chandra Roy, Ramakanta Nandi, Gopi Mohan Basak and Syed Golam Mustafa; the writer Kali Prasanna Ghosh; the zamindar Brojendra Kumar Roy; and the banker-zamindar Ruplal Das. Not much is known about the association's organizational structure, its total membership and finances,[10] but it probably depended heavily upon its wealthy members. Generally it met at the house of one of its members, but on some bigger occasions at the East Bengal Theatre Hall at Patuatuli which served as a town hall for Dacca before the construction of the Northbrook Hall in 1879. The association long survived and served as the chief political platform for East Bengal, organizing numbers of petitions and public meetings.

Thus it was at the People's Association's initiative that a petition, signed by over seven hundred people, was sent to the Lieutenant-Governor Sir Richard Temple on 24 June 1874, requesting him to extend to Dacca, 'the most important place in Eastern Bengal', the privilege of electing its municipal commissioners.[11]

But though an elective system had been legislated for and had the approval of the provincial and central governments, officials at district and divisional level showed no keenness for a change which would so threaten their authority. Often conservative in attitude, they were firm believers in the cult of administrative efficiency, which they saw as threatened should elected commissioners achieve control. Although the association had not specifically demanded the election of the chairman or even the vice-chairman, their prayer for the extension of Act II of 1873 to Dacca was turned down by the Lieutenant-Governor mainly on the basis of an unfavourable report from Francis Richard Cockerell, the Divisional Commissioner of Dacca.

Temple had asked Cockerell 'for a brief note of the merits of and reasons for this application'.[12] Cockerell replied that the interests of the ratepayers of Dacca had not always been properly served or consulted under the existing system in Dacca. Nevertheless he could not recommend the elective system since he did not believe that the electorate would be competent. In a very revealing addendum, he described the petition as having been promoted by 'the so-called People's Association whose object is virtually to substitute... their own nominees for those of the responsible local authorities in the office of Municipal Commissioners', adding that he did not think 'the Municipal administration would gain anything in efficiency by the exchange'.[13]

Meanwhile in August 1874, Sir Richard had himself visited Dacca and inquired into the affairs of the Dacca Municipality. But he was not willing to introduce the elective system against the advice of the local authorities, and he rejected the petition until government had more experience. He did, however, recognize that suitable and competent persons had not always been selected as municipal commissioners and agreed that the association might very properly make representations about suitable candidates to the district officer.[14]

No substantial move was made, however, to reconstitute the municipalities in the mofussil towns on a popular basis until the arrival of Lord Ripon as Viceroy.[15] Ripon issued his famous resolution on local self-government on 18 May 1882, enunciating a reform intended not so much as an aid to administrative efficiency but 'as an instrument of political and popular education'. With the spread of Western education and methods a new class of men, intelligent and public-spirited, had been everywhere rapidly growing up whose talents, he argued, it would not only be bad policy but a gross waste not to employ. This new middle class, moreover, had shown itself eager to participate in the government of the country, and neither blind indifference nor stupid repression must be allowed to make them a discontented source of political danger. The remedy offered by Ripon was 'a training in the working of representative institutions'.[16] In local representative government the new middle class should be offered an outlet and a role.[17]

But as Hugh Tinker records,

> ...in the India of 1882, the Viceroy was alone in his liberalism; the vast majority of local Anglo-Indian officials were conservatives, supporters of a 'paternal' administration, so that the reforms projected by Ripon were attenuated, or even ignored...

In Bengal, the Lieutenant-Governor, Sir Rivers Thompson, certainly made no secret of his opposition to the Viceroy's proposals for local self-government reform.[18] However, Ripon had warm supporters among the population of Bengal. The Dacca People's Association, for example, organized a mammoth public meeting on 24 July 1882 on the premises of the Jagannath School attended by an estimated fifteen to twenty thousand people. So huge a public meeting had never been held in Dacca; almost all the leading citizens and a large number of ordinary people attended it. Several of the prominent zamindars and merchants from other districts of East Bengal also came or sent representatives.

This public meeting, chaired by its president Babu Brojendra Kumar Roy,[19] was the biggest success to date of the Dacca People's Association, and its size, the variety of speeches and the resolutions adopted left no doubt about the sentiment of at least a section of the people of East Bengal. The meeting resolved to urge the Bengal Government immediately to provide that all the members of the municipalities and local boards should be popularly elected, these elected members in their turn electing both chairmen and vice-chairmen.[20]

Despite this demonstration of popular feeling the local British officials were not prepared to accept full local self-government and especially the institution of a non-official chairman. Thus in his reply to a government inquiry of 5 July 1882 A. C. Tute, the officiating Joint-Magistrate, observed,

> There can be no question that if any Bengal community is fit to be entrusted with an elected franchise, that of the city of Dacca is. It is the leading city in Eastern Bengal, and contains a population of men of education, wealth, and intelligence far beyond that contained in

any municipality of which I have had any experience in India, not even excepting the two large towns in the Madras Presidency—Trichinopoly and Salem...

He would not, therefore, hesitate to introduce the elective system into the Dacca Municipality. But he did not believe, after much anxious thought, that the city could either produce or afford to have an elected, non-official chairman. Such was the heavy burden and demand of the job that 'it would be impossible, at any rate at the outset, to carry on the business of the municipality unless the Magistrate or some officials were at the head of it...' He did not think that 'there is a single non-official in Dacca who, without remuneration, would undertake the drudgery and work connected with the office'. In the same vein he continued that the people of Dacca, 'advanced though' in education, were 'apathetic to the most rudimentary requirements of sanitation'. The Indian municipal commissioners were willing enough to acknowledge the blessings of sanitation, and to vote 'at a meeting and away from their surroundings, for most sweeping sanitary reforms', but they were very reluctant personally to make themselves obnoxious to their neighbours, 'and report or take action upon any breach of sanitary law of which they may be guilty'. Yet they were all nominated members; when the elective system would be operative, they would be even more reluctant. It was here then the clinical hand of an outsider, a non-political civil servant would be direly needed. Otherwise, 'I am convinced that Dacca would relapse from even the small advance it has made. Well-privies and other abominations that have been closed would be re-opened, and sanitation become a thing of the past'. He, therefore, strongly advocated 'that for the present, at any rate, the Magistrate of the district should be the Chairman and chief executive authority of the Municipality of Dacca'.[21]

Like Tute, Edward Vasey Westmacott, the District Magistrate, was ready to accept the principle of popularly elected municipal commissioners, although he made no secret of his feelings towards the English-educated class now agitating for an elective system. This section, he added, consisting of pleaders, clerks, schoolteachers and the like, formed almost the only class which made its wants known by public declamation or by writing in the newspapers. But he added,

I must not, however, conceal the fact that there is in the background a large mass of people, with less English education, but by no means wanting in intelligence, and including the principal portion of the Muhammedan citizens, who view the movement with distrust if not with dislike. These people are averse to coming forward in public affairs, and I think it very doubtful whether they will exert themselves to obtain a share in representation, and whether they will not at least at first, leave a monopoly of representation to the Hindoos who have received an English education, but who possess by no means so large a stake in the country as others who do not make themselves so prominent.[22]

This expression of strong feeling towards the silent majority, the less advanced and the underprivileged was a typical bureaucratic reaction to the possibilities of the elective system taking root. The municipal history of Dacca had hitherto reflected no particular sensitivity by magistrates towards the need of the common people, as the most neglected parts of the city were where the majority of them lived. Nor was any one from among the ordinary Muslim population ever nominated to the municipal committee. The truth was that the British officials were reluctant at this stage to share power with the rising Indian middle class.

It is notable that the people of Dacca themselves, Muslims included, expressed no particular anxiety over possible electoral domination by the English-educated Hindus. Indeed, at a public meeting convened on 3 August 1882 by Westmacott to explain government's plans, Syed Golam Mustafa—a prominent Muslim lawyer-zamindar and a municipal commissioner—declared that the Hindus of Dacca had become the more advanced section of the community chiefly by educating themselves. If they should secure a preponderance in the elected municipality, why should the Muslim community resent it? Rather they should be proud of their fellow citizens, who through education and knowledge, had become administrators of their city too.[23] Not everyone might have shared these liberal views, but there was no evidence of antagonism at this period between the Western-educated and the ordinary people, or between Hindus and Muslims in Dacca.

Westmacott, however, expressed serious reservations. He warned the audience that they must show greater judgement in choosing their municipal commissioners so that local self-government did not become 'a failure or a sham'. With splendid rudeness he made clear that he preferred men of business and property as municipal commissioners rather than the merely educated—although of course he bore no personal animosity against the latter. The educated were not generally men of substance and often suffered from financial problems, and he wondered whether they would be able to overcome the temptation to tamper with the public funds entrusted to their charge. He also dwelt upon the laboriousness of the municipal chairmanship and with cheerful effrontery observed that none of the native inhabitants of Dacca possessed either the ability or the experience to bear the burden. His advice was: 'introduce your elective system but retain your official Chairman.'[24]

His speech brought immediate protests from the audience, Babu Ananda Chandra Roy and Kali Prasanna Ghosh both vigorously refuting and critizing Westmacott's unfortunate remarks. The educated people were the backbone of society, Ghosh declared, friends of the rich as well as the poor of the country, a bridge between the two. Roy's comment was that though the educated class might not be rich they were certainly the most capable of representing the native population. He also stressed that it would be for the elected representatives of the people to decide the question of having an elected chairman or not. What did it matter, he asked, if the elected representatives did choose a non-official chairman who in his first months in office made errors of judgement or showed some lack of efficiency? Lord Ripon's reforms were not primarily aimed at increasing administrative efficiency but at educating the people in the art of government.[25]

Westmacott's speech became something of a *cause célèbre* among Western-educated Bengalis, the subject of fierce discussion and bitter comment in the press.[26] Westmacott, however, remained unrepentant in his opposition to any immediate grant of an elected chairmanship for Dacca, under which, he prophesied, administration would break down.[27]

For the time being it was Westmacott's attitude which prevailed, although when the Lieutenant-Governor Sir Rivers Thompson visited Dacca in August 1882 he was presented with an impressive petition in favour of an elective municipal chairmanship.[28] However, after two years' deliberation and much popular pressure, the Bengal Government passed Act III of 1884 which provided for the election of two-thirds of the municipal commissioners, including the vice-chairman and chairman in all but twenty-six of the scheduled municipalities.[29]

In Dacca, under this Act, there were twenty-one municipal commissioners of whom two-thirds or fourteen were to be elected. The city was divided into seven constituencies or wards, electing commissioners roughly according to the size of their respective electorates. The franchise was based mainly on a property qualification, and though some educated groups who were not strictly ratepayers were allowed to vote, their plea for special representation was turned down.[30] The citizenry of Dacca seemed to be quite satisfied, however, with the limited franchise. All adult males, resident in the municipality for at least a year prior to the election, who personally or through landlords paid at least one rupee eight annas a year in municipal taxes were qualified to vote. In addition, any university graduate or licentiate, any pleader or mooktar, or any other person who earned from any employment more than fifty rupees per month, who lived as a member of a joint family, one of the members of which had paid the necessary municipal tax, was also entitled to vote. Electors could also stand or nominate others as candidates for a municipal commissionership.[31] On this basis the number of electors entitled to vote in the first municipal election at Dacca was 7,202 or nearly 9 per cent of the total population of the city, then about 82,210. Since this number must have amounted to nearly forty per cent of all adult males, there could not have been many with either property or education who had expected to receive the vote but did not do so. The first municipal election under these rules was held on 24 November 1884. Whatever the subsequent fortunes of this alien system of local self-government, in Dacca it all began with great promise.

The election was not, however, without incident. Originally 113 individuals were nominated to contest the 14 seats. They represented all shades of importance and influence except that no European or Armenian participated in the contest.[32] There was no organized block, faction or party; each individual aspirant risked his luck at the poll independently, with only a few loyal supporters. But very soon, as the officiating Magistrate, Frank Hunter Barrow, recalled, a caucus was formed of the most prominent citizens, mostly Hindus, headed by Babu Brojendra Kumar Roy, the president of the Dacca People's Association.[33] This caucus selected its own candidates and threw the entire weight of the wealth and influence of its members into an electoral campaign.[34]

This move was followed by the surfacing of Hindu-Muslim tension. The contributory factors were no doubt broadly common to the whole subcontinent. The prime cause was the altered political relationship, following the decline of Mughal authority, between an historically ruling community and its subjects. Under the Mughals the Muslim ruling class by virtue of its power reserved for itself a key place in the bureaucracy, but bureaucratic control was nevertheless shared with a collaborating Hindu élite. Under the British, however, the two élites, Muslim and Hindu, were left to compete for posts in the bureaucracy, under rules laid down by the British. The prime requirement was a mastery of the English language, and with that such elements of British culture as law, history, politics and science. The Hindus, less attached to the Persianized culture of the Mughals, were able to accommodate with much more ease than the Muslims to the demands of the new masters. A Muslim middle class was late in appearing, therefore, and when it did, found Hindus already in possession of place and power. Large-scale or rapid industrialization might have accommodated the aspirations of both Hindus and Muslims; but in its absence only the professions, the bureaucracy or politics remained as acceptable fields for middle-class enterprise. Given the inelasticities in social formation and economic development, it was almost inevitable that group competition should at certain points turn into conflict. In Dacca it was the efforts of the wealthy and educated Hindus, led by Brojendra Kumar Roy, to get their mainly Hindu caucus candidates elected which sparked off Muslim fears. If the efforts of the caucus paid off, then, the Muslims felt, they would be left unrepresented. Hence they started a campaign to persuade Muslims to vote only for Muslim candidates, thus ensuring their victory in at least some of the wards.

The district officials say no more than that it was the Muslim claim to have a fair share of the municipal seat, which led to the communal tension. The *Dhaka Prokash*, however, is more forthright. In a leader not long before the election the editor expressed great sorrow at hearing a 'rumour' of communal antagonism and of certain Muslim ratepayers having vowed not to vote for any Hindu candidate. This, he suspected, was the result of the evil counsel of those who feared loss of power and privilege and the intrigues of certain cunning foreigners who fomented civil strife between the two communities.

On a larger plane, he argued that the Hindus and Muslims of India had lived peaceably together for many centuries and in recent times had been subjected to the same sufferings and neglect. If now in the municipal election—planned for the good of the common people—communal antagonism was allowed to spread, both communities would suffer while the hands of those opposed to the elective system would be strengthened.[35]

It is not known whether this well-meaning advice, published just before the poll, had any effect. But for whatever reason, prominent Hindus and Muslims backed by the caucus and probably also by the Nawab family, finally settled for compromise. It was decided that the two communities should each have a fair share of the municipal seats. In some wards an equal number of Hindu and Muslim candidates were to be nominated and supported, in others, where Muslims or Hindus strongly predominated, a balance was struck between wards. A typical example was provided by Ward V, where one Hindu and one Muslim candidate were nominated and supported by all the leading inhabitants of Dacca and their followers. So successful was this compromise that the two candidates were returned unopposed.

However, the election was not totally controlled by the caucus, nor was a compromise reached in all the wards. There were men of wealth and local influence who for reasons of personal prestige, honour and interest wanted to become municipal commissioners. They chose to test their strength at the polls despite pressure from the caucus and other groups. So though most nominations were withdrawn, twenty-two candidates finally entered the contest for the fourteen seats, seven of them Muslims and the rest Hindus.

The election was held in orderly but most colourful fashion. Processions were organized on behalf of the candidates; carriages were hired to bring voters to the election booths, and refreshments were served—very much in the present-day manner. Northbrook Hall, the East Bengal Theatre at Patuatuli, Purana Paltan Maidan, and the squares of Lalbagh, Chauk Bazar, Bangshal and Armanitola were selected as polling centres. The two halls were beautifully decorated, and large tents and colourful *shamianas* (pavilions) were put up at the four other places to provide room for the assembled voters, the candidates and their supporters. The hurly-burly of election speeches and counter-speeches soon followed.[36]

In Wards IV and V, no poll was demanded, but in the five others votes were taken either by show of hands or *viva voce*.[37] The successful candidates were Ruplal Das, Purna Chandra Banerjee and Khwaja Amirullah in Ward I; Radhika Mohan Basak and Rama Kanta Nandi in Ward II; Chandra Mohan Basak and Moulvie Reza Karim in Ward III; Khwaja Muhammad Yusuf and Haji Abdur Rashid in Ward IV; Babu Ananda Chandra Roy and Syed Golam Mustafa in Ward V; Shaikh Haidar Bux in Ward VI; and Brojendra Kumar Roy and Koilash Chandra Das in Ward VII.

Two successful candidates, Khwaja Muhammad Yusuf and Syed Golam Mustafa, were unseated as not qualified to vote or stand. Unfamiliar with the technicalities of election procedures they had failed to register themselves properly as candidates. Since both candidates had been returned unopposed there were no defeated candidates who could be declared elected, and under clause two of section sixteen of Act III commissioners were therefore nominated by the government. Although Khwaja Muhammad Yusuf was replaced by W. Connan, the Executive Engineer, Syed Golam Mustafa was appointed for Ward V, for which he had stood; the Divisional Commissioner reporting 'that the Syed is a very influential gentleman and a great favourite with the Mahommedan community; which formed the bulk of the population in the ward.'[38] The other seven nominated members included high government officials, distinguished academics, wealthy zamindars, and respected community leaders.[39]

The election results brought into play significant social changes within Dacca. It also reflected the economic prosperity of certain groups of Dacca's inhabitants and a growing awareness that the future of Indian society in the final reckoning lay with the Indians themselves. This awareness was itself a product of the influence of Western education, a symbol of the cultural cross-fertilization that was taking place among sections of the Indian middle-class élite.

The fears of the British officials had been proved groundless. Most of the elected candidates were men of property, wealth and rank; seven were leading zamindars, some of whom in addition to their zamindaris had banking and other businesses; two were members of the Dacca Nawab family; two were leading merchants of the city; one was a most respectable Muslim figure. Only two of their numbers were English-educated lawyers. Wealth and status which many Dacca families had acquired with the city's economic recovery and through the British connection had created a sphere of influence in which was rooted their power and authority. Hence the overwhelming success of the zamindars and merchants at the election. Similarly the traditional caste and community leaders had their spheres of influence too. Indeed the election proved a disappointment to the *Dhaka Prokash* because of what it considered to be the relatively indifferent performance of the educated candidates.[40] Nevertheless in one way the election did bring out the growing maturity of the Daccaites who saw in the whole exercise an affirmation of local government which transcended parochial loyalties of caste, community and traditional forms of patronage. The District Magistrate Frank Hunter Barrow saw these events thus:

> I should consider that very suitable selections have been made. Some very good and prominent men have, it is true, been excluded, but it must be remembered that 'good and prominent men' are not always representative, and it is a forgetfulness of this which leads some critics to condemn the results.

He also confirmed that the elective system would work an improvement, and bring about an effective demand for better sanitation and better municipal government generally.[41]

The election had undoubtedly led to some adjustment of power within the city. This shift was evident even before the election. No longer would the wealthy, land-owning aristocracy and their traditional allies qualify for automatic selection in the running of municipal affairs. So the Khwajas, Dases and Basaks who between them owned and controlled the majority of the businesses and properties of Dacca could no longer expect to have an assured place on the municipal committee. Henceforth their seats had to be won and held against the increasingly skilful challenge of the new English-educated class of lawyers and professional men. This group whose numbers and influence had been growing with the administrative and educational development of the city and the country as a whole achieved, however, no significant breakthrough in Dacca's first municipal election, the reason being that their roots were yet to take firm hold in society. They were after all a new class and the bulk of the citizenry had yet fully to accustom themselves to their existence, mores and values. In the long run the dominance of this middle class was inevitable, given the far reaching changes in government, administration and education that had taken place since the establishment of British power in India. As a corollary of this, the predominant influence of the old ruling class based principally on land was bound to decline. Indeed, Babu Ananda Chandra Roy, the leading lawyer of Dacca,[42] emerged as the new star, and was duly elected the Dacca Municipality's first non-official chairman, foreshadowing the rise of the Gandhis, Jinnahs, Nehrus, Dases, Suhrawardes and Boses all over the subcontinent.

The question of having an official or a non-official chairman had not been seriously discussed by the people of Dacca before the election. After the election it became apparent, however, that the newly-elected commissioners wanted to elect one of their own members as the chairman. It was equally apparent that they were quite apprehensive about official reactions to such a move, for under Act III of 1884 it was still possible to appoint the District Magistrate as chairman. However, Magistrate Frederick Wyer acted very fairly leaving the matter completely in their hands. Still the commissioners handled the matter very delicately. Thus while nominating Ananda Chandra Roy for the chairmanship, Syed Golam Mustafa paid a rich and graceful tribute to the Magistrate. Wyer had done much good work for Dacca, and his kindly manner had made him very popular. With such a man at the head of the Municipality, there was no need to have a non-official chairman. But in later times other individuals would be appointed as magistrates, not all of whom might take so keen an interest in municipal affairs. But if the magistrate was now selected as chairman, it would be seen as a slight by later magistrates if the same honour was not bestowed on them. For this reason he proposed the name of Ananda Chandra Roy for the chairmanship, and Roy was then elected unanimously.[43]

The decision to have an elected non-official vice-chairman was thereafter taken without much hesitation, Khwaja Amirullah—the son-in-law of Khwaja Abdul Ghani—was proposed as vice-chairman by Ruplal Das and unanimously elected.[44] The choice of a Muslim vice-chairman followed the pattern of the electoral compromise.

On 20 April 1885, the Dacca Municipality sat for the first time under its new non-official chairman. After that the history of the Municipality and that of the city passed into a new era. It was also an apt reflection of the larger developments that were taking place elsewhere in the country with the inauguration of the Indian National Congress in that very same year.

NOTES TO CHAPTER VIII

1 Tinker, *Foundations of Local-Self-Government*, 41, *et passim.*
2 See Misra, *Administrative History of India*, 569–91.
3 Ibid., 598.
4 For an account of such press criticism see *DP*, 25 Phalgun 1276 (4 March 1870); *BT*, 26 July 1876 and 7 August 1878; and *Hindu Hitoishini*, 1 January 1876 in RNN, 8 January 1876, 1–2.
5 See *BT*, 18 April 1877.
6 See [Graham, G], *Life in the Moffussil*, II, for the view of a District Magistrate on the difficulties of dealing with Dacca's problems with the limited funds at the disposal of the Municipality, 132–7.
8 K. M. Asghar eventually became the first Indian vice-chairman of the Municipality in 1879.
8 For details see B. C. Pal, *Memoirs of My Life and Times*, I, 234.
9 Report on the proceedings of the First Annual Meeting of the Dacca People's Association held in May 1873, *DP*, 23 Baisakh 1280 (4 May 1873).
10 It is, however, reported that about three hundred and fifty people attended its first annual meeting in May 1873, see *DP*, 23 Baisakh 1280 (4 May 1873).
11 Petition of the Municipal Ratepayers and People of Dacca, Temple Papers, Mss. Eur. F. 86, vol. 214 (no page mark or document numbers, located at the end of the volume).
12 Ibid.
13 Cockerell to Temple, 8 August 1874, Ibid. Francis Cockerell who joined the civil service in 1850 was an experienced officer. Immediately before his appointment as Commissioner of Dacca, he was the Bengal Government's Superintendent and Remembrancer of Legal Affairs.
14 Temple's note on the petition, Ibid.
15 Tinker, *Foundations of Local Self-Government*, 38.
16 L. S. S. O'Malley (ed), *Modern India and the West*, quoted in Tinker, *Foundations*, 44.
17 For further details on Ripon's local government reforms see Tinker, *Foundations*, 43–73 *et passim:* also Misra, *Administrative History*, 601–8, *et passim.*
18 Tinker, *Foundations*, 43–4, 46. For comments of the vernacular press on the attitude of the Lieutenant-Governor to Ripon's reforms, see RNN, June-July 1883, 313–14.
19 Brojendra Kumar Roy was a member of the famous zamindar family of Baliati in the Manikganj subdivision of Dacca. The family also had properties in Dacca itself where its younger members lived while attending the city's schools and colleges. It appears that Borjendra Kumar was the president of the Dacca People's Association from 1881 to 1884.
20 *DP*, 15 Sraban 1289 (30 July 1882), supplement to *BT* 26 July 1882.
21 'Note on Self-Government As Applied to the Dacca Municipality' by A. C. Tute, being appendix B in Magistrate to GB, 12 September 1882, BMP, 2028, January 1883, Collection 1, Nos. 18–19, pp. 91–4.

22 Magistrate to GB, 12 September 1882, BMP, 2028, January 1883, Collection 1, No. 18.
23 *DP*, 22 Sraban 1289 (6 August 1882); also *BT*, 16 August 1882.
24 *DP*, 22 Sraban 1289 (6 August 1882); also *BT*, 16 August 1882.
25 *DP*, 22 Sraban 1289 (6 August 1882).
26 See, for example, *Amrita Bazar Patrika*, (no date) September 1882, quoted in *BT*, 16 September 1882.
27 Westmacott to Div. Comm. 12 September 1882. BMP, 2028, January 1883, Collection 1, No. 19.
28 *BT*, 19 August 1882.
29 Act III of 1884, *The Acts Passed By the Lieutenant-Governor of Bengal in Council* for 1884, 12–17.
30 For details see F. R. S. Collier, *The Bengal Municipal Manual*.
31 *DP* 11 Kartik 1291 (26 October 1884).
32 *DP*, 25 Kartik 1291 (9 November 1884).
33 *DP*, 18 Kartik 1291 (2 November 1884).
34 Unfortunately no written documents on the activities of this caucus are available apart from press reports, nor any list of all the candidates which it chose.
35 Leader, *DP*, 25 Kartik 1291 (9 November 1884).
36 *DP*, 16 Aghrayan 1291 (30 November 1884).
37 In all these wards over fifty per cent of the electorate recorded their votes.
38 Div. Comm. to GB, 27 February 1885, BMP, 2492, March 1885, Collection, 6, No. 97.
39 Ibid., Nos. 99–100.
40 *DP*, 16 Aghrayan 1291 (30 November 1884).
41 Report enclosed in Magistrate to Div. Comm., 8 December 1884; BMP, 2492, March 1885, Collection, 6, Nos. 82–3.
42 Roy was also a very popular figure in Dacca. See the presidential address by Satyendra Nath Basu at the inaugural ceremony of Jagannath College and Jagannath Hall Reunion, 1930, *A Short History of Jagannath College and Jagannath Hall*... 11.
43 Municipal Proc., 27 March 1835; also *DP*, 17 Chaitra 1291 (29 March 1885).
44 Municipal Proc., 27 March 1885.

CONCLUSION

The history of urban centres in India in the late eighteenth and early nineteenth centuries is a story of decline and renewal. The decline, particularly in the north, followed the collapse of the Mughal Empire, while the beginnings of the British order represented a period of germination.

There was, however, no uniform pattern of rise and fall: certain cities experienced both phases; others fell never to recover, and some like Bombay, Calcutta and Madras —all seaports and well linked to their hinterland—bore from the start the stamp of their British creators, as at a later date did New Delhi.

Dacca belonged to the first category: for it the nineteenth century opened on an unpromising note. Once the metropolis of Bengal, Bihar and Orissa, and the most important centre of trade, commerce and handicrafts in eastern India, the city wore a faded look, its suburbs victims of an encroaching tropical jungle, its notable landmarks in a state of advanced decay. As Dacca's star waned so Calcutta's rose; a natural development in view of its status as capital of British India. In the early decades of the nineteenth century Dacca was a city shorn of noteworthy administrative and military functions; its trade and commerce stagnant; its textile manufactures, once the envy of the civilized world and the basis of its wealth, buried under the weight of cheap machine-made cloth from Britain. As thousands of weavers and others lost their livelihood and moved to the countryside to eke out a living from agriculture, much of the heart and life went out of the city.

Visiting Dacca in 1824, Bishop Reginald Heber observed:

> Dacca ... is merely the wreck of its ancient grandeur. Its trade is reduced to the sixteenth part of what it was, and all its splendid buildings, the castle of its founder ..., the noble mosque he built, the palaces of the ancient Nawabs, the factories and churches of the Dutch, French and Portuguese nations are all sunk into ruin, and overgrown with jungle.[1]

The process of decline thus seemed irreversible. However, the assets of Dacca's geographical location, and the richness of its hinterland remained, and were responsible in the period after 1840 for providing the base for the forces of renewal. These forces were administrative, educational and commercial. It is interesting to note that Murshidabad—a city with a similar past—never recovered from its decline. Not only did it lose its overall political and economic importance to Calcutta, but it also lost its regional administrative role to neighbouring Berhampore which became an educational and a commercial centre of modest proportions.

In contrast to Murshidabad, Dacca grew administratively into an increasingly important seat of regional government, and by the end of the nineteenth century it had become an obvious choice as the capital of any new province which might be carved out of the unwieldy Bengal Presidency.[2]

While the newly-erected administrative framework rekindled the political importance of Dacca, the advent of English education provided the city with yet another opportunity for re-exerting its prominence in Bengal. The people of Dacca and East Bengal generally responded enthusiastically to the government's efforts to disseminate Western education, which led to the establishment of important educational institutions in the city, soon turning it into a major centre of intellectual activity in the province. With the steady advance of education the teaching fraternity, Europeans as well as Indians, together with many of their pupils, enlightened officials and sections of the Dacca public, joined in the struggle for social and religious reform, thereby helping to create an intellectual and moral climate which made their city a stronghold of the Bengal renaissance. Societies, associations and debating clubs devoted to the educational, social, cultural and religious regeneration of the country multiplied. This wind of change powered by the written and spoken word blew into every corner of East Bengal. Books, pamphlets, magazines and newspapers called for the eradication of illiteracy, denounced Kulinism, argued for the right of Hindu widows to remarry, and advocated the cause of female education. These socio-religious movements which were the direct result of Western education and Western ideas contradict the conventional view that nineteenth-century Dacca was a dull and stagnant city.

Even the economic life of Dacca, chiefly through the recovery of its trade and commerce, experienced a considerable revival. The greatest impetus to this commercial revival was provided by the Crimean War (1854–1856), which stopped the supply of raw materials and food grains to England from Russia, and forced British merchants and industrialists to look to India as an alternative source for their flax, fibre, oil seeds, hides, skins and food grains. The resulting upsurge in demand increased production in India, particularly in East Bengal, where a considerable extension in the cultivation of jute brought new life to the economy of the region. Dacca seized the opportunity of handling this growing volume of jute export trade from East Bengal, together with that in hides, skins, oil seeds and food grains, resuming thus its traditional role in the commercial life of the region. The introduction of railways and steamers from the mid-nineteenth century in India also opened up a wider domestic market for these products. European as well as Indian merchants journeyed to Dacca and Narayanganj to procure East Bengal's jute and agricultural products. The Armenian and Indian merchants of Dacca were also involved in this new commerce. With the rise of exports came increased demands for imported goods and commodities; the people of East Bengal with more money now in their pockets, were just as eager to buy as they were to sell, thus adding enormously to the volume of Dacca's trade and commerce. In 1876–7 the total value of Dacca's import and export trade amounted to Rs. 11,832,200.[3] As merchants, traders, shopkeepers and bankers throve in this new economic climate, the problem of unemployment in the city eased considerably. This renewal moreover provided fresh opportunities for skilled weavers and their compeers in other fields who had suffered from the declining economy of the earlier decades caused by the influx of machine-made goods from abroad. Nevertheless, although the textile manufactures showed some signs of recovery, as did certain other manufactures such as gold and silver work, and although a few new jute baling and pressing mills were established, Dacca by the end of the period under review had virtually ceased to be a major manufacturing centre; its economy came to be basically dependent on the import and export trade. The city was now essentially an entrepôt (many contemporaries even described Dacca as a large warehouse[4]), its economic fortunes resting on the export of agricultural products and the import of foreign as well as Calcutta and Bombay-made factory goods.

However, by the end of the nineteenth century Dacca had sufficiently grown in stature, as an important administrative, educational and commercial centre, to be well-prepared to take on a more significant role in the following century. Its choice as the capital of a new province in 1905 and then of independent East Pakistan in 1947 might not have been so easily made had not these significant changes in its character been carried out previously.

This revival, moreover, produced fundamental changes within Dacca society. Owing both to natural increase and immigration, Dacca's Hindu population increased faster than the Muslim. A considerable English-educated middle class emerged from within the former, and much later also among the latter.

This new middle class was a characteristic of nineteenth-century urban life and a direct by-product of British rule. While modern and forward-looking in many respects, this bourgeoisie despite moments of note failed on the whole socially and economically to transform Indian society. Unlike their compeers in Europe, whose ascendancy was based on their control of finance, industry and political authority, the bourgeoisie in the subcontinent, more particularly in Bengal, owed their wealth and social power almost exclusively to land rents and to their dominating position in the bureaucracy and professions. This, and their subordinate political status in a colonial structure, presented a restricted field of middle-class activity and made it impossible to accommodate the ever-increasing numbers seeking to move up the social scale. In the inevitable scramble for positions, considerable social tension was generated, thus affecting Hindu–Muslim relations.

In Dacca, for example, the Hindus having gained control of the city's economic life attempted through the initiative of their rising middle class to obtain an exclusively controlling influence over its administration in the first municipal election of 1885. The result was that strong feelings were aroused among the Muslims who feared the loss of their influence and power. Happily on this occasion good sense prevailed, the municipal election being settled through a compromise among the leadership of the Hindu and the Muslim communities. But the residual hostility which remained was cruelly exploited in later years by communal forces with tragic results.

The quality of life in Dacca also improved largely through the efforts of the Municipality; and by the end of the nineteenth century the city had become a healthier and more comfortable place to live in. This was yet another outcome of institution-building under British rule. The concept of local self-government was a foreign one and the institution of municipalities run by officials and citizens and in the subsequent period exclusively by the latter was an experiment introduced throughout India with the hope that it would take root in a foreign environment. The hope was not without foundation and municipalities like Dacca achieved a great deal. The success of each individual municipality, however, varied, but the exercise in urban development through the municipal institution was a positive and healthy one. Dacca, Patna, Ahmedabad and Allahabad, for example, greatly benefited from it. Moreover, the history of Dacca Municipality's development showed that financial difficulties were not the only obstacles barring the way to improved urban living. The lack of dedication and hard work on the part of the municipal administrators and the want of civic consciousness among sections of the public were other contributory factors.

So continued a process of which the culmination was the transformation of Dacca into a modern, forward-looking metropolis. Newspapers and books in Bengali and English, wheeled transport, medical centres, post offices, telegraphs, all symbolized the dawn of a new age. The scourges of cholera, smallpox and malaria were largely controlled. People had more leisure to go to the public libraries, theatres and musical soirées; they played cricket and football with gusto, as well as participating in traditional Muharram and Janmashtami processions. Dacca's architecture also reflected the old and the new: Mughal designs existing side by side with Anglo-Indian styles. So while Dacca was no longer as wealthy or as prosperous as it had been in the palmy days of Mughal rule, new forms of trade, commerce and manufactures had laid the foundations of renewed economic life; however, it was Dacca's social regeneration based largely on modern values and ideas that may yet come to be regarded as the more lasting development.

NOTES TO CONCLUSION

1 Bishop Heber, *Narratives of a Journey*, I, 141.
2 In 1884 the Presidency consisted of Bengal, Bihar, Orissa and Chota Nagpur, and four Tributory and one Native states covering an area of 189,823 square miles, see BAR; for 11884–5, Statistical Review, 1.
3 *Report on the Internal Trade of Bengal*, for 1876–7, 169–70.
4 *A Sketch of Eastern Bengal with Reference to its Railways and Government Control*, 8, et passim.

GLOSSARY

Abkari: Excise
Anna, ana: The sixteenth part of a rupee
Bandar, Shah bandar: Inland port, Imperial port
Barkandaz: Guard, watchman; doorkeeper, a matchlockman
Bhisti: A water-carrier
Bhuimali: A sweeper, a scavenger
Bigha: A measure of land—little less than one-third of an acre
Bund: An embankment; a causeway
Char: A sand-bank or island in the bed of a river
Chauk, chouk: A block; an open place in the city where the market is held
Chaukidar: A nightwatchman; a guard
Chaukidari: The office of nightwatchman; a tax levied to defray the cost of a town or village watch.
Chaprasi: A messenger or orderly wearing a *chappas* or a badge; usually a public servant
Cutcherry: A court; an office; the place where any public business is transacted
Dafadar, duffadar: An officer placed over the chaukidars; a person at the head of a number of persons whether labourers or soldiers
Daftari, dufturee: A record-keeper; a registrar
Daroga, darogha: The head of a police, customs or excise station
Darwan: A doorkeeper, a porter
Diwan: The Chief Financial Minister
Diwani: The office of a Diwan
Dome: Sweeper, scavenger
Faujdar: An officer of the Mughal government who was invested with the charge of the police, and jurisdiction in all criminal matters
Gali, galli: A lane; an alley
Ghat, ghaut: A landing place; steps on the bank of a river; a wharf where customs are commonly levied
Gor: A ditch; a pit; a cess-pool
Gumashta, gomasta: An agent, a steward; a native accountant
Hakim: A ruler, a judge; a physician
Hundi: A bill of exchange
Jamadar: The chief or leader of any number of persons; an officer of the police, customs or excise, second to the Darogha
Jamadarni: A headwoman; the chief female warder
Jhamma: A vitrified brick; pumice stone

Jheel, Jhil: A lake; a marsh; a swamp
Kabiraj: A physician
Khal: A creek; a canal
Khas-land, *khasmahal:* Government property; estates held in the management of the government
Kheda, *keddah:* An enclosure in which wild elephants are caught; here used to refer to the Department entrusted with the catching of wild elephants and taming and training them; elephant depot
Kotwal: The chief officer of police for a city or town
Kotwali: The office of a kotwal or anything relating to it
Kutcha, cutcha: Raw; crude; unpaved
Kutcha-roads: Roads of earthwork only
Lakh: One hundred thousand
Madrasah: School, usually attached to a mosque
Mahalla, mohulla: A division of a town; a quarter; a ward
Maktab: Elementary school
Mali: Gardener
Maund: A measure of weight, about forty pounds
Mehtar: A male sweeper or scavenger
Mehtarni, *mehtrani:* A female sweeper or scavenger
Mofussil, *mufassal:* Provincial or suburban; interior of the country
Mouza, mowza: A village; a parcel or parcels of lands having a separate name in the revenue records, and of known limits.
Muharrir, *mohurrie:* A clerk, a writer, a scribe
Mukhtar, *mooktar:* A legal agent not possessing the right to plead in a District Court or above
Munsif: A subordinate judge
Naib: Deputy
Naib-Nazim: Deputy-governor
Niabat: Deputyship, Vicegerancy; the office of a Naib or Nawab; a sub-province
Panchayat, *panchait:* A court of arbitration, consisting of five or more persons, for the determination of petty disputes among the people of a ward, especially in matters affecting the usages of caste or occupation; a body of local assessors
Pargana: A sub-division of a district, usually comprising many villages; a fiscal unit
Pathsala: Primary school
Peshkar: A subordinate officer who is employed to keep the accounts; a subordinate officer employed in offices and courts
Poddar: A cash keeper; a weighman, one whose office it is to weigh and examine money; a petty banker and money lender
Rawanah: Permit

Ryot, rayat, raiyat: A subject; a cultivator; a farmer
Sadr, sadar: The chief seat of government, the presidency, as opposed to the provinces or mofussil; a principal station or a town
Sadr-amin, sadar-amin: A class of civil judges
Sair: Duties on goods, excise, licences, etc. as opposed to land revenue
Sardar: Ward leader
Sarkar: The government; the state; a writer; an accountant
Subah: A province; a government
Subahdar: The governor of a province; a viceroy under the Mughal government
Sunni: One of the two sects of Muslims; the follower of the traditions
Tahsildar: A tax-collector, a collector of revenue
Talukdar, taluqdar: A petty or under-proprietor
Talukdaris, taluqdaris: small estates
Tanti: Weaver
Thana: A police jurisdiction; police station
Vakil: A legal practitioner or pleader
Zamindar: A landholder individually or jointly engaged to pay land revenue and receive rent
Zamindari: The office and rights of a zamindar; estates
Zilla, zillah: District

BIBLIOGRAPHY

A. UNPUBLISHED SOURCES

1. Official records

(a) India Office Library and Records, London.

East India Company and India Office Records:
Despatches to Bengal, 1828–9;
Home Miscellaneous Series, vols. 379, 456 (f), 815.

Government of India Records:
India Public Consultations, 1834–54;
Proceedings of the Legislative Council of India, 1855–8;
Reports on Native Newspapers published in Bengal, 1874–86.

Government of Bengal Records:
Consultations and Proceedings of the Government of Bengal in the Departments of Customs and Excise, Education, Finance, Judicial, Municipal, Police, Public Works, Railway, Revenue, Sanitation and Statistics for the period 1793–1886;
Legislative Council Proceedings, 1862–85.

(b) Public Records Office, London.

Chancery Proceedings relating to the Will of Robert Mitford, Nos. 408–10; T.S. 11/153–408.

(c) Baptist Missionary Society Library and Archive, London.

Papers of the Reverend Owen Leonard, 1816–1844; India/28; Papers of the Reverend William Robinson, India/28.

(d) Bangladesh Secretariat Record Room, Dacca.

Archive section:
Proceedings of the Lieutenant-Governor of Bengal in the General Department especially the following branches: Education, Judicial, Municipal and Miscellaneous, for the period 1859–85;
Miscellaneous Letters Received and sent by the Collector of Dacca, 1837–59.

(e) *National Archives of Bangladesh, Dacca.*

Miscellaneous judicial, revenue and municipal records of the Commissioner of Dacca, 1875–85. (At the time of my research in 1976 these were not systematically arranged or classified.)

(f) *Dacca District Collectorate Record Room.*

Letters Received (in original) by the Collector of Dacca, *c.* 1790–1885;
Register of Letters Received and Sent with regard to Khas Mahal Lands, 1840–68;
Thakbust Survey Reports for the City and District of Dacca, 1858–9.

(g) *Dacca Municipality (now Corporation) Record Room.*

Miscellaneous Papers of the Dacca Municipal Committee, and Letters to and from the honorary secretary, Municipal Committee,1857–1860 (discovered during the course of research; no catalogue number);
Miscellaneous correspondence of the chairman of the Dacca Municipality, Letters Sent, 1866–67 (discovered during the course of research);
Proceedings of the commissioners of the Dacca Municipality, 1864–87;

Collection of Files and Reports on specific Subjects, especially the following: Administration Reports, Buckland Bund, Budget Estimates, Burial Grounds, By-Laws, Committeeganj Lands, Drainage System, Hackney-Carriage Taxes, Mitford Hospital, Municipal Lands, Municipal Boundaries, Northbrook Hall, Privy-Tax, Reassessment, Sanitary Commissioner's Inspection Reports, Street Lighting, Tolls on Buriganga and Dulai Khal Ferries, Trenching Grounds, Vaccination, Waterworks and Wari Khas Mahal (These files and reports have been arranged under various collection numbers e.g., the Annual Administration Reports of the Municipality have been classified as Collection No. 1 of the Record Department.);

'A Short History of the Dacca Water-Works up to 1893 and certain General Information connected with it, 1894', by K. M. Asghar (Collection no. 25);
'A Brief History of the Dacca Municipality,' by J. N. Sil and L. Johnson, December, 1893 (Collection no. XXXII); Proceedings and Correspondence of the Dacca Municipal Committee, 1852–58 (Collection no. XXXII).

(h) West Bengal State Archives

I. Historical Section, 6 Bhowani Dutt Lane, Calcutta
Government of Bengal Records:
Consultations and Proceedings of the Government of Bengal in the Departments of Finance, Judicial, Medical and Municipal and Revenue for the period 1820–86; also Medical and Municipal Department Proceedings, B Series, 1880–86;
Proceedings and Correspondence of the General Committee of Public Instruction, 1823–42.

II. Current Section, Writers' Building, Calcutta Bengal Public Works Department Proceedings, 1862–66; Reports on Native Newspapers published in Bengal, 1862–66.

(i) National Archives of India, Janpath, New Delhi—1

Proceedings of the Government of India in the Department of Home, especially in the following branches: Municipal, Public, and Public Works for the period 1855–86; Proceedings of the Legislative Council (Original and Copies), 1857–59, 1883–85;
Reports on Native Newspapers published in the Bengal Presidency, 1865–74.

2. Private papers

Papers of Sir William Grey: Private Letter Books, 1869–70, India Office Library, Mss. Eur. D. 700; Papers of Lord Halifax: Trade of Dacca, India Office Library, Mss. Eur. F. 78, vol. 44;
Papers of Sir Richard Temple, India Office Library, Mss. Eur. F 86, vols. 23, 30, 135–146 and 210.

B. PUBLISHED SOURCES AND THESES

1. Official reports and publications

Great Britain

Parliamentary Papers:
Report from the Select Committee on East India Produce Together With the Minutes of Evidence, 1840, vol. VIII. *Second Report from the Select Committee on Colonization and Settlement (India), Together With the Minutes of Evidence*, June, 1858.
Parliamentary Branch Collections
Statement Exhibiting the Moral and Material Progress and Condition of India, 1859–85.

India

Publications of the Government of India:
Bengal Administration Reports, 1855–1871.
Census of the Lower Provinces of Bengal, 1891, vols. III–V, Calcutta, 1893.
Imperial Gazetteer of India: Eastern Bengal and Assam, Calcutta, 1909.
India Sanitary Commission and Public Health Reports, Bengal, 1864–68 (NAI).
Report of the Calcutta University Commission, 1917–19, 13 vols., Calcutta, 1919–20.
Report on Communication Between Calcutta and Dacca, Selection From the Records of the Government of India, Public Works Department, Calcutta, 1856.

Government of Bengal

Acts Passed by the Lieutenant-Governor of Bengal in Council, 1863–85.
Administration Reports, 1871–86; also 1921–22.
Report of the Bengal Provincial Banking Enquiry Committee, 1929–30, 3 vols., Calcutta, 1930.
Census of Bengal, 1872 and 1881.
Report of Bengal District Administration Committee, 1913–14, Calcutta, 1915.
Education Reports—Bengal Schools and Colleges, 1848–54.
Report of the General Committee of Public Instruction, 1836–41.
Report of the Department of Public Instruction, 1842–86.
Report of the Bengal (Provincial) Education Committee, 1883, Calcutta 1883.
Report of the Dacca University Committee, 1912, Calcutta, 1912.
Report of the Committee appointed by the Government of Bengal to Consider Questions connected with Muhammedan Education, Calcutta 1915.
Correspondence relating to the Ferry Funds in the Lower Provinces of Bengal, Selections from Records, Calcutta, 1860.
Indigo Cultivation, Selections from Papers on Indigo Cultivation in Lower Bengal, Calcutta, 1860.
Judicial Statistics of the Provinces, Bengal, 1830–40, Calcutta, 1842.
Report on the Administration of Civil and Criminal Justice in the Lower Provinces, 1872–1885.
Decisions of the Zilla Courts... Dacca, 1847–58.
Report on Municipal Taxation and Expenditure in the Bengal Presidency, 1873–86.
Report on the Police—Annual Crime Reports of the Dacca Division, 1863—72.
Prices of Food Grains, Fire Woods and Salt in Bengal, 1866–78, Calcutta 1879.
Proceedings of the Committee of Circuit at Dacca, 30 October to 28 November, 1772, vol. 4, Calcutta, 1926.
Report on the Revenue Administration of the Lower Provinces of Bengal, 1848–86.
Report of the Sanitary Commissioner for the Lower Provinces of Bengal, 1868–89.
Report on the Survey Operations in Bengal, 1852–78, Calcutta 1852–78.,
Report on the Internal Trade of Bengal, 1876–85.

Allen, B. C., *Eastern Bengal District Gazetteers, Dacca*, vol. V, Allahabad, 1912.

Ascoli, F D., *Final Report of the Survey and Settlement Operations in the District of Dacca, 1910–17*, Calcutta, 1917.

Banerji, N. N., *Monograph on the Cotton Fabrics of Bengal*, Calcutta, 1898.

Carnac, C. F., *Report on the New Police in Bengal From the Date of its Organisation Under Act V of 1861 to the Close of 1862*, Calcutta, 1863.

Clay, A. L., *Principal Heads of the History and Statistics of the Dacca Division* (Report on Dacca was written by A. L. Clay the Officiating Collector and Magistrate of Dacca in July 1867), Calcutta, 1868.

Collin, E. W., *Report on the Existing Arts and Industries in Bengal*, Calcutta, 1890.

Connan, W., *Estimate of the Dacca Water-Works Extension, With a Brief History of the Water-Works, 16 June 1886*, Dacca, 1886 (National Library, Calcutta).

D'Oyly, C. and Parker, H. M,. *Observations upon the Transit And Town Duty System of the Bengal Presidency*, Calcutta, 1835.

Green, W. A , *Report on Vaccination Proceedings throughout the Government of Bengal*, Calcutta, 1868.

Halliday, Sir F. J., *Mutiny in Lower Province—Minute of the Lieutenant-Governor*, Calcutta, 1858.

Hunter, W. W., *A Statistical Account of Bengal, Dacca*, vol. V, London, 1875.

Kerr, H. C., Report *on the Cultivation of, And Trade in, Jute in Bengal, and the Indian Fibres Available for the Manufacture of Paper, with Maps*, Calcutta, 1874.

Long, Rev. J., *Adam's Report on Vernacular Education in Bengal and Bihar submitted to Government in 1835, 1836 and 1838 with a brief view of its past and present condition*, Calcutta, 1868.

Mitter, S. C., 'The Conch Shell Industry in Bengal', Industries Department, *Bulletin*, No. 24, Calcutta, 1927.

Sharp, H., *Selections from Educational Records, Part I, 1781–1839*, Calcutta, 1920.

Government of Eastern Bengal and Assam

Report on the Administration of Eastern Bengal and Assam, 1905–06, Shillong, 1907.

Government of Bangladesh

S. N. H. Rizvi (ed.), *Bangladesh District Gazetteers, Dacca*, Dacca, 1975.

2. Newspapers and Gazettes

The Bengal Times, Dacca, 1876–86.
The Dacca News, Dacca, 26 April 1856–13 November 1858.
Dhaka Prokash (Bengali), Dacca, 1863–89 (Dacca University Library).
Calcutta Gazette, 1864–85.
The Pioneer, Allahabad, 1874.

3. Books, Pamphlets and Articles in English

Adam, William, *Reports on the State of Education in Bengal, 1835 and 1838* (ed. by Anath Nath Basu), Calcutta, 1941.

Ahmed, A. F. Saluhuddin, 'The Bengal Renaissance and the Muslim Community' in D. Kopf and S. Joardar (eds.), *Reflections on the Bengal Renaissance*, Rajshahi, 1977.

Ahmed, Sharif Uddin, 'Urban Problems and Government Policies: a case Study of the City of Dacca, 1810–1830', in K. Ballhatchet and J. Harrison (eds.), *The City in South Asia—Pre-Modern and Modern*, London, 1980.

Ahmed, Sufia, *Muslim Community in Bengal, 1884–1912*, Dacca, 1974.

Argal, R. *Municipal Government in India*, Allahabad, 1954.

Ascoli, F. D. *Early Revenue History of Bengal and the Fifth Report, 1812*, Oxford, 1917.

Atiqullah, M and Khan F. Karim, *Growth of Dacca City, Population and Area, 1608–1981*, Dacca, 1965.

Azam, K. M., *The Panchayat System of Dacca*, Dacca, 1911.

Banerjea, Pramatha Nath, *Indian Finance in the Days of the Company*, London, 1928.

————— *A History of Indian Taxation*, London, 1930.

Banerjee, P., *Calcutta and its Hinterland—A Study in Economic History of India, 1833–1910*, Calcutta, 1975.

Bayly, C. A., *The Local Roots of Indian Politics, Allahabad, 1880–1920*, Oxford, 1975.

Bion, Rev. R., *Report on the Dacca and East Bengal (Baptist) Mission for the year 1872*, Calcutta, 1872 (Calcutta National Library).

Bradley-Birt, F. B., *Twelve Men of Bengal in the 19th Century*, Calcutta, 1910.

————— *The Romance of an Eastern Capital*, London, 1910.

Briggs, Asa, *Victorian Cities*, London, 1963.

Buchanan, D. H., *The Development of Capitalistic Enterprise in India*, New York 1934.

Buckland, C. E., *Bengal Under the Lieutenant-Governors... from 1854–1898*, 2 vols., Calcutta, 1901.

Buckland, C. T., *Sketches of the Social Life in India*, London, 1884.

Bysack, B. R. L., *Some Incidents in Bengal During the Eighteenth Century—Before and After*, Dacca, 1906.

Campbell, G., *Memoirs of My Indian Career* (ed. by Sir Charles E. Bernard), 2 vols., London, 1893.

Carpenter, Mary, *Prison Discipline and Female Education in India* (India Office Tract), London, 1867.

---------------- *Six Months in India*, 2 vols., London, 1868.

Chadwick, E. *Report on the Sanitary Condition of the Labouring Population of Great Britain*, 1842 (ed. with an introduction by M. W. Flinn), Edinburgh University Press, 1965.

Chakrabarti, Rai Bahadur Monohan, *Summary of the Changes in the Jurisdiction of Districts in Bengal, 1757–1916*, Calcutta, 1917, (Calcutta National Library).

Chatterjee, Anjali, *Bengal in the Reign of Aurangzib, 1658–1707*, Calcutta, 1967.

Chattopadhya, G. (ed.), *Awakening in Bengal in Early 19th Century—Selected Documents*, Calcutta, 1963.

Chaudhury, Susil, *Trade and Commercial Organisation in Bengal, 1650–1720, with special reference to the English East India Company*, Calcutta, 1975

Cherry, Gordon, E. *Urban Change and Planning—A History of Urban Development in Britain Since 1790*, London, 1977.

Chowdhury, Benoy, *Growth of Commercial Agriculture in Bengal (1757–1900)*, vol. 1, Calcutta, 1964.

Collier, F. R. S., *The Bengal Municipal Manual* (3rd edn.), Calcutta, 1894.

Cooke, C. N., *The Rise, Progress and Present Condition of Banking in India*, Calcutta, 1863.

Crane, Robert I. (ed.), *Transition in South Asia: Problems of Modernisation*, Durham, 1970.

Croft, A., *Review of Education in India, 1888, with special reference to the Report of the Education Commission*, Calcutta, 1888.

Dani, A. H., *Dacca—A Record of its Changing Fortunes* (revised edn.), Dacca, 1962.

---------------- *Peshwar—Historic City of the Frontier*, Peshwar, 1969.

Das, M. N., *Studies in the Economic and Social Development of Modern India, 1848–56*, Calcutta, 1959.

Deb, Raja Binay Krishna, *The Early History and Growth of Calcutta*, Calcutta, 1905.

Dobbin, C. *Urban Leadership in Western India—Politics and Communities in Bombay City 1840–1885*, Oxford, 1972.

Dufferin, Lady, *Our Viceregal Life in India, 1884–1880*, London, 1890.

Dutt, R. Palme, *India Today*, Bombay, 1947.

Dyos, H. J., *The Study of Urban History*, London, 1968.

Forrest, G. W., *Cities of India, Past and Present*, London, 1903.

Gadgil, D. R., *The Industrial Evolution of India in Recent Times, 1860-1939* (fifth edn.) Bombay, 1971.

Gallaghar, John, Gordon Johnson and Anil Seal (eds.), *Locality, Province and Nation—Essays on Indian Politics, 1870–1940*, Cambridge, 1973.

Geddes, Patrick, *Report on Town Planning—Dacca*, Calcutta, 1911.

Geertz, Clifford,, *Peddlers and Princes—Social Change and Economic Modernization in two Indonesian Towns*, Chicago, 1968.

Ghosh, J. M., *Sannyasi and Fakir Raiders in Bengal*, Calcutta, 1930.

Ghosh, M., Alok K. Datta and B. Roy (eds.) *Calcutta—A Study in Urban Growth Dynamics*, Calcutta, 1972.

Ghosh, Suprokash, *The Urban Pattern of Calcutta—Economic Geography*, Calcutta, 1950.

Gillion, Kenneth L., *Ahmedabad—A Study in Indian Urban History*, Berkeley & Los Angeles, 1968.

Goode, S. W., *Municipal Calcutta—Its Institutions in Their Origin and Growth*, Edinburgh, 1916.

Gupta, Atul Chandra (ed.), *Studies in the Bengal Renaissance*, Jadhabpur, 1958.

Gupta, Narayani, *Delhi Between Two Empires 1803–1931, Society, Government and Urban Growth*, Delhi, 1981.

Gupta, Nirmal Kumar, *Dacca—Old and New*, Dacca, 1940. (Bangiya Sahitya Parisad Library, Calcutta).

Haider, Azimusshan, *Dacca: History and Romanence in Place Names*, Dacca, 1967 (Dacca Municipality Record Room).

---------------- (ed.), *A City and its Civic Body—A Souvenir to mark the Centenary of Dacca Municipality* (Published by Dacca Municipality), Dacca, 1966 (DMRR).

Hamilton, Walter, *A Geographical, Statistical and Historical Description of Hindostan and the Adjacent Countries*, 2 vols., London, 1820.

Hardy, P., *The Muslims of British India*, Cambridge, 1972.

Harrison, J. B. & Hunt, R. (eds.), *The District Officer in India 1930–1947*, London, 1980.

Hasan, Sayid Aulad, *Notes on the Antiquities of Dacca*, Dacca, 1912.

Howell, A. P., *Selections From Educational Records of the Government of India*, vol. 1, *Educational Reports*, With a Foreword Note by Prem Kripal, Delhi, 1960.

----------------- *Education in British India Prior to 1854 and in 1870–71*, Calcutta, 1872.

Jagannath College and Jagannath Hall Reunion, *A Short History of Jagannath College and Jagannath Hall Reunion, 1929–32* (Published by R C. Majumdar), Dacca, 1933.

Karim, A., *Muhammedan Education in Bengal*, Calcutta, 1900.

Karim, Abdul, *Dacca the Mughal Capital*, Dacca, 1964.

Khan, Abdul Majid, *The Transition in Bengal, 1756–1775—A Study of Sayid Muhammad Reza Khan*, Cambridge, 1969.

Kinsey, Gillion, *The Growth of London*, London, 1973.

Kirwan, D. J., *Palace and Hovels, or Phases of London Life*, (new edn.), London, 1963.

Kitchen, P., *An Introduction to the Ideas and Life of Patrick Geddes—A Most Unsettling Person*, London, 1975.

Kopf, David, *Nineteenth Century Bengal and Fifteenth Century Europe*, Calcutta, 1963.

Kopf, D. and Joardar, S. (eds.), *Reflections on the Bengal Renaissance*, Rajshahi, 1977.

Leonard, G. S., *A History of the Brahmo Samaj from its Rise to the Present Day*, Calcutta, 1870 (Reprinted and Republished by K. N. Tagore, Calcutta, 1935).

Luhani, G.A.K., *Dacca—Past and Present* (India Office Tract), Allahabad, 1911.

Maddison, Angus, *Class Structure and Economic Growth—India and Pakistan since the Mughals*, London, 1971.

Mahmood, S., *A History of English Education in India (1781–1893)*, Aligarh, 1895.

Majumdar, R. C., *Glimpses of Bengal in the Nineteenth Century*, Calcutta, 1960.

-------------- (ed.) *History of Bengal*, vol. 1 Dacca, 1943.

Marshall, P. J., *East India Fortunes: the British in Bengal in the Eighteenth Century*, Oxford, 1976.

Misra, B. B., *The Central Administration of the East India Company, 1773–1834*, Manchester, 1959.

-------------- *The Judicial Administration of the East India Company in Bengal, 1765–82*, Delhi, 1961.

-------------- *The Administrative History of India 1834–1947*, Bombay, 1970.

-------------- *The Indian Middle Classes: Their Growth in Modern Times*, London, 1961.

Mohsin, K. M., *A Bengal District in Transition—Murshidabad, 1765–1793*, Dacca, 1973.

Moore, R. J., *Sir Charles Wood's Indian Policy, 1853–56*, Manchester, 1966.

Moorhouse, Geoffrey, *Calcutta*, London, 1971.

Morris, D. Morris and Others, *Indian Economy in the Nineteenth Century: A Symposium* (Indian Economic and Social History Association Publication), Delhi, 1969.

Morrison, B. M., *Political Centres and Cultural Regions in Early Bengal*, Arizona, 1970.

North-Field, H. D., *A Front-Line Post—Mission Work in Dacca*, London, 1938.

Park, Richard L. (ed.), *Urban Bengal*, Michigan, 1969.

Park, Robert E., Burgess, E. W. and Mackenzie, R. D., *The City* (4th Impression) Chicago, 1967.

Poddar, A., *Renaissance in Bengal—Quest and Confrontation*, Calcutta, 1970.

Rahman, M., *From Consultation to Confrontation—A Study of the Muslim League in British Indian Politics, 1906–1912*, London, 1970.

Reynolds, Susan, *An Introduction to the History of English Medieval Towns*, Oxford, 1977.

Raychaudhuri, Tapan, *Bengal Under Akbar and Jahangir—An Introductory Study in Social History*, Delhi, 1969.

Risley, H. H., *The Tribes and Castes of Bengal—Ethnographic Glossary* 2 vols., Calcutta, 1891–1892.

Ross, R. L., and Cumming J. G. *Municipal Administration and Reform in Patna City*, Calcutta, 1905.

Ruddock, Grenfell, *Towns and Villages of Pakistan; A Study*, (Planning Commission, Government of Pakistan Publication), Karachi, 1964.

Saran, Paramatma, *The Provincial Government of the Mughals, 1526–1658* (2nd edn.), Bombay, 1973.

Sarkar, J. N. (ed.), *History of Bengal*, vol. 2, Dacca, 1948.

Seth, J. Mesrov B., *History of the Armenians in India*... Calcutta, 1895.

Simson, Frank B., *Letters on Sports in Eastern Bengal*, London, 1886.

Sinha, D. P., *The Educational Policy of the East India Company in Bengal up to 1854*, Calcutta, 1964.

---------------- *Some Aspects of British Social and Administrative Policy in India During the Administration of Lord Auckland*, Calcutta, 1969.

Sinha, J. C., *Economic Annals of Bengal*, London, 1927.

Sinha, N., *Freedom Movement in Bengal, 1818–1904, WHO'S WHO*, Calcutta, 1968.

Sinha, N. K., *The Economic History of Bengal, 1793–1848*, vol. 3, Calcutta, 1970.

---------------- *The Economic History of Bengal From Plassey to Permanent Settlement*, 2 vols., Calcutta, 1956–68.

Sinha, P., *Nineteenth Century Bengal—Aspects of Social History*, Calcutta, 1965.

Sjoberg, G., *The Pre-Industrial Society*, Glencoe, Illinois, 1960.

A Sketch of Eastern Bengal with reference to its Railways and Government Control (Printed anonymously for Private Circulation), Calcutta, 1861.

Smith, John, *Experience of a Landholder and Indigo Planter in Eastern Bengal*, Aberdeen, London, 1859.

Spate, O. H. K. and Learmonth, A. T. A., *India and Pakistan—A General and Regional Geography*, (3rd edn., reprinted), London, 1972.

Spear, P., *The Nabobs, A Study of the Social Life of the English in 18th Century India*, London, 1963.

Stokes, Eric, *The English Utilitarians and India*, Oxford, 1959.

Sutton-Page, Rev. W., *In City and Jungle—A Brief Survey of the Work of the Baptist Missionary Society in the City and District of Dacca, Eastern Bengal*, London, 1907.

Symes-Scutt, G. P., *The History of the Bank of Bengal*... Calcutta, 1904.

Taifoor, S. M., *Glimpses of Old Dhaka* (revised edn.), Dacca, 1956 (Central Public Library, Dacca).

Taylor, James, *A Sketch of the Topography and Statistics of Dacca*, Calcutta, 1840.

---------------- *A Descriptive and Historical Account of the Cotton Manufacture of Dacca*, London, 1851.

Temple, Richard, *Men and Events of My Time in India*, London, 1882.

---------------- *India in 1880*, London, 1880.

Tinker, H., *The Foundations of Local Self-Government in India, Pakistan and Burma* (2nd edn.), London, 1968.

Trevelyan, C. E., *A Report upon the Inland Customs and Town-duties of the Bengal Presidency* (2nd edn.), Calcutta, 1835.

Tripathi, A., *Trade and Finance in the Bengal Presidency*, Calcutta, 1956.

Turner, Roy (ed.), *India's Urban Future*, Berkeley and Los Angeles, 1962.

Tyson, Goeffrey, *Bengal Chamber of Commerce and Industry, 1853–1953—A Centenary Survey*, Calcutta, 1952.

University of Calcutta, *Hundred Years of the University of Calcutta* (Centenary Publication), Calcutta, 1957

Ubaidallah, Al-Ubaidi M., *The Madrasah Scheme*, Calcutta, 1873.

Wirth, Louis, *On Cities and Social Life—Selected Papers*, *Chicago*, 1964.

Wise, J., *Notes on the Races, Castes and Trades of Eastern Bengal*, London, 1883.

4. Works in Bengali

Ahmad, Abuz Zoha Nur, *Unish Sataker Dhakar Samaj Jiban* (A Sketch of the Social Life of Dacca During the Nineteenth Century), Dacca, 1975.

Bandhopadhya, Brojendra Nath, *Bangla Samayik Patra* (Selections from Contemporary Bengali Newspapers, 1818–1867), Calcutta, 1938.

---------------- *Krishna Chandra Majumdar [0] Haris Chandra Mitra* (Krishna Chandra Majumdar and Haris Chandra Mitra), Calcutta, 1945.

Bhadra, Nabin Chandra, *Bhawaler Itihasa* (History of Bhawal in Dacca), Dacca, 1875.

Chattopadhya, Nabakanta, *Dhaka Zelar Bhugal Ebong Shankhep Aitihasik Bibaran* (A Descriptive Geography and Brief History of the Dacca District), Dacca, 1868 (National Library, Calcutta)

Dacca Brahmo Samaj, *Dhaka Brahmo Samajer Itihash* (A History of the Dacca Brahmo Samaj), Dacca, 1875.

Dacca Famine Relief Committee, *Dhaka Durbhikha Nibarani Sabhar Baktrita O Karjo Bibaran* (Proceedings of the Dacca Famine Relief Committee, March 1874), Dacca, 1874.

Das, Govinda Chandra, *Suhridcheda* (Biography of Krishna Kumar Chowdhury—a Zamindar of Sylhet), Dacca, 1875.

East Bengal Mercantile Company Ltd., *East Bengal* (or Prospectus of the East Bengal Mercantile Co.), Dacca, 1877.

Ghosh, Benoy (ed.), *Samayik Patre Banglar Samaj Chitra-Tattabodhini Patrikar Rachana Sankalan, 1840–1905* (Bengali Society as Depicted in the Contemporary Newspaper—*Tattabodhini)*, Calcutta, 1963.

Gupta, Nirmal, *Dhakar Katha* (The History of Dacca), Calcutta, 1960 (Bangiya Sahitya Parishad Library, Calcutta).

Gupta, Yogendra Nath, *Vikrampurer Itihasa* (A History of Vikrampur in Dacca), Calcutta, 1910.

Karim, Abdul, *Dhakai Muslin* (The Muslin of Dacca—A History of the Manufacture and Trade of the cotton textiles of Dacca from the earliest time to *c.* 1840), Dacca, 1965.

Lakhsmimani Charit or *Life Story of Lakhsmimani* (A Social History of the Nineteenth Century City of Dacca and the Reform activities of the Brahmo Samaj), Dacca, 1887.

Majumdar, Kedar Nath, *Dhakar Bibaran* (History of Dacca), Dacca, 1910.

---------------- *Dhaka Sahachar* (A Brief Account of the Geography and History of the Dacca District), Mymensingh (N.D.) (Bangiya Sahitya Parishad Library, Calcutta).

Mitra, Harish Chandra, *Mao Dharbe Ke?* (Who is to bell the cat? A Satire on Social Life in Dacca), Dacca, 1863.

Mukhopadhya, Rash Behari, *Sankhipta Jiban Brittanta* (An Autobiography), Dacca, 1875.

Mukhopadhya, Somnath, *Balya Bibaha* (Child Marriage or Social History of Dacca), Dacca, 1870.

Roy, Lalit Mohan, *Engrajadhikar Varat Barsha* (India Under the British), Dacca, 1870.

Roy, Yatindra Mohan, *Dhakar Itihasa* (A History of Dacca), Calcutta, 1913 (Bangiya Sahitya Parishad Library, Calcutta).

Sen, Dina Nath, *Bangla Desher Lt. Governor O Assamer Chief Commissioner Adhinashta Pradesh Samuher Bibaran* (Descriptive Accounts of the Provinces under the Lieutenant-Governor of Bengal and the Chief Commissioner of Assam), (13th edn.), Calcutta, 1885 (National Library, Calcutta).

Sen, Satyen, *Saharer Itikatha* (Past Events of the City), Dacca, 1974.

Shastri, Siva Nath, *Ramtanu Lahiri O Tatkalin Banga Samaj* (Ramtanu Lahiri and the then Bengali Society; A Social History of Bengal during the Nineteenth Century), Calcutta, 1907.

Vasu, Haridas, *Dhakar Katha* (The History of Dacca), Dacca, 1924.

5. Works in Urdu and Persian

Abul Fazl, *Akbarnama*, III (tr. by H. Beveridge), London, 1902.

Hakim Habibur Rahman, *Dhaka Pachas Sal Pahle* (Dacca Fifty Years Ago) Lahore, 1949 (Dacca University Library).

---------------- *Asudgani-i-Dhaka* (Sketches of Social Life of Dacca), Dacca, 1942 (Dacca University Library, Dacca).

Munshi Rahman Ali Talish, *Tarikh-i-Dhaka* (History of Dacca) ed. by Dr Ahmed Ali, Arrah, 1910.

Nathan, Mirza, *Bahristan-i-Ghaybi* (tr. by M.I. Borah), Gauhati, Assam, 1936.

Nawab Nusrat Jang, *Tarikh-i-Nusratjangi* (ed. by Harinath Dey) in *Memoirs of the Asiatic Society of Bengal*, vol. II, No. 6 (1908, 121–53).

6. *Theses*

Ahmed, Sharif Uddin, 'The History of the City of Dacca, *c.* 1840–1885' (Ph.D., University of London, 1978).

Ali, Muhammad Yousuf, 'Bibliography of Works on the City and District of Dacca' (Library Science M.A., University of Dacca, 1965; Bangla Academy Library, Dacca).

Basu, R., 'Urban Society in Bengal, 1850–1872, with special reference to Calcutta' (Ph.D., University of London, 1974).

Bridges, Harold, 'The Kingdom of Christ in East Bengal' (D.D., Baptist Mission Library, London).

Islam, Mafizul Chaudhury, 'The Regional Geography of Dacca with special reference to its Agriculture and Industrial Activities' (M.A., University of Aligarh, 1944; India Office Library, Mss. Eur. C. 151).

Khatoon, Latifa, 'Some Aspects of the Social History of Bengal with Special Reference to the Muslims, 1854–1884' (M.A., University of London, 1955).

Osmany, S. H., 'Chittagong Port: A Study of its Fortunes, 1892–1912' (Ph.D., University of London, 1978).

Rahman, J. A. 'Some Aspects of the Indian Viceroyalty of Lord Elgin, 1862–63' (Ph.D., University of London, 1971).

7. *Articles in English published in Journals and Newspapers*

Ahmed, Nafis, 'The Landscape of the Dacca Urban Area', *The Oriental Geographer*, Dacca, vol. VII, I (1963), 1–18.

Ali, Abdul, A. F. M., 'Notes on the Early History of the English Factory at Dacca' *Bengal Past and Present*, Calcutta, vol. XXXII (July-Dec 1920), 14–20.

Ascoli, F. D. 'The Jurisdiction of the District of Dacca from the Earliest Times', *The Dacca Review*, Dacca, (1916–17), 15–23 (Barendra Research Museum Library, Rajshahi, Bangladesh).

Bayly, C. A., 'Town Building in North India, 1790–1830', *Modern Asian Studies*, Cambridge, IX, 4 (1975), 483–504.

Bhattasali, N. K., 'Early Days of Mughal Rule in Dacca', *Islamic Culture*, Hyderabad, XVI, 4 (1942), 393–403.

Banerji, S. C., 'Naib Nazims of Dacca during the Company's Administration, 1778–1843', *Indian Historical Record Commission*, Proceedings, vol. XVI (1939), 31–33; also BPP, LIX (July-Dec. 1940), 17–29.

'Dacca Forty Years Ago', (Cuttings from the Newspaper *The East* published from Dacca), *The Dacca Review*, VI, 2 (1916), 66–74 (Varendra Research Museum Library, Rajshahi).

'Dacca the Ancient Capital of Bengal', *Friend of India*, Calcutta 1876.
Gumperz, Ellen McDonald, 'City-Hinterland Relations and the Development of a Regional Elite in Nineteenth Century Bombay', *Journal of Asian Studies*, XXXIII, 4, (1974), 581–601.
Hasan, Sayid Aulad, 'Old Dacca', *Dacca Review*, IV (Aug-Sept. 1909), 146–58.
Hossain, Syud, 'Echoes From Old Dhaka', BPP, III, 2 (1909), 211–237.
Karim, Abdul (ed.), 'An Account of the District of Dacca dated 1800', *Asiatic Society of Pakistan*, VII (Dec. 1962), 289–341.
Khan, M. Siddiq, 'Life in Old Dacca' (Sketches of Social Life in Dacca during the Nineteenth Century), *Pakistan Quarterly*, IX (Summer 1959) 20–7.
Khan, Ghulam Ambia, 'Dacca Past and Present', *East and West*, Bombay, X, Part I, No. III (1911), 58–67.
Mandal, A., 'The Ideology and the Interest of the Bengal Intelligentsia; Sir George Campbell's Education Policy, 1871–74', *The Indian Economic and Social History Review*, Delhi, XII, I (1975), 81–98.
Qanungo, K. R., 'Dacca and its Medieval History', BPP, LXVI, 129 (1946–47), 58–62.
Ruddock, G., 'Capital of East Pakistan', *Pakistan Quarterly*, VII (1957), 49–58.
Sarkar, Jagadish Narayan, 'The Early History of Patna College', BPP, LXII, 125 (1942), 92–115; LXIII, 126 (1943), 31–43; LXIV, 127 (1944), 68–83.
Sinha, J. C., 'The Dacca Muslin Industry', *Modern Review*, Calcutta, XXXVII, 4 (1925), 400–8.
Stapleton, H. E., 'List of Tombs of Historic Interest in Dacca Cemetery', BPP, XXXI, 61–62 (1926), 10–12.
The Times (London), 'The Rehabilitation of Dacca—Past History and Modern Development of the City', 24 May 1909.
Walter, Henry, 'Census of the City of Dacca', *Asiatic Researches*, Calcutta, XVII (1832), 535–558.
Zaidi, Z. H., 'The Political Motive in the Partition of Bengal', *The Journal of the Pakistan Historical Society*, April, 1964.

8. Maps and Directories (India Office Library)

Rennell, J., *Map of the Country Round the City of Dacca*, 1774.
---------------- *Plan of the Environs of the City of Dacca*, 1780.
Surveyor General of India, *A Revenue Survey Map of the City of Dacca Including Cantonments*, 1859.
The Bengal Directory and General Register, Calcutta, annually, 1835–42; compiled, printed and published by Samuel Smith & Co.
The Bengal and Agra Directory and Annual Register, Calcutta, annually 1843–55, Samuel Smith and Co.

The New Calcutta Directory, Calcutta annually, 1856–63; complied by A.G. Roussae and printed and published by Frank Carbery and others.

Thacker's Directory for Bengal, Calcutta annually, 1864–87.

9. Diaries, Travel Accounts, Guide Books, Memoirs, Photographs and Illustrations

Album of Dacca (A collection of Photographic Views and Portraits), Dacca, 1890 (Calcutta National Library—Rare Book Section),.

[Clay, A. L.], *Leaves From a Diary in Lower Bengal* by C.S. (Retired), London, 1896.

Davidson, Lt. Col. C. J. C., 'Dacca in 1840', BPP, XLII, I (1931), 36–48.

D'Oyly, Sir Charles, *Antiquities of Dacca* (With Illustrations), London, 1824–30.

[Graham, George], *Life in the Mofussil, Or The Civilian in Lower Bengal* By An Ex-Civilian, 2 vols. in One, London, 1878.

Heber, Bishop Reginald, *Narratives of a Journey Through the Upper Provinces Of India From Calcutta to Bombay, 1824–1825 (with notes upon Ceylon)*, 2 vols. (new edn.), London, 1849.

Majumdar, H. N., *The Reminiscences of Dacca*, Calcutta, 1926.

Manrique, S., *Travels of Fray Sebastien Manrique, 1629–1643*, 2 vols., The Hakluyt Society, Oxford, 1927.

Mookherjee, Sambhu Chandra, *Travels and Voyages between Calcutta and Independent Tipperah*, Calcutta, 1887.

Murray, John (Publisher), *Handbook of the Bengal Presidency etc.*, London, 1882.

Pal, Bipin Chandra, *Memoirs of My Life and Times, 1857–1900*, 2 vols. in one (new edn.), Calcutta, 1973.

Panorama of Dacca (Coloured Sketches of Buildings and Landscapes of the City of Dacca, Artist Unknown), London, 1847.

Stocquelor, J. H. (Publisher), *The Handbook of India—A Guide to the Stranger, the Traveller and a Companion to the Resident*, London, 1844.

---------------- *The Handbook of British India etc.* (3rd edn.), London, 1854.

C. Interviews

1. Interview with Dr Arun Kumar Basak, a descendant of the famous Basak family of Nawabpur, Dacca, Dacca, June, 1976.
2. Interview with Babu Braja Gopal Das, a direct descendant of Sanatan Das and Ruplal Das—the great banker-zamindars of Dacca during the nineteenth century, Dacca, February 1976.
3. Interview with Maulvi Belayet Hussain, a former Head Maulvi of Calcutta Madrasah and Dacca Madrasah, Dacca, July 1976.

INDEX